# PEACE &
## INTERNATIONAL
# RELATIONS

A Funding Guide for
Independent Groups

A Directory of Social Change publication

Edited by
**Susan Forrester**

**PEACE & INTERNATIONAL RELATIONS**
**Edited by Susan Forrester**

The research for this book has been undertaken with financial support from the Joseph Rowntree Charitable Trust.

Published by the Directory of Social Change, Radius Works, Back Lane, London NW3 IHL (071-284 4364), from whom copies may be obtained.

Designed and typeset by Linda Parker
Printed by Page Bros, Norwich

British Library Cataloguing-in-Publication Data
A catalogue record for this book is available from the British Library.

ISBN 1 873860 58 7

# Acknowledgements

Most particular thanks are given to the Joseph Rowntree Charitable Trust for funding the research for this guide, and also to all those individuals too numerous to name who have helped in providing information for this guide.

# Contents

# Introduction

This guide updates the funding section of the earlier guide *'Peace and Security, a Guide to Independent Groups and Grant Sources'* published in 1988.

## The scope of the book

The title of this new guide reflects the change in emphasis of international affairs since the late 1980s and the frame of reference of the book has been has been altered and extended to echo this shift. The guide has aimed to cover funding sources with an interest in: international affairs, peace, disarmament and arms control, conflict resolution and mediation, civil liberties, human rights and refugees, development education, Northern Ireland and East West partnerships.

Whilst a greater number of trusts and foundations from Britain and the USA have been identified, the response from trusts and foundations in Europe and Japan has been disappointing and it has been difficult to elicit responses even from those which provided information for the previous guide.

Most of the entries give examples of recent grants to organisations working in areas relevant to this guide. It also stretches the boundaries to include grants to organisations working internationally in environmental development and relief work because of the overlapping of global perspectives and the greater likelihood of such organisations to be open to funding approaches. It has not been possible to make a useful estimate of the proportion of funding given by each trust to work relevant to the scope of this guide. It would only be a misleading guestimate. Readers should be careful to look at the examples of grants and their scale within the context of the annual funding given by each trust.

# TRUSTS WITH
# SPECIFIC INTERESTS

## Introduction

The trusts shown in these lists are those which either have a particular policy to support this area of work, or give a significant proportion of their total funding to this area of work.

These lists do not cover all those trusts which are known to have given one or two grants in this field. There is no substitute for a careful browse through all the entries to identity likely trusts to approach.

## Peace and International Relations

(US foundations have not been listed as all those included have some specific policy in this area)

### UK Sources

A S Charitable Trust
Atlantic Peace Foundation
Britten Pears Foundation
Barrow & Geraldine S Cadbury Trust
Barrow Cadbury Fund
Cheney Peace Settlement
J Anthony Clark Charitable Foundation
Roger & Sarah Bancroft Clark Charitable Trust
Dinam Charity
Dulverton Trust
Miss M E Ellis 1985 Charitable Trust
Esmée Fairbairn Charitable Trust
Give Peace a Chance Trust
Hillcote Trust
J G Joffe Charitable Trust
Lansbury House Trust Fund
Maypole Fund
Network Foundation
Noel Buxton Trust
Polden-Puckham Charitable Foundation
Quaker Peace & Service, Peace Committee
Radley Charitable Trust
Eva Reckitt Trust Fund
Sir James Reckitt Charity
Joseph Rowntree Charitable Trust
Scott Bader Commonwealth Ltd
W F Southall Trust
Sir Halley Stewart Trust
Westcroft Trust

**Others**

European Cultural Foundation

European Youth Foundation

Niwano Peace Foundation

NORDSAM

Olof Palme Memorial Fund

Saskawa Peace Foundation

# International Development and Aid/Development Education

### UK Sources

A S Charitable Trust

Keith & Freda Abraham Charitable Trust

Alchemy Foundation

Allachy Trust

Batchworth Trust

Benfield Motors Charitable Trust

Bower Trust

Broad Oak Trust

Edward Cadbury Charitable Trust

Henry T & Lucy B Cadbury Charitable Trust

Richard Cadbury Charitable Trust

William Adlington Cadbury Charitable Trust

CAFOD

Charity Projects

Christian Aid

Wallace Curzon Charitable Trust

Delves Charitable Trust

Wilfred & Elsie Elkes Charity Fund

Franklin Trusts

Fray's Charitable Trust

Gatsby Charitable Foundation

Headley Trust

Hilden Charitable Fund

J C Joffe Charitable Trust

Inchcape Charitable Trust fund

Morel Charitable Trust

Paget Charitable Trust

Rowan Charitable Trust

Strathspey Charitable Trust

Edmund Vinson Charitable Trust

Mary Webb Trust

**Others**

Commission of the European Communities

# Northern Ireland

### UK Sources

Avenue Charitable Trust

Barrow & Geraldine S Cadbury Trust

Barrow Cadbury Fund Ltd

J & L A Cadbury Charitable Trust

Roger & Sarah Bancroft Clark Charitable Trust

Community Relations Council

Ernest Cook Trust

Co-operation North

Enkalon Foundation

Hambland and Lankelly Foundations

Charles Hayward Trust

Inter-Church Emergency Fund for Ireland

Irish Ecumenical Church Loan Fund Committee

Allen Lane Foundation

Lawlor Foundation

Esmé Mitchell Trust

John Moore's Foundation

Noel Buxton Trust

Northern Ireland Voluntary Trust

Eva Reckitt Trust Fund

Joseph Rowntree Charitable Trust

Sir Halley Stewart Trust

Wates Foundation

Women Caring Trust

**Others**

The Ireland Funds

# East/West Relations

### UK Trusts

Charity Know How

Esmée Fairbairn Charitable Trust

Franklin Trusts

Nuffield Foundation
Partners in Europe
Wates Foundation
Westminster Foundation for Democracy

## Governmental Support

Know How Fund, Joint Assistance Unit of the Foreign & Commonwealth Office
NATO Linkage Fund
PHARE
TACIS
TEMPUS

## USA Foundations

Lynde & Harry Bradley Foundation, Inc
Carnegie Foundation of New York
Eurasia Foundation
Ford Foundation
German Marshall Fund
William & Mary Greve Foundation, Inc
John D & Catherine J MacArthur Foundation
Andrew W Mellon Foundation
Charles Stewart Mott Foundation
Joyce Mertz-Gilmore Foundation
National Endowment for Democracy
John M Olin Foundation
Pew Charitable Trusts
Rockefeller Brothers Fund
Soros Foundations (some 20 set up in Central and Eastern Europe, countries of the former Soviet Union)
United Way International

## Others

King Baudouin Foundation
Heinz-Schwarzkopf-Stiftung Junges Europa
Sasakawa Central Europe Fund – See Sasakawa Peace Foundation
See The Soros Foundations for addresses of foundations in Central and Eastern Europe, etc.
Volkswagen-Stiftung

# Human Rights (*support to refugees)

## UK Trusts

1970 Trust
Aid to the Church in Need*
Ajama Charitable Trust
Lord Ashdown Charitable Trust
Avenue Charitable Trust
Besom Foundation
Bromley Trust
Barrow & Geraldine S Cadbury Trust
Barrow Cadbury Trust Fund Ltd
Christopher Cadbury Charitable Trust
G W Cadbury Charitable Trust
Chownes Foundation
City Parochial Foundation*
Stephen Clark Charitable Settlement
Cobb Charity
Miriam Dean Refugee Trust Fund*
Ericson Trust*
Walter Guinness Charitable Trust
Harbour Foundation Ltd*
Hilden Charitable Fund
Housing Associations Charitable Trust*
Neil Kreitman Foundation
Laing Foundations
Allen Lane Foundation*
Leigh Trust
Lyndhurst Settlement
Mackintosh Foundation *
Network Foundation
Oakdale Trust
Onaway Trust
Hugh Pilkington Charitable Trust *
Polden-Puckham Charitable Foundation
Mr C A Rodewald's Charitable Settlement
Rowan Charitable Trust
Joseph Rowntree Charitable Trust*
Henry Smith's (Kensington Estates) Charity
Tudor Trust*

## Others

European Cultural Foundation
European Human Rights Foundation

# UK SOURCES

## UK Trusts

**Contents**

The Cumber Family Charitable Trust
The Wallace Curzon Charitable Trust
Daiwa Anglo-Japanese Foundation
The Margaret Davies Charity
The De La Rue Jubilee Trust
Miriam Dean Refugee Trust Fund
Delves Charitable Trust
Delves Charitable Trust
Dinam Charity
Dolphin Charitable Trust
The Dulverton Trust
Wilfred and Elsie Elkes Charity Fund
The John Ellerman Foundation
   (formerly the Moorgate Trust Fund and
   the New Moorgate Trust Fund)
Miss M E Ellis 1985 Charitable Trust
Enkalon Foundation
Ericson Trust
European Educational Research Trust
Esmée Fairbairn Charitable Trust
Ferguson Benevolent Fund Limited
Allan and Nesta Ferguson Charitable Trust
Firbank Charitable Trust
Fitton Trust
The Flow Foundation
Jill Franklin Trust
Norman Franklin Trust
Fray's Charitable Trust
Fulbright Commission
Fund for Human Need
The Gatsby Charitable Foundation
J Paul Getty Jr General Charitable Trust
Give Peace a Chance Trust
GNC Trust
Godinton Charitable Trust
The Goldsmiths' Company's Charities
S & F Goodman Trust Fund
The Grand Charity
The Great Britain-Sasakawa Foundation
Walter Guinness Charitable Trust
Gunter Charitable Trust
The Hadrian Trust
The Hambland and Lankelly Foundations
Harbour Foundation Ltd
The Mrs J S Harcus Charitable Trust

L G Harris & Co Ltd Charitable Trust
The Hayward Foundation
The Charles Hayward Trust
The Headley Trust
Hickinbotham Charitable Trust
Walter Higgs Charitable Trust
Hilden Charitable Fund
Hillcote Trust
P H Holt Charitable Trust
Housing Associations Charitable Trust (HACT)
Inchcape Charitable Trust Fund
Inter-Church Emergency Fund for Ireland
Irish Ecumenical Church Loan Fund Committee
The Jerusalem Trust
The Jessel, Toynbee and Gillett Charitable Trust
J G Joffe Charitable Trust
The Ian Karten Charitable Trust
Kleinwort Benson Charitable Trust
Sir Cyril Kleinwort Charitable Settlement
Ernest Kleinwort Charitable Trust
Neil Kreitman Foundation
The Kulika Trust
Beatrice Laing Trust
The Kirby Laing Foundation
Maurice Laing Foundation
The Allen Lane Foundation
Lansbury House Trust Fund
The Lawlor Foundation
Edgar Lee Foundation
The Leigh Trust
Lester Trust Fund
The Leverhulme Trust
Livingstone Trust
Lloyd's Charities Trust
The Lyndhurst Settlement
The Mackintosh Foundation
Linda Marcus Charitable Trust
The Marsden Charitable Trust
The Marsh Christian Trust
The Maxco Trust
Maypole Fund
The Mercers' Charitable Foundation
Mercury Provident plc
The Millfield Trust
The Millicope Foundation

Victor Mishcon Trust
Esmé Mitchell Trust
The Moores Family Charity Foundation
John Moores Foundation
Morel Charitable Trust
S C and M E Morland's Charitable Trust
Network Foundation
Noel Buxton Trust
Northern Ireland Voluntary Trust
Nuffield Foundation
Oakdale Trust
Oakmoor Trust
Onaway Trust
Oppenheimer Charitable Trust
Oxfam
P F Charitable Trust
Paget Charitable Trust
Partners in Europe
Harry Payne Trust
Hugh Pilkington Charitable Trust
G S Plaut Charitable Trust Limited
The Polden-Puckham Charitable Foundation
Simone Prendergast Charitable Trust
Quaker Peace & Service, Peace Committee
Radley Charitable Trust
Rank Foundation Ltd
The Eleanor Rathbone Charitable Trust
Albert Reckitt Charitable Trust
Eva Reckitt Trust Fund
The Sir James Reckitt Charity
Rest-Harrow Trust
Ripple Effect Foundation
Mr C A Rodewald's Charitable Settlement
Mrs L D Rope's Third Charitable Settlement
Rotary International in Great Britain and Ireland
The Rothley Trust
Rowan Charitable Trust
Joseph Rowntree Charitable Trust
Joseph Rowntree Reform Trust
A and B Sainsbury Charitable Trust
Sainsbury Family Charitable Trusts
Peter Samuel Charitable Trust
Save & Prosper Foundation
Schroder Charitable Trust
Scott Bader Commonwealth Ltd

Scouloudi Foundation (formerly known as the Twenty-Seven Foundation)
Henry Smith's (Kensington Estates) Charity
W F Southall Trust
Sir Sigmund Sternberg Charitable Foundation
Sir Halley Stewart Trust
Still Waters Charitable Trust
Eric Stonehouse Trust Ltd
Strathspey Charitable Trust
The Sumray Charitable Trust
The Bernard Sunley Charitable Foundation
Joan Tanner Charitable Settlement
C B & H H Taylor Trust
Thompson Charitable Trust
The Tudor Trust
Tyne & Wear Foundation
Tzedakah
Van Neste Foundation
Edward Vinson Charitable Trust
Howard Walker Charitable Trust
Anne Wall Trust
Warbeck Fund Ltd
The Wates Foundation
Mary Webb Trust
Weinberg Foundation
The Weinstock Fund
Welton Foundation
The Westcroft Trust
Westminster Foundation for Democracy
The Garfield Weston Foundation
The Westward Trust
The Whitaker Charitable Trust
Humphrey Whitbread's First Charitable Trust
The H D H Wills 1965 Charitable Trust
Women Caring Trust
Zephyr Charitable Trust
Zochonis Charitable Trust

# 1970 Trust

*(handwritten: w)*

*(handwritten: see DGMT p.454)*

**GRANT TOTAL:** Around £15,000

**MAIN AREAS OF WORK:** See below

**ADDRESS:** ~~68 Crescent Road, London N22 4RZ~~

**CORRESPONDENT:** D G Rennie

**TRUSTEES:** D Rennie

**BENEFICIAL AREA:** National

**GENERAL:** This small trust, which pays out a total of some £15,000 a year to beneficiaries, is not a registered charity. It supports a range of radical causes. Its objects are to support groups doing innovative work in the fields of:

- Civil liberties (e.g. freedom of information; democracy; humanising work; children's welfare);
- Public interest in the face of vested interest groups (e.g. advertising, alcohol, roads, war, pharmaceuticals, and tobacco industries);
- Disadvantaged minorities;
- Multiracial initiatives;
- Environment (e.g. taming road traffic; ecologically sound food production; preventing pollution);
- Intermediate technology;
- Public transport, pedestrians, bicycling, road accident prevention;
- Preventive health;
- Prison reform.

The trust is interested in smaller groups in their formative days, particularly those which are innovatory rather than local branches of an existing body. Grants are usually between £100 and £1,000 a year for at least 3 years.

**APPLICATIONS:** There is no application form. Proposals should be summarised in about 100 words and be accompanied by supportive information.

# A S Charitable Trust

**GRANT TOTAL:** £17,500 (1990/91)

**ADDRESS:** 31 Green Street, London W1Y 3FD

**CORRESPONDENT:** R St George Calvocoressi

**TRUSTEES:** R St George Calvocoressi, C W Brocklebank, Sir Thomas Hare

**GENERAL:** The trust has general charitable objects and a national and international scope. The trust is sympathetic to projects for Third World development; peacemaking and reconciliation; training in Christian Lay Leadership; Christ-centred social action; charismatic Christian groups involved in any of the above. Preference is for charities known to the trust or in which they have a special interest or knowledge. Appeals by large charities and individuals are not considered.

Over recent years CHIPS, Christian International Peace Service, has been the major beneficiary, receiving £11,500 in 1991/92. Christian Engineers in Development received £2,500. Small grants have been made to Traidcraft, International Ecumenical Fellowship and Dunamis.

**APPLICATIONS:** Correspondence cannot be answered as funds are fully committed.

# Keith and Freda Abraham Charitable Trust

**GRANT TOTAL:** £22,000 (1991/92)

**MAIN AREAS OF WORK:** General

**ADDRESS:** 30 Bear Street, Barnstaple, Devon EX32 7DD

**TELEPHONE:** 0271-75271

**CORRESPONDENT:** R J Stanbury

**TRUSTEES:** K N Abraham, Mrs F Abraham, H J Purnell, C D Squire, C T Mill

**BENEFICIAL AREA:** National and international

**INFORMATION:** Accounts are on file at the Charity Commission.

**GENERAL:** The trust gives in particular 'to major national charities to which the trustees have a personal leaning and local projects'. In 1991/92 resources were underspent: 'the trustees are actively considering some major projects and this is why substantial income has been retained". The 26 grants which were given included the following with relevance to this guide:

Sightsavers (£2,500);

Bangladesh Appeal (£1,000);

Albanian Children's Appeal (£1,000);

Oxfam (£1,000).

**APPLICATIONS:** In writing to the correspondent.

# Aid to the Church in Need

**GRANT TOTAL:** £924,000 (1991)

**MAIN AREAS OF WORK:** Oppressed Christians and refugees

**ADDRESS:** 124 Carshalton Road, Sutton, Surrey SM1 4RL

**TELEPHONE:** 081-642 8668

**CORRESPONDENT:** The Director

**TRUSTEES:** Members of the Board

**BENEFICIAL AREA:** National and international

**INFORMATION:** An annual report with details of grant-aid, and a newsletter 'The Mirror' which gives details of individual projects are available.

**GENERAL:** This charity aims to relieve need and suffering in the Church wherever it is oppressed or in poverty. It is a Universal Public Association within the Catholic Church dependent on the Holy See. Whilst support is given particularly for Roman Catholics, refugees are assisted regardless of their religious belief.

**APPLICATIONS:** In writing to the correspondent.


# The AIM Foundation

**GRANT TOTAL:** £278,000 (1992/93)

**ADDRESS:** Peter Fitt, Chartered Accountants, 15 High Street, West Mersea, Essex CO5 8QA

**CORRESPONDENT:** Peter Fitt

**TRUSTEES:** Ian Roy Marks, Mrs Angela D Marks, Charles F Woodhouse.

**BENEFICIAL AREA:** National and international

**INFORMATION:** Accounts are on file at the Charity Commission but the grants are not listed after 1990/91.

**GENERAL:** This trust was called until 1993, the Ian Roy Marks Charitable Trust. In 1990/91, the most recent year for which a schedule of grants is available with the accounts at the Charity Commission, grants with relevance to this guide were made to:

Network Foundation (£21,100);

Intermediate Technology Development Group (£20,000);

Gaia Foundation, Natural Justice, World Conservation (£15,000 each);

Earthwatch Europe (£6,000).

Donations of up to £1,000 totalling £11,645 were not listed. Ian Roy Marks is also a trustee of the Ripple Effect Foundation (see separate entry).

**APPLICATIONS:** A note with the accounts states that the trustees initiate their own contacts with projects and do not encourage or respond to applications. This point has been emphasised by the correspondent.


# Ajahma Charitable Trust

**GRANT TOTAL:** £138,000 (1991/92)

**MAIN AREAS OF WORK:** General

**ADDRESS:** P O Box 103, Watford WD1 7SF

**CORRESPONDENT:** Miss J A Sheridan

**TRUSTEES:** Jennifer Sheridan, Elizabeth Simpson, James Sinclair Taylor, Michael Horsham.

**BENEFICIAL AREA:** Undefined

**INFORMATION:** Accounts are on file at the Charity Commission.

**GENERAL:** This trust was formerly known at the Jennifer Sheridan Charitable Trust. It has assets of some £1.2 million. The accounts show grants relevant to this guide were given:

In 1991/92 –

Oxfam (£9,300, with grant of £5,000 and £9,300 in the 2 previous years);

Gaia Foundation (£2,000);

Population Concern (£3,600);

Prisoners Abroad, Family Rights Group and Third World First (£500 each);

In 1990/91 –

The Medical Foundation for the Victims of Torture (£1,500);

Somali Anglo Association (£500);

In 1998/90 –

Nicaraguan Health Fund (£2,000);

Civil Liberties Trust (£1,000).

It is understood that the Civil Liberties Trust was given support again in 1992.

**APPLICATIONS:** In writing to the correspondent.

# The Alchemy Foundation
(formerly the Starlight Foundation)

**GRANT TOTAL:** £525,000 (1992/93)

**MAIN AREAS OF WORK:** General

**ADDRESS:** Trevereux Manor, Limpsfield Chart, Oxted, Surrey RH8 OTL

**TELEPHONE:** 0883-730800 (Fax)

**CORRESPONDENT:** Richard Stilgoe

**TRUSTEES:** Richard Stilgoe, Annabel Stilgoe, Rev D Reeves, Dr M Smith, Esther Rantzen, A Armitage, A Murison

**BENEFICIAL AREA:** National and international

**INFORMATION:** Accounts are on file at the Charity Commission.

**GENERAL:** The foundation focuses on 'long-term projects in the third world involving water supply, irrigation and improvements using appropriate technology' as well many areas of work in the UK. These particularly concentrate on children, the homeless and young people with special needs. The accounts for 1991/92 at the Charity Commission show the most substantial support was given to Oxfam and Save the Children for a series of projects. The totals allocated are given below:

Save the Children (£250,000);

Oxfam (£95,000);

Ockenden Venture, for disabled refugees (£2,000);

WaterAid (£1,000);

Pestalozzi Trust (£500).

A grant was also given to Coleraine Community Project (£1,000).

**APPLICATIONS:** In writing to the correspondent

# Alliance Family Foundation Limited

**GRANT TOTAL:** £81,000

**MAIN AREAS OF WORK:** Relief of poverty, religion, education, medicine

**ADDRESS:** c/o 12th Floor, Bank House, Charlotte Street, Manchester MI 4ET

**CORRESPONDENT:** Miss J M Ridgeway, Secretary.

**DIRECTORS:** Sir David Alliance, N Alliance, G N Alliance, Mrs S D Esterkin.

**BENEFICIAL AREA:** National

**INFORMATION:** Accounts are on file at the Charity Commission but with no schedule of grants since 1988.

**GENERAL:** From much earlier lists of grants it appears that this trust gives mainly to Jewish charities. However it is known that a grant was given to Cooperation Ireland (GB) in 1992.

# The Appledore Trust

**GRANT TOTAL:** £47,000 (1992/93)

**MAIN AREAS OF WORK:** People in UK, people abroad, birds, animals and habitats

**ADDRESS:** 8 Church Lane, Middleton Cheney, Banbury, Oxfordshire OXI17 2NR

**CORRESPONDENT:** Mrs Diana Myers

**TRUSTEES:** Diana Myers, Merrilyn Myers, M Bernard Moreton.

**BENEFICIAL AREA:** National, international and local e.g. hospices

**INFORMATION:** Accounts are on file at the Charity Commission.

**GENERAL:** Grants with relevance to the scope of this book have been given:

In 1992/93 –

Disaster Emergency Committee (£5,000);

Amnesty International (£1,500);

International Refugee Year Trust (£1,000);

Intermediate Technology Development Trust (£1,000 and in the previous year);

Aid to Russian Christians, UNICEF, Greenpeace, FOE (£500 each);

In 1991/92 –

Friends of the Earth (£4,000, 2 grants);

Care Britain (£2,000, 3 grants);

Christian Aid Gulf Crisis Appeal (£1,000);

Sightsavers (£1,000).

**APPLICATIONS:** In writing to the correspondent. However the trust has written that it deeply regrets being listed in any directory because it receives such large numbers of applications. The trust makes regular donations to five charities which absorb more than half its income so that only a small amount is available for other charities.

# Lord Ashdown Charitable Trust

**GRANT TOTAL:** £1.7 million (1992/3)

**MAIN AREAS OF WORK:** General

**ADDRESS:** c/o Clive Marks FCA, 44a New Cavendish Street, London W1M 7LG

**CORRESPONDENT:** C M Marks

**TRUSTEES:** C M Marks, G F Renwick, Dr R M E Stone, J M Silver

**BENEFICIAL AREA:** National

**INFORMATION:** Accounts are on file at the Charity Commission, but those for 1991/92 do not include a schedule of grants.

**GENERAL:** The trust gives to a wide range of organisations and has a particular interest in Jewish initiatives. There is no schedule of grants given with the most recent accounts available on public record. Instead allocations are recorded in the following broad categories:

Community £492,000

Education £410,000

Children £119,000

Prevention of Illness £101,000

Medical £34,000

Hospice and Aged £70,000

Arts £41,000

Students £21,000

Small Grants £24,000

Grants for special consultancy to individual charities £23,000

Grant Research & Advisory Services to Donees £27,000

Exceptional grant (Arts) £350,000

It is known that the Civil Liberties Trust and the Refugee Council have received support in 1991/92. A review of the schedules of grants in earlier years showed the following with relevance to the scope of this guide:

In 1990/91 –

Institute Revival, for Soviet Jewry revival activity (£21,000);

International Council of Christians and Jews (£15,000);

Group Relations Educational Trust (£13,500);

Foundation for the Care of the Victims of Apartheid, Council of Christians and Jews (£10,000 each);

International Alert, for Third World mediation (£5,000);

One World Action, Refugee Support Centre (£2,500 each);

In 1989/90 –

Cambodia Trust (£15,000);

Anti-Slavery Society (£2,500);

United World College of the Atlantic (£1,000);

Survival International (£150);

Enniskillen Community Development Project (£100).

**EXCLUSIONS:** No second degrees. No postgraduate studies. No elective or intercalcated courses. No sponsorship for expeditions.

**APPLICATIONS:** 'Trustees support registered charities only. Students with disabilities may be considered, as well as a strictly limited number of causes unlikely to find funding from other sources.'

'Sadly, the trustees can no longer respond to unsolicited applications. Only applicants known to the trustees will be considered. Applications will not be considered unless accompanied by a SAE.'

'Absolutely no personal callers or telephone enquiries.'

# Atlantic Peace Foundation

**GRANT TOTAL:** Not known.

**ADDRESS:** Bertrand Russell House, 45 Gamble Street, Nottingham NG7 4ET

**TELEPHONE:** 0602-784 504

**CORRESPONDENT:** Ken Fleet

**TRUSTEES:** Ken Fleet, Ann Kestenbaum, Michael Barrett Brown.

**GENERAL:** The foundation makes occasional

grants for research into peace and conflict. In 1987 the foundation had a total fund of about £20,000 with some £1,500 annual interest as income. It has not replied to repeated requests for up-to-date information.

# Avenue Charitable Trust

**GRANT TOTAL:** £206,000 (1991)

**ADDRESS:** c/o Messrs Sayers, Butterworth, 18 Bentinck Street, London W1M 5RL.

**CORRESPONDENT:** S G Kemp

**TRUSTEES:** Hon F D L Astor, Hon Mrs B A Astor, S G Kemp.

**BENEFICIAL AREA:** National and international

**INFORMATION:** Accounts are on file at the Charity Commission.

**GENERAL:** The trust has general charitable objects. Grants relevant to the scope of this guide were given:

In 1991 –

Anti-Apartheid Movement (£7,026);

Anti-Slavery Society (£1,000 with £2,000 in the previous year);

Medical Foundation for the Care of Victims of Torture (£500);

Northern Ireland Voluntary Trust (£1,000 with £800 given in the previous year);

Parliamentary Human Rights Trust (£500, a regular grant);

Prison Charity shops (£18,000);

Runnymede Trust (£350, with £350 and £500 in the 2 previous years);

Writers and Scholars Education Trust (£500 with £483 in the previous year);

In 1990 –

Africa Now (£110);

Canon Collins Educational Trust for Southern Africa (£250);

South Africa Townships Health Fund (£1,000).

**APPLICATIONS:** In writing to the correspondent, but applicants should note that income is already fully committed to existing beneficiaries.

# The Baring Foundation

**GRANT TOTAL:** £7,936,000 (1992)

**MAIN AREAS OF WORK:** Social welfare, education, health, conservation/environment, arts

**ADDRESS:** 8 Bishopgate, London EC2N 4AE

**TELEPHONE:** 071-280 1348

**CORRESPONDENT:** David Carrington, Director

**TRUSTEES:** Lord Ashburton, Nicolas Baring, Mrs Tessa Baring, R D Broadley, Lord Howick, Lady Lloyd, Professor Lord Adrian, M J Rivett-Carnac, Sir Crispin Tickell, Martin Findlay.

**BENEFICIAL AREA:** National with a special interest in London, Merseyside, Tyne and Wear, and Cleveland areas.

**INFORMATION:** Annual report and guidelines for applicants are available from the foundation.

**GENERAL:** The foundation only supports local organisations in the specific areas noted above. In 1992 the foundation's grant payments were allocated as follows:

Social welfare £4,749,000;

Education £816,000;

Health £684,000;

Conservation/environment £618,000;

Miscellaneous £222,000.

In 1992 the following grants with relevance to the scope of this guide were given under the following categories to:

Under Education –

Intermediate Technology Development Group (£30,000);

Sussex University Institute of Development Studies for costs of Chinese exchange scheme (£17,364);

Newcastle University for Russian archivist (£15,000);

Ditchley Foundation for international conferences (£10,000);

Under Social Welfare –

University of Oxford Refugee Studies (£74,000);

Runnymede Trust (£52,000);

Minority Rights Group (£21,000);

Under International –

VSO (£150,000);

Oxfam (£50,000 in 2 grants);

Catholic Institute for International Relations (£36,000);

Charity Know How Fund (£30,000);

Fontmell Group for its work promoting the use of military resources for disaster relief (£5,000);

Under London –

Windmill Project for Refugee Women (£6,000);

A grant of £150,000 was given to Northern Ireland Voluntary Trust (see separate entry).

**EXCLUSIONS:** No grants to local charities outside the specific regions in which the foundation takes a particular interest.

**APPLICATIONS:** The foundation publishes guide-lines for applicants and these should be obtained before any further approach is made.

## Batchworth Trust

**GRANT TOTAL:** £164,000 (1992)

**MAIN AREAS OF WORK:** General, Medical, Social Welfare

**ADDRESS:** Cooper Lancaster, Chartered Account-ants, 33-35 Bell Street, Reigate, Surrey RH2 7AW

**TELEPHONE:** 0737-221311

**CORRESPONDENT:** Martin Neve, Accountant.

**BENEFICIAL AREA:** National and international.

**INFORMATION:** Accounts are on file at the Charity Commission.

**GENERAL:** In 1992 the trust had assets of some £1.97 million and it gave the following grants with some relevance to this guide:

Oxfam (£20,000);

Oxfam, African Farm Projects (£1,549);

Sierra Leone (£7,500);

Save the Children Fund (£20,000);

Christian Aid (£10,000);

Prisoners Abroad, V S O, (£3,000 each);

Hungarian Student Bursary at Trinity College, Cambridge (£3,000);

Prospect Burma (£1,000).

**APPLICATIONS:** The correspondent has written

that postal applications are very rarely selected for grants and does not wish an entry in this guide to lead applicants to think they will be considered in any serious way.

## Philip Baxendale Charitable Trust

**GRANT TOTAL:** £26,300

**MAIN AREAS OF WORK:** General

**ADDRESS:** 34 Margaret Road, Penworthen, Preston PR1 9QT

**CORRESPONDENT:** Ms Olive Watson

**TRUSTEES:** Philip Baxendale, T C Campbell, Olive Watson.

**BENEFICIAL AREA:** National and international

**INFORMATION:** Accounts are on file at the Charity Commission.

**GENERAL:** The trust gives to a wide range of interests and many of its grants are recurrent. Grants relevant to this guide in 1992 were:

Intermediate Technology Development Group (£1,000 and in the 2 previous years);

Population Concern (£1,200, also in the previous year).

**APPLICATIONS:** It is understood that the trust's funds are fully committed and unsolicited applications are unlikely to receive a reply.

## The Beaverbrook Foundation

**GRANT TOTAL:** £332,000 (1993)

**ADDRESS:** 11 Old Queen Street, London SW1H 9JA

**TELEPHONE:** 071-222 7474

**CORRESPONDENT:** Michael Marshall, General Secretary

**TRUSTEES:** Timothy M Aitken (Chairman), Lady Violet Aitken (Deputy Chairman), Hon Laura Levi, Lady Susan Beaverbrook, J E A Kidd

**BENEFICIAL AREA:** UK and Canada

**INFORMATION:** Accounts are on file at the Charity Commission.

**GENERAL:** The foundation was set up with

general charitable purposes in the UK and Canada. In recent years the following grants with some relevance to the scope of this bookwere given:

In 1993 –

Raleigh International (£10,000);

British Aerial Museum, American Air Museum in Britain Campaign (£5,000 each);

Save the Children Fund (£3,000);

Women Caring Trust (£500 with £600 in 1991);

In 1992 –

Empire and Commonwealth Museum (£30,000);

Population Concern (£2,000);

Royal Air Force Benevolent Fund (£1,100);

SOS Yugoslavia (£1,000);

Battle of Britain Memorial Trust (£870);

Pestalozzi Children's Village Trust (£250);

In 1991 –

English Speaking Union (£1,000)

**APPLICATIONS:** In writing to the correspondent.

# Benfield Motors Charitable Trust

**GRANT TOTAL:** £64,000 (1991/92)

**MAIN AREAS OF WORK:** General

**ADDRESS:** Newcastle Business Park, Newcastle-upon-Tyne, NE4 7YD

**CORRESPONDENT:** Mrs L Squires

**TRUSTEES:** John Squires, Malcolm Squires, Stephen Squires

**BENEFICIAL AREA:** National and international with a particular interest in the North East.

**INFORMATION:** Accounts are on file at the Charity Commission.

**GENERAL:** In 1991/92 grants with relevance to the scope of this guide were given to:

The CROP Fund (£5,000);

Christian Aid (£3,000);

Gloria Hunniford Appeal for Bangladesh (£2,000);

Amnesty International (£100).

**APPLICATIONS:** In writing to the correspondent.

# Benham Charitable Settlement

**GRANT TOTAL:** £120,000 (1992/93)

**ADDRESS:** Hurstbourne, Portnall Drive, Virginia Water, Surrey GU25 4NR

**CORRESPONDENT:** Mrs M M Title

**TRUSTEES:** Mrs M M Title, Mrs R A Nickols, E. D. D'Alton, P. Schofield, E N Langley

**BENEFICIAL AREA:** National with a special interest in Northamptonshire

**INFORMATION:** Accounts are on file at the Charity Commission.

**GENERAL:** In 1992/93 the following grants with some relevance to the scope of this guide were given:

Save the Children Fund (£300);

V S O, Y Care International, Irish School of Ecumenics (£200 each);

Marie Stopes International, Howard League, International Christian Relief (£150 each);

Population Concern (£100).

**APPLICATIONS:** In writing to the correspondent.

# Besom Foundation

**GRANT TOTAL:** £41,400 (1992/93)

**MAIN AREAS OF WORK:** See below

**ADDRESS:** 42 Burlington Road, London W4 4BE

**TELEPHONE:** 081-742 1779

**CORRESPONDENT:** Mrs H L Odgers

**TRUSTEES:** James R B Odgers, Fiona J Ruttle, John M E Scott.

**BENEFICIAL AREA:** National and international

**INFORMATION:** Accounts are on file at the Charity Commission.

**GENERAL:** This charity which was set up in 1987 has as its slogan 'Sweep away Suffering – Fund the Future'. Recent grants relevant to this guide were given:

In 1992/93 –

Prisoners Abroad (£1,962);

WaterAid (£1,680);

Enniskillen Together (£895);

In 1991/92 –

 Medical Foundation for Care of the Victims of Torture (£1,629);
 Echo Romania (£1,517);
 Survival International (£1,000).

**APPLICATIONS:** In writing to the correspondent.

## The Blair Foundation

**GRANT TOTAL:** £289,000 (1990/91)

**MAIN AREAS OF WORK:** General and Jewish causes

**ADDRESS:** Smith and Williamson, Onslow Bridge Chambers, Bridge Street, Guildford, Surrey GU1 4RA

**CORRESPONDENT:** G J Healy

**TRUSTEES:** Robert C Thornton, Alan D Thornton, Jennifer Thornton, Graham Healy

**BENEFICIAL AREA:** National and international

**INFORMATION:** Accounts are on file at the Charity Commission.

**GENERAL:** The foundation doubled its grant expenditure in 1990/91. Most of its 51 grants were given to Jewish causes.

The following grants relevant to this guide were made:

 Centre for Holocaust Studies, Leicester University (£5,000);
 Interns for Peace (£5,000).

**APPLICATIONS:** In writing to the correspondent.

## The Bower Trust

**GRANT TOTAL:** £8,430 (1992/93)

**MAIN AREAS OF WORK:** General

**ADDRESS:** New Guild House, 45 Great Charles Street, Queensway, Birmingham B32 LX

**TELEPHONE:** 021-212 2222

**CORRESPONDENT:** Roger Harriman

**TRUSTEES:** Roger Harriman, Christina Benfield, Graham Benfield, Frederick Slater

**BENEFICIAL AREA:** National, international, Wales

**INFORMATION:** Accounts are on file at the Charity Commission.

**GENERAL:** The trust's main interest is in charities connected with the Third World and charities with activities in Wales.

 The trust has not been spending all its available funds and may well be accumulating for a special project. Grants relevant to this guide have been made in recent years:

In 1992/93 –

 Intermediate Technology Development Trust (£2,000 with grants also given in the 2 previous years);
 Save the Children, Somalia appeal, Amar appeal (£1,000 each);
 ActionAid (£1,335);

In 1991/92 –

 CARE Britain (£2,000 and in the previous year);
 UNA Trust Kurdish appeal (£1,000);

In 1990/91 –

 Disaster Emergency Committee at Crisis (£2,000);
 Oxfam Cambodia appeal (£2,000).

**EXCLUSIONS:** Generally the trustees are not interested in regional requests from charities.

**APPLICATIONS:** In writing to the correspondent.

## C T Bowring (Charities Fund) Ltd

**GRANT TOTAL:** £150,000 (1993)

**ADDRESS:** The Bowring Building, Tower Place, London EC3P 3BE

**TELEPHONE:** 071-357 3032

**CORRESPONDENT:** F R Rutter, Director

**TRUSTEES:** The Directors.

**INFORMATION:** Accounts are on file at the Charity Commission.

**GENERAL:** The fund gives to a wide range of organisations, but only to those which are registered charities. Most of its grants are small in scale and very few are £1,000 or more.

 The following grants with some relevance to the scope of this guide have been given:

In 1991-

 Ulster Defence Benevolent Fund (£500 and in the previous year);

Voluntary Service Belfast, Lagan College, British Executive Service Overseas, Pestalozzi Children's Village Fund, Save the Children (£350 each).

**APPLICATIONS:** In writing to the correspondent.

## E & H N Boyd & J E Morland Charitable Trust

**GRANT TOTAL:** £2,500 annually

**MAIN AREAS OF WORK:** General and the work of the Religious Society of Friends

**ADDRESS:** 19 Queenswood Road, Moseley, Birmingham B13 9AU.

**CORRESPONDENT:** H N Boyd

**TRUSTEES:** H N Boyd, Esther Boyd, Janet Morland.

**BENEFICIAL AREA:** National and international

**INFORMATION:** No accounts are on file at the Charity Commission since 1989.

**GENERAL:** Grants are usually from £50 to £150. Grants made in 1992/93 relevant to this guide included:

WMM Peace Education Officer, Oxfam (£100 each);

Cape Town Peace Centre, Ulster PEO, Tools for Self Reliance, ITDG, Northern Friends Peace Board (£50 each);

British Refugee Council, Survival International, UNAIS, UNICEF, Anti-Slavery Society, Prisoners Of Conscience Appeal Fund, (£30 each).

**APPLICATIONS:** Applications are usually considered quarterly.

## The British Academy

**ADDRESS:** 20-21 Cornwall Terrace, London Nil 4QP

**TELEPHONE:** 071-487 5966

**CORRESPONDENT:** Assistant Secretaries for Research Grants, Research Posts or Overseas Exchanges, as appropriate

**INFORMATION:** An information guide is published.

**GENERAL:** Founded in 1901, The British Academy is the premier national learned society devoted to the promotion of advanced scholarship in the humanities and social sciences. The purposes of the Academy's Charter are promoted in the following ways:

**Research Grants:** Since 1926 the Academy has received Government funds for the support of research, and these are complemented by a number of private funds administered by the Academy for special purposes. They take many forms; grants are made both to individual scholars ordinarily resident in the United Kingdom and of post-doctoral or equivalent status – for their private research and to learned bodies and other groups.

**Exchange Agreements:** There are now some 25 agreements with other academies and academic institutions overseas. These provide for fixed number of exchange visits of the kind that might be difficult for individual scholars to arrange without official help.

**Appointments:** The Academy administers two competitions: Readerships and Post-doctoral Fellowships.

**Research Projects:** The Academy sponsors 30 collective research undertakings of its own.

- Sponsorship of British schools and institutes overseas.

- Lectures, discussion meetings and the award of Prizes and Medals for outstanding work in various fields of the humanities.

- Publication, primarily of fundamental texts and research aids prepared under the direction of Academy committees. There are limited schemes for supporting publications.

**Postgraduate Sponsorships:** Since 1991 the Academy has had full responsibility for the scheme for the Postgraduate Studentships in the Humanities, which from 1984 it administered on behalf of the Secretary of State for Education and Science. Full details are available from The British Postgraduate Studentships Office (081-951 5188).

**APPLICATIONS:** All applicants should first obtain the Academy's guide.

# Britten-Pears Foundation

**GRANT TOTAL:** £213,000 (1991)

**MAIN AREAS OF WORK:** See below

**ADDRESS:** The Red House, Aldeburgh, Suffolk, IP15 5PZ

**TELEPHONE:** 072885-2615

**CORRESPONDENT:** The administrator

**TRUSTEES:** Marion Thorpe (Chair), Isador Caplan, Dr Donald Mitchell, Dr Colin Matthews, Noel Periton, Hugh Cobbe, Peter Carter, David Drew, Sir John Tooley, Andrew Potter

**INFORMATION:** Accounts are on file at the Charity Commission but without a schedule of grants.

**GENERAL:** The foundation has assets to some £5.7 million. Its objects are:

- to promote the knowledge of the works of Benjamin Britten and Peter Pears;

- to promote and encourage the knowledge, study, teaching and performance of music an the arts generally;

- to advance education in matters related to peace;

- to encourage charitable objects close to the interests of the founders. The correspondent has written: ' Only a relatively tiny percentage of total grants is paid annually to non-music activities and then seldom in response to new applicants; mainly to those whose activities were supported by the founders in the past'.

**APPLICATIONS:** See above.

# Broad Oak Trust

**GRANT TOTAL:** £7,600 (1991/92)

**MAIN AREAS OF WORK:** General

**ADDRESS:** The Broadhurst, Brandeston, Woodbridge, Suffolk IPI3 7AG

**CORRESPONDENT:** Lord Cunliffe

**TRUSTEES:** Lord Cunliffe, Lady Cunliffe.

**BENEFICIAL AREA:** National and international

**INFORMATION:** Accounts are on file at the Charity Commission.

**GENERAL:** The trust has a particular interest in the Third world and the environment, the elderly and the handicapped.

In 1991/92 the trust made the following grants with relevance to this guide:

British Red Cross (£2,250, 2 grants);

Oxfam (£1,000, a standing order);

Friends of the Earth (£300, a standing order);

Feed the Minds (£300, a standing order).

**EXCLUSIONS:** Anything other than UK registered charities.

**APPLICATIONS:** Funds are committed. Applications are not acknowledged.

# The Bromley Trust

**GRANT TOTAL:** Not known, about £60,000

**MAIN AREAS OF WORK:** Human rights, conservation

**ADDRESS:** Ashley Manor, King's Somborne, Stockbridge, Hampshire SO20 6RQ

**CORRESPONDENT:** Mr Keith Bromley

**TRUSTEES:** Keith Bromley; Anna Home; Nicholas Measham; Alan Humphries; Lady Ann Wood

**BENEFICIAL AREA:** National and overseas.

**INFORMATION:** Accounts are on file at the Charity Commission.

**GENERAL:** The trust in the main gives grants to charitable organisations that:

- combat violations of human rights; and help victims of torture, refugees from oppression and those who have been falsely imprisoned.

- Help those who have suffered severe bodily or mental hurt through no fault of their own, and if need be help their dependants: try in some small way to off-set man's inhumanity to man.

- Oppose the extinction of the world's fauna and flora and the destruction of the environment of wildlife and for mankind worldwide.

Annual income for 1993/94 is expected to be in the region of £95,000.

The correspondent has noted that by far the greatest part of income goes to those charities concerned with human rights. Grants are paid to their following 'mainstream' charities in quarterly payments: Medical Foundation for the Care of Victims of Torture; Anti-Slavery International; Survival International; Prisoners of Conscience Appeal Fund; Amnesty International (British

Section) Charitable Trust; Ockenden Venture; Asylum Aid; Prisoners Abroad; Writers and Scholars Educational Trust; Minority Rights Group; Justice Educational and Research Trust; Childhope UK; The International Childcare Trust; Population Concern; Greenpeace Environmental Trust; Birdlife International; Fauna and Flora Preservation Society; Wildfowl & Wetlands Trust; Aldeburgh Foundation; Manic Depression Fellowship.

**EXCLUSIONS:** Any organisation not covered by the stated objectives.

**APPLICATIONS:** In writing to the correspondent.

# T B H Brunner's Charitable Trust

**GRANT TOTAL:** £38,000 (1992/93)

**ADDRESS:** 24 Bedford Gardens, London W8

**TELEPHONE:** 071-727 6277

**CORRESPONDENT:** T. B. H. Brunner

**TRUSTEES:** T B H Brunner, Helen Y Brunner.

**BENEFICIAL AREA:** National and international

**GENERAL:** The trust has general charitable objects with a special interest in arts, particularly music. Recipients of grants in 1992/93 included:

Minority Rights Group (£1,000, also in the previous year);

CARE Britain (£1,000).

*Apply see p. 86 Vol 2 Directory Grant Making Trusts*

# Denis Buxton Trust

**GRANT TOTAL:** £6,000 (1992/93)

**MAIN AREAS OF WORK:** General

**ADDRESS:** Messrs Smith & Williamson, 1 Riding House Street, London W1A 3AS

**CORRESPONDENT:** The Secretary

**TRUSTEES:** Paul Buxton, Cecilia Dick, Richenda Buxton, Mary Buxton, Cressida Dick, Francis Yelin.

**BENEFICIAL AREA:** National and international with a particular interest in Northern Ireland, East Africa, India as well as Essex, Norfolk and East London within England.

**INFORMATION:** Accounts are on file at the Charity Commission.

**GENERAL:** The trust gives many small grants, many of which are recurrent. Those relevant to this guide in 1992/93 were:

Save the Children Fund (£525);

Oxfam (£280);

Anti-Slavery International (£125);

Prisoners Abroad (£70);

Runnymede Trust (£50);

Victim Support (£50);

ITDG (£50);

BELTIE, Belfast (£50);

Voluntary Service, Belfast (£35);

Minority Rights Group (£20).

**EXCLUSIONS:** No grants to individuals or to general appeals.

**APPLICATIONS:** In writing to the correspondent. An acknowledgement cannot be expected if the application is unsolicited.

# C M B Charities Ltd

**GRANT TOTAL:** £94,000 (1990)

**ADDRESS:** Metal Box plc, Queen's House, Forbury Road, Reading RG1 3JH

**TELEPHONE:** 0734-581 177

**CORRESPONDENT:** Miss P Axtell, Secretary

**TRUSTEES:** G. J. Armstrong (Chairman), E. Cameron, F. Lyttle, G. C. Zanbuni.

**INFORMATION:** Accounts are on file at the Charity Commission but with no schedule of grants since 1982.

**GENERAL:** The trust supports national charities for general charitable purposes. The most recent accounts filed at the Charity Commission were for 1982 and showed the following grants which have relevance to the scope of this book:

European Educational Research Trust (£1,000);

Quaker Peace and Service (£1,000).

**APPLICATIONS:** The Council of Management meets quarterly.

# Barrow & Geraldine S Cadbury Trust (BGSC Trust)

# Barrow Cadbury Fund Ltd (BC Fund Ltd)

**GRANT TOTAL:** £1,349,000 for BGSC Trust; £328,000 for BC Fund Ltd (1992/93)

**ADDRESS:** 2 College Walk, Selly Oak, Birmingham B29 6LQ

**TELEPHONE:** 021-472 0417

**CORRESPONDENT:** Eric Adams, Secretary.

**TRUSTEES:** Charles Cadbury (Chairman), Catherine R Hickinbotham, (Vice Chairman), Geraldine M Cadbury, Rachel E Cadbury, Edward P Cadbury, Philippa H Southall, Roger P Hickinbotham, Anna C Southall, Richard G Cadbury, Erica R Cadbury, Ruth M Cadbury, James E Cadbury (all are also directors of the fund).

**BENEFICIAL AREA:** Unrestricted

**INFORMATION:** A detailed annual report with statistical analysis and listings of grants is available. A basic information leaflet outlines the trusts and gives guidelines for applicants.

**GENERAL:** The trustees seek to support projects of an innovatory nature which would have particular difficulty in obtaining funds from public appeals. Grants may be for capital or revenue purposes. The Barrow Cadbury Fund Ltd is a registered company and is not restricted to grant-making for charitable purposes. Grants are made in the same fields as the trust if there are grounds for assuming that the activity would not be deemed 'charitable' in the legal sense.

It should also be noted that the Paul S Cadbury Trust which operates under the same administration no longer supports work in Northern Ireland.

The BGSC trust has general charitable objects. Whilst details of its policy and practice are given below readers should note that following changes in chairmanship and staffing all trust and fund policies are currently under review and present practices may **not be in operation from 1995.**

In 1992/93 grants were made in the following categories:

- Civil Rights and Social Justice – fostering projects which bear on rights and responsibilities which go beyond equal opportunities.
- Disability – projects promoting self-advocacy, independent living and improved employment for those with learning difficulties.
- Ethnicity – projects contributing to racial justice and equal opportunities in the public, private and voluntary sectors.
- Gender – projects addressing gender inequality and women's rights in the public, private and voluntary sectors.
- Penal Affairs – promotion of research, new thinking and good practice in the field.
- Reconciliation – backing for projects which foster reconciliation and which are compatible with trustees' Quaker approach to issues of peace and war, including support for organisations promoting mutual understanding and justice in Northern Ireland.

A selection of grants made in 1992/93 which are relevant to the scope of this guide is given below (the full list would be too extensive).

**Under Peace and international Relations**

*International – BGSC Trust*

Centre for Inter-Group Studies, Cape Town University (£10,000);

Quaker Council for European Affairs (£10,000);

*National – BGSC Trust*

Department of Peace Studies, Bradford University (£28,500);

Nuclear Non-Proliferation Project, Southampton University (£20,000);

European Dialogue (£14,000);

All-Party Parliamentary Group on Overseas Development (£11,000);

Working Party on Chemical and Biological Weapons (£10,250);

British American Security Information Council, Verification Technology Information Centre (£10,000 each);

Oxford Research Group (£7,500);

*BCF Ltd*

Saferworld (£10,000).

**Under Equal Opportunities**

*BGSC Trust*

Parliamentary All Party Group on Race and Community (£10,000);

Midlands Refugee Council (£10,000).

**Under Civil Rights and Social Justice**

*BGCS Trust*

Joint Council on the Welfare of Immigrants, West Midlands (£23,500);

Joint Council on the Welfare of Immigrants, London (£17,000);

Refugee Council (£16,000);

Refugee Studies Programme (£1,500 2 grants);

*BCF Ltd*

Human Rights Sub-Committee of European Parliament (£10,000);

**Under Northern Ireland**

Independent Commission of Inquiry for Northern Ireland (£50,000);

Committee on Administration of Justice, Belfast (£20,000);

Community of the Peace People, Belfast (£7,000);

Ulster Quaker Service Committee (£7,500);

Ulster Quaker Peace Education Project (£4,000);

**APPLICATIONS:** An information leaflet is available. There are no deadlines for relevant applications and no application form. The trustees like to receive copies of minutes, accounts, budgets and working papers which indicate the thinking which has gone into making the application. Unsolicited applications which do not relate to the trust's published criteria will not normally be acknowledged.

# Christopher Cadbury Charitable Trust

**GRANT TOTAL:** £138,700 (1992/93)

**ADDRESS:** New Guild House, 45 Great Charles Street, Queensway, Birmingham B3 2LX

**TELEPHONE:** 021-212 2222

**CORRESPONDENT:** Roger Harriman

**TRUSTEES:** J C Cadbury, Dr C J Cadbury, R V J Cadbury, Mrs V B Reekie, Mrs C V E Benfield, Dr T N D Peet, P H G Cadbury

**BENEFICIAL AREA:** National with a particular interest in the Midlands.

**INFORMATION:** Accounts are on file at the Charity Commission

**GENERAL:** In 1992/93 the trust gave the following grants with relevance to the scope of this guide:

Intermediate Technology Development Group (£2,000 with £1,250 in the previous year);

International Planned Parenthood Federation (£2,000);

Survival International (£1,000);

British Red Cross Bosnia (£400);

Anti-Slavery Society, Minority Rights Group (£250 each with grants also given in the previous year);

UNICEF (£150).

**APPLICATIONS:** It is understood that this trust has committed its funds in advance so that unsolicited applications are unlikely to be considered.

# Edward Cadbury Charitable Trust Incorporated

**GRANT TOTAL:** £509,500 (1992/93)

**ADDRESS:** (see also the Edward and Dorothy Cadbury Trust (1928)), Elmfield, College Walk, Birmingham B29 6LE

**TELEPHONE:** 021-472 1838

**CORRESPONDENT:** Mrs M. Walton, The Secretary.

**TRUSTEES:** C E Gillett, C S Littleboy, C R Gillett, A S Littleboy, N R Cadbury

**BENEFICIAL AREA:** National and international with a particular interest in the West Midlands.

**INFORMATION:** Accounts are on file at the Charity Commission.

**GENERAL:** The trust's gives a statement of its aims with its accounts: ' to continue to support the interest of the founders and the particular charitable interests of the trustees. The voluntary sector in the West Midlands Christian Mission, the ecumenical movement and interfaith relations, the oppressed and disadvantaged in this country and the developing world, education, arts and the environment. The trustees prefer to support small and new organisations and projects rather than large national organisations'. Grants are mainly between £250 and £2,500. Those with relevance to the scope of this guide were:

In 1992/93-

Oxfam (£25,000);

Population Concern (£3,000 and in the previous year);

Africa Now (£5,000 and in the previous year);

World University Service (£5,000 and in the 2 previous years);

Runnymede Trust (£750);

Youth Action, Northern Ireland (£2,500);

In 1991/92 –

Church Relief International (£1,200);

Skillshare Africa, Pestalozzi Children's Village Trust (£1,000 each);

ARMS, VSO, Ranfurly Library (£500 each);

Relief Society of Tigray (£150);

Amnesty International, CND (£100 each);

In 1990/91 –

Society of Friends (£38,190);

Cambodia Trust (£5,000);

Medical Foundation for the Care of Victims of Torture, UNA Trust (£1,000 each).

**EXCLUSIONS:** No grants to individuals.

**APPLICATIONS:** In writing to the correspondent.

# Edward and Dorothy Cadbury Trust (1928)

**GRANT TOTAL:** £94,000 (1992/93)

**MAIN AREAS OF WORK:** General

**ADDRESS:** (see also the Edward Cadbury Charitable Trust), Elmfield, College Walk, Selly Oak, Birmingham B29 6LE

**TELEPHONE:** 021-4721838

**CORRESPONDENT:** Mrs M Walton, The Secretary.

**TRUSTEES:** Mrs P A Gillett, Dr C M Elliott, Mrs P S Ward.

**BENEFICIAL AREA:** National and international with a particular interest in the West Midlands.

**INFORMATION:** Accounts are on file at the Charity Commission.

**GENERAL:** The trust gives a large number of small grants of less than £1,000. A review of the trust's

accounts showed the following grants with some relevance to the scope of this guide:

In 1992/93 –

Oxfam (£500);

Ethiopiaid (£250);

Marie Stopes International (£150 and in the previous year);

Canon Collins Educational Trust for Southern Africa (£100 and in the previous year);

Survival International (£200 with £100 in the previous year);

Northern Friends Peace Board (£100);

In 1991/92 –

Society of Friends (£27,000);

Selly Oak Colleges (£465);

Project Orbis International (£300);

Africa Now (£250);

West Midlands Quaker Peace Education Project, Save the Children Fund (£200);

**APPLICATIONS:** In writing to the correspondent.

# G W Cadbury Charitable Trust

**GRANT TOTAL:** £78,600 (1992/93)

**MAIN AREAS OF WORK:** General with a particular interest in population control and conservation.

**ADDRESS:** New Guild House, 45 Great Charles Street, Queensway, Birmingham B3 2LX

**TELEPHONE:** 021-212 2222

**CORRESPONDENT:** Roger Harriman

**TRUSTEES:** G W Cadbury, Mrs C A Wood Woodroffe, Mrs L E Boal, Miss J C Boal, P C Boal, Miss J L Woodroffe, N B Woodroffe.

**BENEFICIAL AREA:** National and international with a particular interest in Canada.

**INFORMATION:** Accounts are on file at the Charity Commission.

**GENERAL:** In 1992/93 the trust gave the following grants with relevance to this guide:

Amnesty International (£5,000);

International Planned Parenthood Federation (£2,000);

Intermediate Technology Development Group, Marie Stopes International (£200 each);

CARE (£50).

**APPLICATIONS:** Unsolicited applications are unlikely to be accepted as trustees usually respond to their own continuing interests including Canada and the United States of America.

# Henry T & Lucy B Cadbury Charitable Trust

**GRANT TOTAL:** £16,000 (1990)

**MAIN AREAS OF WORK:** General

**ADDRESS:** Pont d'Ouche, 21360 – Thorey sur Ouche, France.

**TELEPHONE:** 80 33 03 37

**CORRESPONDENT:** Miss B S Cadbury

**TRUSTEES:** Mrs E M Hambly, M B Gillett, C Gillett, K M Charity, E Rawlins, R Charity, B S Cadbury.

**BENEFICIAL AREA:** National and international.

**INFORMATION:** Accounts are on file at the Charity Commission up to 1990.

**GENERAL:** The trust has general charitable objects. In 1990 the following grants with relevance to this guide were given:

Quaker Peace and Service, Columbia (£2,000);

Oxfam Vietnam (£500);

Oxfam Gulf Emergency Appeal (£500);

Oxfam Tigray (£500);

Tools for Self Reliance (£500);

Intermediate Technology Development Group (£500);

British Red Cross, Romania (£200);

British Red Cross, Ethiopia (£500);

**APPLICATIONS:** The trust's income is committed each year and unsolicited applications should not expect to receive a reply.

# J & L A Cadbury Charitable Trust

**GRANT TOTAL:** £17,500 (1991/92)

**MAIN AREAS OF WORK:** General

**ADDRESS:** 2 College Walk, Birmingham B29 6LE

**TELEPHONE:** 021-4721464

**CORRESPONDENT:** Mrs Sylvia Gale, The Secretary

*no longer in existence*

**TRUSTEES:** Mrs L A Cadbury, Mrs S M Gale, W J B Taylor.

**BENEFICIAL AREA:** National with a particular interest in the West Midlands.

**GENERAL:** The trust had assets of £578,000 in 1991/92. Its grantmaking had dropped from £25,000 in 1990/91 to £17,500 in 1991/92. Its practice is to make many small grants. Those relevant to this guide in 1991/92 were:

Ulster Quaker Service Committee, Woodbrooke College (£200 each);

Centre for Black and White Christian Partnership, Belfast Charitable Trust for Integrated Education, Youth Action for Northern Ireland, Population Concern (£100 each).

**APPLICATIONS:** In writing to the correspondent.

# Richard Cadbury Charitable Trust

**GRANT TOTAL:** £66,660 (1991/92)

**MAIN AREAS OF WORK:** General

**ADDRESS:** 6 Middleborough Road, Coventry CV1 4DE

**CORRESPONDENT:** Mrs M M Slora.

**TRUSTEES:** R B Cadbury, Mrs M M Slora.

**BENEFICIAL AREA:** National and international.

**INFORMATION:** The accounts are on file at the Charity Commission.

**GENERAL:** In 1991/92 the trust made the following grants with relevance to this guide:

Christian Aid, Oxfam, Greenpeace, Quaker Peace and Service, Save the Children Fund, Woodbrooke College, Voluntary Service Overseas (£1,000 each);

Intermediate Technology Development Group, LEAP (£500 each);

Population Concern (£300);

Survival International (£250);

Marie Stopes International, Trans World Radio (£200 each).

**EXCLUSIONS:** Individuals and students.

**APPLICATIONS:** Applications should be sent by February, June and October each year.

# William Adlington Cadbury Charitable Trust

**GRANT TOTAL:** £314,000

**MAIN AREAS OF WORK:** General

**ADDRESS:** 2 College Walk, Birmingham B29 6LE

**TELEPHONE:** 021-472 1464

**CORRESPONDENT:** Christine Stober, Secretary.

**TRUSTEES:** Mrs Hannah Henderson Taylor, Alan Cadbury, Brandon Cadbury, Mrs Sarah Stafford, W James Beech Taylor, Rupert A. Cadbury, Mrs C Margaret Salmon, Mrs Katherine M Hampton.

**BENEFICIAL AREA:** National and international with a particular interest in the West Midlands.

**INFORMATION:** Accounts are on file at the Charity Commission.

**GENERAL:** The trust which has assets of some £3.9 million, has general charitable objects and gives support nationally. It has a particular interest in the West Midlands. The trust has now categorised its grants under the following headings:

- Society of Friends;
- Churches and Christian Projects;
- Health and Social Welfare;
- Education & Training;
- Environment and Conservation;
- Preservation;
- The Arts;
- Penal Affairs;
- Northern Ireland;
- Overseas Projects.

The trust's schedules of grants showed the following allocations with relevance to the scope of this guide:

In 1992/93-

Quaker Peace and Service Moscow Appeal (£2,000);

Quaker Peace and Service (£5,000 also in the previous year);

West Midlands Quaker Peace Education Project (£1,000);

The Extern Organisation, Ormeau Centre, NI (£2,000);

International Voluntary Service, NI (£500);

Cannon Collins Educational Trust for Southern Africa (£1,000);

Charity Know How (£5,000);

Save the Children Fund £15,000);

Voluntary Service Overseas (£4,000 with £200 in the previous year);

Oxfam (£20,000).

In 1991/92 –

Save the Children Fund, Oxfam (£40,000 each);

Medical Foundation for the Victims of Torture (£5,000);

Quaker Peace Studies Trust (£2,000);

Marie Stopes International, Prisoners of Conscience Appeal Fund, Cambodia Trust, WaterAid (£1,000 each);

Laois Community Games, Northern Ireland (£800);

Howard League (£500);

United Nations Association (£300).

**APPLICATIONS:** In writing to the correspondent.

# Vera and Maxwell Caplin Charitable Trust

**GRANT TOTAL:** Not known

**ADDRESS:** 6 Post Office Avenue, Southport, Merseyside PR9 OUS.

**CORRESPONDENT:** A M Caplin.

**TRUSTEES:** A M Caplin, Mrs V D Caplin, E B Caplin, D K Malies.

**GENERAL:** The trust was established in 1976 with the following objects: 'to advance education in the art or science of government and other branches of political and economic science and in particular the study of relationship to one another of the United Kingdom of Great Britain and Ireland and the other countries of the British Commonwealth'.

Since its establishment no accounts have been lodged with the Charity Commission.

# Catholic Fund for Overseas Development (CAFOD)

**GRANT TOTAL:** £208,000 for development education funding within the UK.

**ADDRESS:** Romero Close, Stockwell Road, London SW9 9TY

**TELEPHONE:** 071-733 7900; Fax: 071-274 9630

**CORRESPONDENT:** Brian Davies, Head of Education Department; Denise Carter

**BENEFICIAL AREA:** England and Wales

**INFORMATION:** Education Fund Guidelines leaflet.

**GENERAL:** CAFOD's Development Education programme makes support in four areas:

- *Justice and Peace Co-funding* to a number of dioceses for J&P workers. Such funding is a priority for CAFOD and applications from new Commissions are always welcomed as long as parallel funding is being provided from within the diocese.

Eight grants, ranging between £8,500 and £300, in 1992/93 included:

National Liaison Committee, for support work for the Commissions (£8,500);

Southwark J&P Commission, for f/t worker (£5,250);

- *Programme Funding* for a number of national programmes – One World Week, Development Education Association, Action for World Development Fund, Volunteer Missionary Movement, Young Christian Workers. Many of these programmes are also funded by Christian Aid, Oxfam and Save the Children Fund and these agencies work closely with CAFOD on education funding. Projects in this category have programmes sometimes of two or three years' duration. Funding for second and subsequent years is subject to satisfactory reporting on the previous year's work.

Seven grants given in 1992/93 ranging between £100 and £7,000 included:

Tourism Concern, education work in relation to Third World tourism (£5,500);

MA Curriculum Project, for a 2 year project in Environment and Development Education at South Bank University (£4,050);

Intermediate Technology for a 3 year education programme related to the National Curriculum (£7,000).

- *Project Funding* to a wide range of one-off projects often operating at a local level. Priority is given to education in CAFOD's own Catholic constituency and funding is not normally available for local Development Education Centres.

Sixteen grants ranging between £200 and £5,500 in 1992/93 included:

IIED Education for Sustainability Project, for a project following up the Rio Earth Summit (£5,500);

National Curriculum Monitoring Project, an inter-agency project (£3,000);

Alternative for India Development, development education programme by Indians among their community in Birmingham (£3,000);

JABBOK, towards production/running costs of new drama on racism/refugees (£2,000);

Oxford DE Exchange, to develop a North/South DE exchange programme organised by Oxford DEC.

- *Media projects*, for which part of the annual budget is set aside. These projects are administered by the Head of the Communications Department.

Two grants were given in 1992/93:

Old Street Films, for film on Guatemala for Channel 4 (£1,000);

International Broadcasting Trust, film on Africa (£3,000).

As the agency of the Catholic Church in England and Wales, CAFOD gives priority to awareness raising within the Catholic community and to programmes and projects which set out to influence sectors of the community not reached by other efforts. More specifically, preference is given to programmes and projects which:

- Have clearly defined objectives and can be accomplished within a specified time limit;

- Have a well thought-out strategy and a tried and tested methodology;

- Attempt to break new ground or reach a new public;

- Involve 'multipliers' – educators, animators and those who will in turn influence others.

CAFOD expects an annual written report on completion and that evaluation procedures will be built into the programme.

**EXCLUSIONS:** Programmes in the formal sector for which there is official funding; buildings; programmes normally funded from commercial sources; projects outside England and Wales.

**APPLICATIONS:** An application form is provided. Applications must be submitted at the beginning of January and the beginning of July to be able to reach Education Funding Committee meetings in February and July each year. Details of information expected from applicants is provided in the Education Fund Guidelines leaflet.

# Charity Know How

**GRANT TOTAL:** £945,400 (Nov 1991/Mar 1993)

**MAIN AREAS OF WORK:** Support to the voluntary sector in Eastern Europe

**ADDRESS:** 114/118 Southampton Row, London WC1 5AA

**TELEPHONE:** 071-831 7798; Fax 071-831 0134

**CORRESPONDENT:** Ian Bell, Director.

**TRUSTEES:** Trustees of the Charities Aid Foundation; Grants Committee: Robert Hazell, the Nuffield Foundation (Chairman), and representatives from the fund contributors.

**INFORMATION:** Detailed annual report and guidelines for applicants available from the trust.

**GENERAL:** Charity Know How (CKH) was established in 1991, the joint initiative of a group of British trusts and the Joint Assistance Unit of the Foreign and Commonwealth Office which administers the main Know How Fund (see separate entry). Its purpose is to provide assistance and support to the re-emerging voluntary sector in the countries of Central and Eastern Europe, the Baltic states, the Republics of the former Soviet Union, Albania and Slovenia. It supports initiatives, whether local or by UK based charities.

The programme is administered by the Charities Aid Foundation. A complementary service, East-West Link, was launched in November 1992 to provide assistance to organisations and individuals seeking suitable counterparts. Grants of up to £500 towards travel costs of an introductory visit are available.

Grants are provided for the following:

- advice on the legal, fiscal and regulatory framework necessary for voluntary organisations to operate effectively;
- advice and support for co-ordinating bodies seeking to promote and represent the voluntary sector;
- study visits between voluntary organisations in the UK and their counterparts in the region;
- training programmes for voluntary sector personnel, including seminars, workshops and, occasionally, conferences;
- translation of training/information materials.

In 1993/94 CKH offered special consideration to organisations and projects seeking to address problems in social policy, ethnic tension and the rights of minorities and disadvantaged social groups.

Funding is available for travel and subsistence and for the administration costs incurred by the UK partner. At the request of one of the participating trusts, a proportion of the fund will be used for the support of projects involving young people under the age of 26. Most grants are small and part-funding is considered, Special consideration will be given to applications which contain an element of co-funding in money or in kind from either the receiving organisation or its UK partner. Follow-up applications will be welcomed subject to satisfactory reports on progress. Grants are relatively small and the majority are offered part funding only. The annual report for 1992/93 notes that the increasing number of grants below £1,000, by Chairman's Action, contribute to an average of less than £3,000 in the financial year.

Provision for a small number of larger grants up to £25,000 was introduced in September 1992. These Special Project Grants are for model projects which can be adapted of replicated by others and whose main purpose is to develop the voluntary sector as a whole or in a particular field. Capital projects are not eligible and long term core funding is excluded. These grants are made at only two meetings each year, in March and September.

A limited number of small grants, known as Exploratory Grants, up to £500 can also be made to pay the travel costs of a visit to facilitate a link where all the background work has been done and personal contact is required to complete preparations.

Grants given between November 1991 and March 1993 with particular relevance to this guide were:

**Bulgaria**

Women's Democratic Union of Bulgaria/ Mothers for Peace, for costs of a Bulgarian delegate (£200);

**Hungary**

Interjustice Hungary and others/ Interights UK, for representatives to attend a London meeting on migration and refugee issues as they relate to the European Convention of Human Rights and EC law. (£965);

Martin Luther King, Hungary/ Interights, for briefing papers legal advice and nominal legal fees to develop the foundation's work (£6,550);

Fides/Department of Peace Studies, University of Bradford, attendance at a conference (£382);

**Romania**

Church leaders in Romania/Community for Reconciliation, conflict resolution training by UK team (£1,800);

**Russia**

Centre for Applied Conflictology, Moscow/ Quaker Peace and Service and Mediation, for visit to mediation centres in England (£1,700);

Institute of Psychology, Moscow/Responding to Conflict Programme, for a 3 month training course in Birmingham (£1,000);

Russian Lawyers Committee in Defence of Human Rights/ Interights, for lectures in Moscow (£2,000);

**Ukraine**

Ukraine Peace Council/Responding to Conflict Programme, for Director of UPC to attend 3 month conflict course (£2,000).

**EXCLUSIONS:** Grants will not normally be available for the following:

- the teaching of English as a foreign language;
- the administration of schemes for UK volunteers (eg working holidays);
- activities considered by the Committee to be for personal rather than institutional development;
- core funding in the region or the UK;
- attendance at conferences where the benefit to institutional development is not clearly demonstrated;
- the provision of offices or equipment (including fax machines and other communications equipment);
- full professional fees for any consultancy.

**APPLICATIONS:** On a form available from the correspondent. The Grants Committee meets five times a year. Closing dates for 1993/94 were: 8th February, 10th May, 16 August, 5th November, 4th February. Potential applicants should first read the Guidelines for Applicants available from the fund.

# Charity Projects

**GRANT TOTAL:** Africa grants: over £8 million; UK grants: £6.4 million (1992)

**ADDRESS:** 1st Floor, 74 New Oxford Street, London WC1A 1EF

**TELEPHONE:** 071-436 1122; Fax: 071-436 1541

**CORRESPONDENT:** Richard Graham, Africa Grants Officer; Tania Bronstein, UK Grants Officer

**BENEFICIAL AREA:** Africa and the UK

**INFORMATION:** Annual report; guidelines for applicants.

**GENERAL:** Charity Projects gives grants to organisations working in Africa and the UK.

**Africa Grants:** The following is taken from the Africa grant-making criteria for 1993/94. Grants will only be made to UK registered charities with development as a primary aim. Proposals are particularly welcomed for:

- work that is innovative and may therefore involve a higher level of risk;
- work that is unattractive to other donors on the grounds of political considerations or the

sensitivity of the projects' activities, and where Charity Projects' funds can be used to access other donors' funds;

- programmes of small related projects based around a common theme (e.g. pastoralist land rights) rather than for one specific project. The programme need not be limited to one country;
- projects that can demonstrate their commitment to equal opportunities throughout their work.

All proposals are assessed against the following criteria as to whether they would be:

- promoting African organisations;
- responding to locally-felt needs;
- thinking in the long-term;
- targeting disadvantaged groups;
- measuring impact and learning from experience.

Grants are given throughout Africa including Southern Africa. In 1992 two grants totalling £170,000 were made in Southern Africa.

**UK Grants:** Four funding programmes operate: a grants programme for organisations working with older people, and the other three programmes for organisations working with young people specifically in the fields of homelessness, alcohol and drug abuse, and disability.

The following information has been supplied by the UK Grants Officer following a request for information about Charity Projects' support for refugees:

'We do not have a programme specifically targeted at refugee groups. However we recognise that refugees in this country experience a number of problems and that community organisations helping them have great difficulties gaining financial support ... We currently fund a number of refugee organisations and most have received funding from the homelessness programme. (Homelessness and housing problems being a major problem experienced by the communities here in the UK.)'

Because of the large number of young refugees from the Horn of Africa, Charity Projects commissioned in 1993 an Eritrean consultant to examine their particular problems and look at ways in which Charity Projects could help refugee organisations in a pro-active way. Charity Projects is committed to helping this group and funds have

been earmarked to implement whichever proposals are decided upon.

**APPLICATIONS:** The grant-making guidelines for the Africa Grants Programme should be obtained prior to making an application. This includes their grant-making timetable. Similar information should be obtained about guidelines, criteria and deadlines from the UK Grants Programme.

# The Charterhouse Charitable Trust

**GRANT TOTAL:** £98,000 (1992/93)

**ADDRESS:** 1 Paternoster Row, St Paul's, London EC4M 7DH

**CORRESPONDENT:** The Secretary

**TRUSTEES:** M V Blank, E G Cox

**BENEFICIAL AREA:** National with a particular interest in London.

**INFORMATION:** Accounts are on file at the Charity Commission.

**GENERAL:** In 1992/93 the following grants with some relevance to the scope of this guide were given:

Runnymede Trust, Friends of the Earth (£1,000 each);

Cooperation Ireland, Airey Neave Trust (£500 each).

**APPLICATIONS:** In writing to the correspondent.

# The Chase Charity

**GRANT TOTAL:** £260,000 (1992/93)

**ADDRESS:** 2 The Court, High Street, Harwell, Didcot, Oxfordshire OX11 0EY

**TELEPHONE:** 0235-820044

**CORRESPONDENT:** Peter Kilgarriff

**TRUSTEES:** A Ramsay Hack, G Halcrow, R Mills, Mrs R A Moore, Mrs C Flanders, K Grant, A Stannard.

**BENEFICIAL AREA:** National with a particular interest in rural areas

**INFORMATION:** Accounts are on file at the Charity Commission.

**GENERAL:** The charity gives to social welfare, the arts, heritage and education. Some grants have been made in Northern Ireland in recent years: In 1990/91 –

North Down and Ards Home-Start (£3,000);

Age Concern, Northern Ireland (£2,750);

Praxis Mental Health (£2,500);

In 1991/92 –

Mullaghdun Community Association (£3,000);

In 1992/93 –

Derrygannon Community Association (£2,500).

**APPLICATIONS:** Preliminary enquiries may be made by telephone or short letter. Applications can be made at any time and must include the latest available accounts and a full information about the project.

## Cheney Peace Settlement

**GRANT TOTAL:** About £10,000 annually

**ADDRESS:** Aylesmore Farm, Shipton-on-Stour, Warwickshire

**TELEPHONE:** 0608685 279

**CORRESPONDENT:** Howard Cheney

**TRUSTEES:** Harry Mister, Geoffrey Tattersall. Harry Mister, Trustee, 3 Upperhead Row, Huddersfield, Yorkshire HD1 2JL (0484-23622).

**GENERAL:** The settlement was started by Howard Cheney in 1976. It is not a registered charity. Support is given to a broad range of groups in the vanguard of work to improve human relationships and conditions between themselves and their environment.

**APPLICATIONS:** The settlor did not want an entry in this guide. The funds are small and already committed.

## The Chownes Foundation

**GRANT TOTAL:** £115,000 (1989/90)

**MAIN AREAS OF WORK:** General

**ADDRESS:** 94 Church Road, Hove, East Sussex BN3 2EF

**CORRESPONDENT:** Mr R A Brooker

**TRUSTEES:** Charles Stonor, Joan Stonor, the Abbot of Worth.

**INFORMATION:** Accounts are on file at the Charity Commission but without a grants list.

**GENERAL:** The foundation has wide interests and its objects include making grants to social non-political causes with explicit reference to Amnesty International.

## Christian Action

**GRANT TOTAL:** £86,000

**MAIN AREAS OF WORK:** Christianity in all its aspects

**ADDRESS:** St Anselm's Church Hall, Kennington Cross, Kennington Road, London SE11 5DU

**TELEPHONE:** 071-735 2372

**CORRESPONDENT:** Rev Canon Eric James, Honorary Director; Mrs Jane Spurr, Secretary

**TRUSTEES:** Members of Council: Very Rev Trevor Beeson (Chairman), Rev J Quill (Treasurer).

**BENEFICIAL AREA:** National

**INFORMATION:** Accounts are on file at the Charity Commission but without a schedule of grants. A quarterly journal of information about the work of the organisation is available.

**GENERAL:** Christian Action made grants of £86,000 in 1992. This total divided into:

General £32,000;

Contracted £54,000.

It is understood that all the funds are committed for the foreseeable future.

**APPLICATIONS:** Applications should be submitted to the Honorary Director.

## Christian Aid

*[handwritten annotation: Does not fund education except through churches + does not fund my kind of work in UK, diminishing funding in peace + justice]*

**GRANT TOTAL:** About £650,000 a year for development education

**ADDRESS:** PO Box 100, London SE1 7RT or Interchurch House, 35 Lower Marsh, London SE1 7RT

**TELEPHONE:** 071-620 4444 x 2345

**CORRESPONDENT:** Barbara Vellacott, Head of Education Sector (for development education grants)

**INFORMATION:** Information on criteria for development education assistance is available.

**GENERAL:** Christian Aid supports development education work. Its funding is arranged via its Development Education Grants Committees: a committee comprising board members and other advisers makes decisions on national grants. Regional Development Education Committees (five in England and one each in Scotland, Wales and Ireland) encourage imaginative local initiatives.

UK/Ireland grants for development education awarded between March and November 1993 included the following:

Action for World Development Fund (£23,220);

One World Week (£18,390);

Development Education Association (£18,000);

International Broadcasting Trust (£17,289);

Trade Union International Research and Education Group (£13,520);

Farmer Third World Network (£6,150);

World Studies 8-13 Project (£5,535);

Ecumenical Committee for Corporate Responsibility (£5,288);

Third World First (£2,560);

Hull Development Education Centre (£820);

Puppetworks (£300).

**APPLICATIONS:** The National Committee meets in March, June/July and November. Applications need to be received eight weeks in advance. The Regional Committees meet at different times and information on these should be found out as necessary. There is no application form, but detailed guidelines are prepared.

# The City Parochial Foundation

**GRANT TOTAL:** £5,744,000 (1992)

**MAIN AREAS OF WORK:** Social welfare in London

**ADDRESS:** 6 Middle Street, London EC1A 7PH

**TELEPHONE:** 071-606 6145

**CORRESPONDENT:** Timothy Cook, Clerk

**TRUSTEES:** 21 trustees nominated by 10 bodies including the Crown, the University of London, the Church Commissioners, the Bishopsgate Foundation and the Cripplegate Foundation.

**BENEFICIAL AREA:** The Metropolitan Police District of London and the City of London.

**INFORMATION:** Leaflet on policies and procedures, annual report, and the review of policy for the years 1992-96 available from the foundation. Full accounts on file at the Charity Commission.

**GENERAL:** The foundation undertook a major review of its grant-making policies in 1991. It has developed its approach to Strategic Funding for issues best looked at across London. As part of this programme applications are invited to focus on:

• Training opportunities;

• Implementation of equal opportunities policies;

• Support structures for refugee communities;

• Proposals which help groups of voluntary organisations to develop a more coherent strategy;

• Proposals which address London-wide issues concerning the poor.

In 1992 the foundation made the following grants of relevance to this guide:

Training and Support Unit for Refugee Organisations (£250,000);

The Refugee Council, to appoint community development Worker/Financial Adviser (£45,000);

London Hazards Centre, for p/t post for outreach worker (£26,000);

Bromley Refugee Network (£20,500);

Tamil Refugee Action Group, for a women's welfare worker (£20,000);

City and East London College, towards the travel costs of refugee and asylum-seeking students (£20,000);

Minority Rights Group, for publishing reprinting costs (£3,000).

**EXCLUSIONS:** These are set out in the published procedures of the foundation.

**APPLICATIONS:** There are no application forms. Before submitting a detailed application it is advisable to discuss the proposed application with one of the staff. All applicants should obtain a copy of the application procedures set out by the foundation. (No application should exceed 3 sides of A4 plus necessary appendices. Most applications must be finalised by: 31st January for April; 30th April for July meeting; 15th August for October meeting; 15th October for January meeting.

# J Anthony Clark Charitable Foundation

**GRANT TOTAL:** £423,000 (1991/92)

**MAIN AREAS OF WORK:** See below

**ADDRESS:** Peat Marwick, 15 Pembroke Road, Bristol, Avon BS8 3BG

**CORRESPONDENT:** A E Hill

**TRUSTEES:** T A Clark, Caroline Pym, D M Parkes, L P Clark, J C Clark.

**BENEFICIAL AREA:** National

**INFORMATION:** Accounts are on file at the Charity Commission.

**GENERAL:** The trust states that its charitable objects are 'oriented towards social change in areas of health, education, peace, preservation of the earth and the arts. Trustees are particularly interested in supporting the work of small, new and innovative projects.'

In 1991/92 it made the following grants with relevance to this guide:

Oxfam (£20,000, with £81,000 given in the previous year);

Survival International (£8,000, with £5,000 given in the previous year);

ActionAid 2000 (£3,000);

Prisoners Abroad (£1,000 with £5,000 given in the previous year);

Quaker Peace and Service (£2,000);

In 1990/91 the following grants were given:

Better Belfast, British Refugee Council (£3,000 each);

Trust for Research and Education in Arms Trade (£1,000).

**APPLICATIONS:** Applications can made at any time but the trustees do not reply to unsolicited approaches unless they are able to make a grant or wish for further information.

# The Stephen Clark Charitable Settlement 1965

**GRANT TOTAL:** £6,000 (1991)

**ADDRESS:** 112 Rodenhurst Road, London SW4 8AP

**CORRESPONDENT:** Harriet Hall

**TRUSTEES:** Harriet Hall, Henry G Clark

**BENEFICIAL AREA:** National and international

**INFORMATION:** Accounts are on file at the Charity Commission.

**GENERAL:** In 1991 the settlement gave £6,000 in grants and the year before its total grant-making had been more than double this amount at £16,400. Grants with relevance to the scope of this guide were:

In 1991 –

Oxfam (£2,000 with £2,400 in the previous year);

Nicaragua Health Fund (£200 also in the previous year);

Refugee Council (£200; Iran Aid (£100);

In 1990 –

Survival International, Friends of the Earth (£1,000 each);

Amnesty International (£500 and in the previous year);

Civil Liberties Trust (£200 with £500 in the previous year);

Medical Foundation for the Care of Victims of Torture, Disasters Emergency Committee (£200 each).

**APPLICATIONS:** In writing to the correspondent.

# Roger & Sarah Bancroft Clark Charitable Trust

**GRANT TOTAL:** £72,000 (1991)

**MAIN AREAS OF WORK:** General

**ADDRESS:** 40 High Street, Street, Somerset BA16 OYA

**CORRESPONDENT:** Mrs B L Gunson

**TRUSTEES:** Priscilla Johnston, Eleanor C Robertson, Mary P Lovell, S Clark, S Caroline Gould.

**BENEFICIAL AREA:** National and international

**GENERAL:** The trust has a time-limit to 2020. Its assets in 1991 were £1 million, its net income, £92,000 and undistributed income, £178,000. It has a particular interest in the Society of Friends, education and local appeals.

In 1991 the following grants relevant to this guide were made:

Quaker Peace and Service, Oxfam (£1,500 each);

Quaker Social Responsibility, South Africa Scholarship Trust (£1,000);

Ulster Quaker Service Committee (£750);

Friends World Committee for Consultation (£250);

Save the Children Fund, Centre for Neighbourhood Development, Belfast (£200 each);

Belfast Trust for Integrated Education, International Young Quakers, Marie Stopes International, Quaker Peace Studies Trust, Ulster Quaker Peace Committee (£100).

**APPLICATIONS:** Applications are reviewed three times a year and will be acknowledged if a SAE is enclosed. It should be noted that the trust's funds are fully committed and unsolicited applications are unlikely to be successful. The trust has written that it did not wish to be included in this guide, and was not prepared to update or revise this entry which they have said is inaccurate.

# Hilda and Alice Clark Charitable Trust

**GRANT TOTAL:** £27,500 (1990)

**MAIN AREAS OF WORK:** General, Education and the Society of Friends

**ADDRESS:** KPMG Peat Marwick, 15 Pembroke Road, Bristol, Avon BS8 3BG

**CORRESPONDENT:** The trustees.

**TRUSTEES:** R B Clark, J A Clark, P T Clothier, S Clark, M P Lovell, A T Clothier.

**BENEFICIAL AREA:** National

**INFORMATION:** Accounts have not been filed at the Charity Commission since 1982.

**GENERAL:** Whilst this trust has general charitable objects it is likely that it gives mainly to the

Society of Friends. Its schedule of grants in 1982 showed grants to Quaker Peace and Service, the Quaker Home Service Council, and Quaker Social Responsibility and Education.

**APPLICATIONS:** Applications are reviewed each year in December.

# Co-operation North

**ADDRESS:** 7 Botanic Avenue, Belfast BT7 1JG/37 Upper Fitzwilliam Street, Dublin 2

**TELEPHONE:** Belfast 0232-321462; Dublin 01-661 0588

**CORRESPONDENT:** Tony Kennedy, Chief Executive

**BENEFICIAL AREA:** Republic of Ireland and Northern Ireland

**INFORMATION:** An annual report and information about grants for exchange schemes.

**GENERAL:** The aims of Co-operation North which also includes Co-operation Ireland, are: 'To advance mutual understanding and respect by promoting practical co-operation between the people of Northern Ireland and of the Republic of Ireland'. It was founded as a registered charity in 1979 by leaders in business, trade unions and academic life. Its main offices are in Belfast and Dublin.

Co-operation North works through:

• Exchange schemes, residential conferences and camps, Co-operation North brings together mainly young people, to establish long-term permanent links.

• Cross-community and cross-border links between opinion leaders in business, the media and cultural groups, and encourage these links to become self-sustaining.

• A Special and Fundraising Events programme encourages thousands of people to participate in cross-border fun events such as Maracycle, and raise funds for the organisations.

**APPLICATIONS:** A Guide to Cross-Border Exchanges is published and an application form is available.

# Cobb Charity

**GRANT TOTAL:** £24,500 (1991/92)

**MAIN AREAS OF WORK:** Environment, social welfare, peace, education in innovative projects

**ADDRESS:** 5 Station Road, Fulbourn, Cambridge CB1 5ER

**CORRESPONDENT:** C Cochran

**TRUSTEES:** C Cochran, Eleanor Allitt, F Appelbe.

**BENEFICIAL AREA:** National and international

**INFORMATION:** Accounts are on file at the Charity Commission.

**GENERAL:** The trust gives to a wide range of humanitarian and ecological causes. Smaller charities are favoured. All its grants were for £500 in 1992/93. Grants relevant to this guide were given to: Civil Liberties Trust, Natural Justice Charity, National Council for the Welfare of Prisoners Abroad, Radical Alternative Prison, Marie Stopes International, Survival International, Population Services, Natural Energy Project, ITDG, Friends of the Earth, Greenpeace, Earth Resources, Research, Inniskillin Community Development Project. All organisations must be registered charities.

**APPLICATIONS:** Unsolicited approaches by letter or telephone are not answered.

# Leslie Cohen Trust Fund

**GRANT TOTAL:** £9,600 (1992)

**MAIN AREAS OF WORK:** General

**ADDRESS:** 14 Lakeland Drive, Leeds LS17 7PH

**TELEPHONE:** 0532-685404

**CORRESPONDENT:** The Secretary

**TRUSTEES:** Mrs D Cohen, Mrs P Mack

**BENEFICIAL AREA:** National

**INFORMATION:** Accounts are on file at the Charity Commission.

**GENERAL:** The fund made the following grants in 1992 which are relevant to this guide:

Oxfam, Nicaragua (£500);

Oxfam, Cambodia (£500);

Cambodia Trust (£380).

In the previous year it made grants of £500 each to Amnesty International and to Oxfam.

**APPLICATIONS:** The trustees regret that applications cannot expect a reply. They have written 'No postal application will be considered. It is a waste of your time and money in sending'.

# Cole Charitable Trust

**GRANT TOTAL:** £40,000

**MAIN AREAS OF WORK:** Education, community in Birmingham

**ADDRESS:** 128 Tamworth Road, Sutton Coldfield, West Midlands B75 6DH

**CORRESPONDENT:** Dr J G L Cole

**TRUSTEES:** Mrs Joy Cole, Dr T J Cole, G N Cole, Dr J G L Cole.

**BENEFICIAL AREA:** National and Birmingham

**INFORMATION:** Accounts are on file at the Charity Commission.

**GENERAL:** The following grants relevant to this guide were made:

In 1993 –

Intermediate Technology Development Group (£600, also given in the previous year);

Medical Foundation for the Victims of Torture, Prison Reform Trust, (£300 each, also given in the previous year);

Charity Know How, Books Abroad, (£300 each).

In 1992 –

VSO (£600);

Population Concern (£300);

First Steps to Freedom (£150).

**EXCLUSIONS:** Individuals

**APPLICATIONS:** Applications should be made in writing with clear details of the projects and its budget. Acknowledgements cannot be expected although further information may be requested. Please do not send a SAE.

# The Canon Collins Educational Trust for Southern Africa

**GRANT TOTAL:** £502,200 (1991)

**MAIN AREAS OF WORK:** See below

**ADDRESS:** 22 The Ivories, 6-8 Northampton Street, London N1 2HX

**TELEPHONE:** 071-354 1462

**CORRESPONDENT:** Ethel de Keyser, Director

**TRUSTEES:** Diana Collins, Phyllis Altman, John Prevett, Dame Alix Meynell, Lord Walston, Joel Joffe, Dr Helen Hudson.

**BENEFICIAL AREA:** South Africa and Namibia

**GENERAL:** The objects of the trust are: 'The advancement of education of the people of Southern Africa and in particular refugees and prisoners suffering a legal restriction on their liberty'. Scholarships are provided in the UK to postgraduate students from Southern Africa to study disciplines which are most urgently needed in that region; To assist the development of staff skills at the historically black universities and expand its tertiary education programme in South Africa itself.

**APPLICATIONS:** In writing to the correspondent.

# Combined Charities Trust

**GRANT TOTAL:** £76,000

**MAIN AREAS OF WORK:** Relief of poverty, general

**ADDRESS:** Barclays Bank Trust Co Ltd, Trust Management Office, P O Box 27, Octagon House, Godbrook Park, Northwick, Cheshire CW9 7RE

**CORRESPONDENT:** Barclays Bank Trust Co Ltd

**TRUSTEES:** Barclays Bank Trust Co Ltd

**GENERAL:** Seventeen grants were given in 1990/91, 13 of which were for £5,000, whilst the others were between £2,000 and £2,500. A grant was given to the Medical Foundation for the Care of the Victims of Torture.

**APPLICATIONS:** In writing to the correspondent.

# Commonwealth Foundation

**GRANT TOTAL:** Annual income: £1.9 million

**ADDRESS:** Marlborough House, Pall Mall, London SW1Y 5HY

**TELEPHONE:** 071-930 3783

**CORRESPONDENT:** Dr Humayun Khan, Director

**INFORMATION:** A briefing leaflet and guide to conference organisers.

**GENERAL:** The foundation is an autonomous body

with a Board of Governors nominated by the 44 Commonwealth Governments which contribute to it. The Foundation works among the unofficial bodies of the Commonwealth. It co-operates in the activities of professional Commonwealth Associations and has supported the establishment of a series of interdisciplinary professional centres and Commonwealth non-governmental organisation liaison units. It is responsible for a range of Commonwealth Foundation Fellowship and Bursary Schemes e.g. the Fellowship Scheme to Promote Commonwealth Understanding whereby twelve Fellowships are awarded annually to professionals of influence to undertake a one month programme on Commonwealth affairs. Fellowships are not available on personal application.

The following Ad Hoc Awards are available on personal application to the Foundation: Bursaries for short-term study, refresher courses, advisory visits and training attachments; Grants for attendance at conferences, seminars and workshops. These awards are available to professional women and men and members of non-governmental organisations throughout the Commonwealth. Bursaries are tenable for periods not exceeding three months in a Commonwealth country other than the applicant's own.

**APPLICATIONS:** In writing, there is no application form. Three months' notice is required.

# Commonwealth Relations Trust

**GRANT TOTAL:** £202,000 (1992)

**ADDRESS:** 28 Bedford Square, London WC18 3EG

**TELEPHONE:** 071-6310686

**CORRESPONDENT:** Ms Sarah Lock, The Secretary.

**TRUSTEES:** The trustees of the Nuffield Foundation now are automatically trustees of this Trust i.e. Lord Flowers, (Chairman), Professor B M Hoggett, Professor R C 0 Matthews, Sir John Banham, Professor R May, Professor Sir Michael Rutter, Mrs A Sofer

**INFORMATION:** An information sheet is available.

**GENERAL:** The trust, formerly the Imperial Relations Trust, was set up in 1937 by an anonymous gift to the first Earl Baldwin of Bewdley to strengthen ties which bind together the United Kingdom and other independent countries of the Commonwealth. Fellowships, travel bursaries and grants are given. As its name implies the Trust covers all member countries of the Commonwealth (initially it had only covered a selected few). At the present time Fellowships and Travelling Bursaries are awarded as follows:

**Fellowships:** One each year to Australia, Canada and to New Zealand to enable an experienced teacher from each country to spend a year at the University of London Institute of Education, or any other college in the UK; these are 'matched' with additional Fellowships provided by Australia, Canada and New Zealand.

**Travelling Bursaries:** Bursaries are offered annually to eight national broadcasting organisations of Commonwealth countries for three-month visits to the UK by members of staff; four UK broadcasters from the BBC and the independent sector receive awards for visits to Commonwealth countries overseas, with an emphasis on visits to developing countries.

Similar schemes exist for trade unionists, adult educators, print journalists and workers in local enterprise development to visit the UK and from similar individuals from the UK to visit a Commonwealth country overseas.

Adult Education Bursaries £30,254;

London University £9,000;

Trades Union Travelling Bursaries £24,647;

Bursaries for broadcasters £70,330;

Bursaries for print journalists £12,476.

Support is also available for people travelling from the UK to Commonwealth countries and vice versa. Awards are advertised by the national organisations concerned and applications should be addressed directly to them. Details may be obtained from the Secretary.

# Commonwealth Youth Exchange Council

**GRANT TOTAL:** £164,000 (1992/93)

**ADDRESS:** 7 Lion Yard, Tremadoc Road, Clapham, London SW4 7NQ

**TELEPHONE:** 071-498 6151; Fax 071-720 5403

**CORRESPONDENT:** Vic Craggs, Director

**INFORMATION:** Guidelines are available.

**GENERAL:** The aim of this financial support is to promote reciprocal exchanges which will develop contact and better understanding between the young people of the UK and other Commonwealth countries.

Priority is given to funding:

- New or particularly innovative exchange programmes;
- Exchanges with Commonwealth countries in Africa, Asia and the Caribbean;
- British organisations which have not been previously very active in this field;
- Exchanges involving young Britons who would not normally have the opportunity to take part.

An exchange may begin with a visit overseas by a British group or with a visit to Britain by another Commonwealth group. In either case there should be the prospect of a reciprocal visit taking place within a reasonable time scale in the future. Projects must be organised by an established organisation in the UK and in the partner country and led by a responsible person. Exchanges, particularly outside Europe are expected to last at least 21 days. The participants should be aged between 16 and 25 years and groups should be between 5 and 15 in number.

In 1992/93 the council supported 957 young people who took part in 78 group visits. Of these 40 were out-going from Britain and 38 incoming. The geographical spread was: Africa 30; Asia 19; The Caribbean 16; Other Countries 13.

**APPLICATIONS:** An application form is available and applications should be submitted at least 9 months before the project begins. The grants sub-committee is made up of representatives of central government, local education authorities and voluntary youth organisations. Applications should be made in the Autumn before the financial year in which the project takes place.

# Community Relations Council

**GRANT TOTAL:** £1,144,000 (1992/93)

**MAIN AREAS OF WORK:** Community relations work to increase understanding and co-operation between groups in Northern Ireland

**ADDRESS:** 6 Murray Street, Belfast BT16DN

**TELEPHONE:** 0232-439953; Fax 0232-235208

**CORRESPONDENT:** Dr Mari Fitzduff, Director; Ray Mullan, Information Officer

**TRUSTEES:** Council members: James Hawthorne (Chairman), Professor Paul Arthur, Glen Barr, Terence Donaghy, Caroline Ferguson, Hugh Frazer, Maurice Hayes, Jackie Hewitt, Anne McCorkell, Donal McFerran, Maura Maginn, Alasdair Maclaughlin, Chris Ryder, David Stevens, Paul Sweeney. Additional members to be appointed end January 1994.

**INFORMATION:** Full annual reports are obtainable from the Council.

**GENERAL:** The Council was established in 1990 as a registered charity and limited company, with the main aim to increase understanding and co-operation between political, cultural and religious communities in Northern Ireland. It operates a number of grant schemes to support community relations work. The Council receives the greater part of its funding from the Central Community Relations Unit of the Northern Ireland Government and from the European Regional Development Fund. It has also received funding for particular projects from the International Fund for Ireland.

The Council is responsible for the administration of core-funding grants to a number of reconciliation and community groups. In 1992/93, 18 groups received core-funding totalling £563,400 and groups supported in this way included:

Colombanus Community,
Community of the Peace People,
Cornerstone Community,
Corrymeela Community,
East Belfast Development Centre,
Harmony Community Trust,
Irish School of Ecumenics,
L'Derry Peace and Reconciliation Group,

Protestant and Catholic Encounter,
Ulster Quaker Service Committee,
Women Together.

The Council runs a series of grants schemes which in 1992/93 awarded a total of £581,000 in grants. The schemes operational in October 1993 were:

**1. Inter-Community Grant scheme:** £230,000 in 1993/94

Assists local groups involved in cross-community reconciliation work and the many other work and community organisations which have the potential for increasing communal understanding and reducing sectarian tension in Northern Ireland. Grant-aid for programmes designed to increase understanding and acceptance of diversity as well as those which involve actual cross-community contact.

**2. Development Grant Scheme:** £6,000 in 1992/93

For groups primarily concerned with community relations which have identified a need to improve their management/development. Grants cover consultation fees, staff development and professional advice on financial management.

**3. Local Cultural Traditions Grant Scheme:** £75,000 in 1993/94

Aimed at community and voluntary groups wishing to develop projects which encourage cultural confidence and an acceptance of cultural diversity. Projects may involve groups in single-identity work as well as work exploring local traditions other than their own. Many such projects will also have a cross-community base.

In the above schemes the maximum grant per application is £6,000 and most grants have been under £1,500.

**4. Publications Grant Scheme:** £76,000 in 1992/93

To subsidise publications which have already found a publisher and which promote the cultural traditions objectives of the Council. The purpose of the grant is to help the publication reach a wider audience. Applications may be made by Northern Ireland publishers only.

**5. Media Grants:** £96,000 in 1992/93

Supports professional, independent television/film projects which will contribute to a better understanding of cultural diversity and community issues within Northern Ireland. Since 1992 this scheme has taken the form of an annual competition, advertised in the local press. There were six winners in 1993.

**6. Cultural Traditions Fellowships**, available for one year, are advertised annually. Six Fellowships, to the value of approximately £6,000 each, were awarded in 1993.

EXCLUSIONS: The grant schemes do not extend to schools or youth clubs for which the Department of Education (N I) has responsibility. Neither will grants be given for travel outside the British Isles, or to groups outside N I.

APPLICATIONS: Application for core-funding may be made in writing to the Council. For schemes 1–3 application forms and detailed criteria forms are available from the address above. Grant applications up to £1,500 are considered within several weeks of receipt. Larger applications are considered by committees which meet four or five times a year.

# Ernest Cook Trust

GRANT TOTAL: £417,500 (1992/93)

ADDRESS: Estate Office, Fairford Park, Fairford, Gloucestershire GL7 4JH

TELEPHONE: 0285-713 273

CORRESPONDENT: J. G. L. Malleson, Secretary

TRUSTEES: W R Benyon (Chairman), Lord Saye and Sele, Sir Jack Boles, C F Badcock, M C Tuely, A W M Christie-Miller

INFORMATION: Accounts are on file at the Charity Commission. A leaflet listing recent grants and outlining policy is available.

GENERAL: The major part of the trust's support is for projects concerned with education in the countryside including programmes interpreting the countryside for city dwellers and for research into issues affecting rural society or concerned with conservation of the countryside.

Support is also given to organisations assisting travel overseas by young people particularly where the aim is to develop understanding between people of different countries. In 1992/93 the trust gave a total of £24,000 in this field and examples of grants were:

Interface (£2,000);

Project Trust (£2,000).

Grants were also given to colleges and schools for particular projects. Following a recent re-appraisal of the trust's policies very limited funding will be committed for educational travel in the future.

The trust also has an ongoing policy to support cross-community work in Northern Ireland. In 1992/93 a total of £16,000 was given in this field and grants included:

Lagan College (£5,000);

Northern Ireland Children's Holiday Scheme (£3,000);

Ulster Quaker Peace Project (£2,000).

APPLICATIONS: Applications may be submitted at any time. Trustees meet in Spring and Autumn to consider proposals whilst requests for smaller grants are considered at more frequent intervals. Applications should be no longer than four sides of A4 and submitted by the person directing the project. Applications should be accompanied by a SAE as only the proposals submitted to the trustees are acknowledged.

# Craps Charitable Trust

GRANT TOTAL: £121,000 (1991/92)

MAIN AREAS OF WORK: General

ADDRESS: Messrs Tarloe Lyons, Watchmaker Court, 33 St John's Lane, London EC1M 4DB

CORRESPONDENT: See above

TRUSTEES: C E Shanbury, Miss C S Dent, J P M Dent.

BENEFICIAL AREA: National and international

INFORMATION: Accounts are on file at the Charity Commission.

GENERAL: The trust gives to a wide range of causes and Jewish charities. The following grants relevant to this guide were given in 1991/92 and in the previous year:

Greenpeace, Friends of the Earth, Amnesty International (each received £1,000).

APPLICATIONS: Applications cannot expect an acknowledgement.

# John and Edythe Crosfield Charitable Trust

**GRANT TOTAL:** £25,300 (1991/92)

**ADDRESS:** Grove Lodge, Admiral's Walk, London NW3 6RS.

**CORRESPONDENT:** J F. Crosfield

**TRUSTEES:** J F Crosfield, Mrs E M Crosfield, R J Crosfield.

**BENEFICIAL AREA:** National and international

**INFORMATION:** Accounts are on file at the Charity Commission

**GENERAL:** The trust's objects are 'To help deprived children and deprived adults who are sick or old. To support medical research and preserve the ecology'. In 1991/92 the following grants with relevance to this guide were given:

Save the Children Fund, Sightsavers (£1,000 each);

Belfast Trust for Integrated Education, Oxfam, VSO, Population Concern (£500 each).

**APPLICATIONS:** The trust is understood to give regular support to particular charities and does not consider new applications.

# The Cumber Family Charitable Trust

**GRANT TOTAL:** £50,000 annually

**ADDRESS:** Manor Farm, Marcham, Abingdon, Oxon OX13 6NZ

**TELEPHONE:** 0865-391327

**CORRESPONDENT:** Mrs M J Cumber

**TRUSTEES:** Miss M Cumber, A R Davey, W Cumber, Mrs S Cumber, Mrs M J Cumber

**BENEFICIAL AREA:** Overseas and national with a preference for Berkshire and Oxfordshire.

**INFORMATION:** Accounts are on file at the Charity Commission.

**GENERAL:** The following grants with relevance to the scope of this guide included:

In 1993 –

APT Design and Development (£3,000);

Refugee Council, SOS Sahel, Romanian Orphanage Trust, Tear Fund (£2,000 each);

Prisoners of Conscience (£1,000);

In 1992 –

Marie Stopes International, SOS Sahel, Farm Africa, Send a Cow, (£1,000 each);

In 1991 –

Tear Fund (£7,000);

Christian Aid for churches appeal in Eastern Europe (£3,000);

Romanian Orphanage Trust (£2,000).

**APPLICATIONS:** In writing to the correspondent. Applications are considered in May and November.

# The Wallace Curzon Charitable Trust

**GRANT TOTAL:** £18,500 (1991/92)

**MAIN AREAS OF WORK:** Children

**ADDRESS:** Homanton House, Shrewton, Near Salisbury, Wilts SP3 4ER

**CORRESPONDENT:** F D Curzon, Secretary

**TRUSTEES:** Peter Curzon, Fritz Curzon, Robert Spooner.

**BENEFICIAL AREA:** National and international

**INFORMATION:** Accounts are on file at the Charity Commission.

**GENERAL:** This trust mainly supports UK children's charities, development agencies and disaster appeals in developing countries and Eastern Europe. In 1991/92 Save the Children Fund received a grant of £10,000 with £5,000 given in the previous year. Other grants in 1990/91 included: Britain-Nepal Medical Trust (£5,000) and the Blue Peter Appeal for Romania.

**EXCLUSIONS:** Individuals

**APPLICATIONS:** In writing to the correspondent. Only organisations the trust is able to support can expect to receive a reply.

# Daiwa Anglo-Japanese Foundation

**GRANT TOTAL:** £500,000 (1992)

**MAIN AREAS OF WORK:** Anglo-Japanese Relations

**ADDRESS:** 13/14 Cornwall Terrace, London NW1 4QP

**TELEPHONE:** 071-548 8302

**CORRESPONDENT:** C H D Everett, Director General

**TRUSTEES:** Lord Roll of Ipsden, Y Chino, Lord Adrian, Lord Carrington, Akio Morita, N P Clegg.

**BENEFICIAL AREA:** Britain, Japan.

**INFORMATION:** Full accounts are on file at the Charity Commission.

**GENERAL:** The foundation's aims are to:

- enhance the UK's and Japan's understanding of each others' people and culture;
- enable British and Japanese students and academics to further their education by travel;
- make grants to charities engaged in education or research in the UK and Japan.

The foundation was set up with an initial grant of £10 million in 1988 and further donations of £5 million in 1989 and 1990. The foundation's programme consists of three elements: Daiwa Scholarships, General Grants and Activities centres on the Daiwa Foundation Japan House.

**Daiwa Scholarships:** Since 1991 the foundation has given five or more scholarships a year to outstanding British graduates between the ages of 21 and 28 to enable them to learn Japanese for two years first in the UK and then in Japan. These scholarships are advertised every autumn.

**General Grants:** Each year the foundation makes general grants to the total value of £500,000 to £600,000. Since 1988 these grants have included the establishment of lectureships in Japanese Studies at British Universities and 250 or so general grants ranging from £150 to £7,000 to a range of individuals and institutions, in Japan and the UK. Recipients have included Japanese and British groups and artists performing in each others countries, Japanese teaching in British schools, exchange visits between schools, and many professional and academic visits and exchanges. The foundation sees itself as pump-priming rather than providing permanent finance and does all it can to work in conjunction with other donors.

**Daiwa Foundation Japan House:** The foundation has purchased a house in Regent's Park which will become the centre for its activities,

and a focus and meeting place for all those with a general interest in Japan and Anglo-Japanese relations. The foundation has not supplied any details of the specific grants that it has given. It is known, for instance, that support has been given in 1992/93 to the Royal Institute of International Affairs for its Asia-Pacific programme and its International Security programme.

**APPLICATIONS:** Applicants are encouraged to write in their own style and explain their project, and should include a budget and any other sources of help available. Applicants are interviewed before recommendations are made to the trustees. Applications from Japan should be sent to Masanobu Mark Nakamura, Daiwa Anglo-Japanese Foundation, 1-2-1 Kyobashi Chuo-ky, Tokyo 104, Japan.

# The Margaret Davies Charity

**GRANT TOTAL:** Over £100,000 (1992)

**ADDRESS:** Perthybu Offices, Sarn, Newtown, Powys SY16 4EP

**TELEPHONE:** 0686 670404

**CORRESPONDENT:** Mrs S Hamer

**TRUSTEES:** I E E Davies, J H Davies, Dr J A Davies, T A Owen, R D Davies

**BENEFICIAL AREA:** National with a preference for Wales

**INFORMATION:** Accounts are on file at the Charity Commission.

**GENERAL:** Regular support has been given to the National Museum of Cardiff, the University of Wales, hospitals, hospices and the Temple of Peace, Cardiff.

**APPLICATIONS:** In writing to the correspondent.

# The De La Rue Jubilee Trust

**GRANT TOTAL:** £66,500 (1991/92)

**ADDRESS:** 6 Agar Street, London WC2N 4DE

**CORRESPONDENT:** Appeals Secretary

**TRUSTEES:** P F Orchard, B J Isted, P R E Conisbee, F J Richardson, D L Hosie.

**BENEFICIAL AREA:** National

**INFORMATION:** The accounts on file at the Charity Commission have not been accompanied by a schedule of grants since 1990/91.

**GENERAL:** Grants have been made in 1990/91 to:

Save the Children Fund (£10,000 and in previous years);

UK Centre for Economic and Environmental Development (£2,000 and in previous years).

It is known that Co-operation Ireland (GB) received support in 1992.

**APPLICATIONS:** It is understood that unsolicited applications are unlikely to be considered.


# Miriam Dean Refugee Trust Fund

**GRANT TOTAL:** £77,000 (1992)

**MAIN AREAS OF WORK:** Community and self-help projects among the poorest

**ADDRESS:** Little Oxleas, Woolton Hill, Newbury, Berkshire RG15 9XQ

**TELEPHONE:** 0635-253391

**CORRESPONDENT:** Rev and Mrs T E Dorey

**TRUSTEES:** H Capon, T Dorey, V Dorey, J Budd, G Livermore

**BENEFICIAL AREA:** International, mainly East Africa and India

**INFORMATION:** Accounts are on file at the Charity Commission.

**GENERAL:** The trust's objects are: For the benefit of such persons abroad whether orphans, sick aged or otherwise, who are in need of assistance by reason of war, disaster, pestilence or otherwise or any organisation engaged in the relief of suffering humanity abroad.

The trust has assets of some £269,000 and in 1992 made the following grants:

Tibetan refugees, for 5 projects (£38,158);

India, for 4 projects (£28,555);

Tanzania, for 3 projects (£6,970);

Three other projects were supported including projects in Beruit and Burma (£3,027).

**EXCLUSIONS:** No grants are made to students travelling abroad.


# Delves Charitable Trust

**GRANT TOTAL:** £142,750 (1992/93)

**MAIN AREAS OF WORK:** General with a particular interest in medial research, hospices, overseas aid, social welfare and the environment

**ADDRESS:** New Guild House, 45 Great Charles Street, Queensway, Birmingham B3 2LX

**TELEPHONE:** 021-212 2222

**CORRESPONDENT:** R Harriman

**TRUSTEES:** Mrs M Breeze, J Breeze, G Breeze, Miss E Breeze, Dr C Breeze, C Breeze, R Harriman.

**BENEFICIAL AREA:** National and international

**INFORMATION:** Accounts are on file at the Charity Commission.

**GENERAL:** The trust has assets of some £3.8 million and in 1992/93 gave the following grants which are relevant to this guide:

Quaker Peace and Service, Intermediate Technology Development Trust (£8,000 each);

Save the Children Fund (£7,000);

LEPRA (£5,000);

Survival International (£4,000);

International Planned Parenthood Federation (£2,000);

Amnesty International (£1,000).

**APPLICATIONS:** The trust's funds are heavily committed so new applications are not considered.


# Dinam Charity

**GRANT TOTAL:** £107,000 (1992)

**MAIN AREAS OF WORK:** General

**ADDRESS:** 8 Southampton Place, London WC1A 2EA

**CORRESPONDENT:** Hon J H Davies

**TRUSTEES:** Hon Mrs Mary M Noble, Hon Mrs G R Jean Cormack, Hon Edward D G Davies, Hon Jonathan H Davies, J S Tyres.

**BENEFICIAL AREA:** National and international

**INFORMATION:** Accounts are on file at the Charity Commission.

**GENERAL:** The trust was set up in 1926 by David Davies. Its particular interests include the development of international understanding.

The most recent accounts on file at the Charity Commission for 1992 showed that the major part of its grant-making continued to be allocated to the David Davies Memorial Institute of International Studies (£85,600, with £83,528 in the previous year). In 1991 The Welsh Centre for International Affairs received £25,000.

**APPLICATIONS:** In writing to the correspondent.

## Dolphin Charitable Trust

**GRANT TOTAL:** £12,000 (1990/91)

**MAIN AREAS OF WORK:** General

**ADDRESS:** Kleinwort Benson Trustees Limited, PO Box 191, 10 Fenchurch Street, London EC3M 3LB

**CORRESPONDENT:** See above

**TRUSTEES:** Kleinwort Benson Trustees Limited

**BENEFICIAL AREA:** National

**INFORMATION:** Accounts are on file at the Charity Commission.

**GENERAL:** In 1990/91 the trust give 30 grants with two relevant to this guide:

Prisoners of Conscience Appeal Fund (£300);

Amnesty International (£200).

**APPLICATIONS:** Applications will not usually be acknowledged. Grants are given to causes known to the trustees.

## The Dulverton Trust

**GRANT TOTAL:** £2,182,000 (1992/93)

**MAIN AREAS OF WORK:** General, see below

**ADDRESS:** 5 St James's Place, London SWlY lNP

**TELEPHONE:** 071-629 912; Fax 071-495 6201

**CORRESPONDENT:** Major General M. J. Tomlinson, Secretary.

**TRUSTEES:** Hon Robert Wills (Chairman), Lord Carrington, Lord Dulverton, Colonel D V Fanshawe, Sir David Wills, Colonel S J Watson, C A H Wills, Dr Catherine Wills, J W Watson, Sir Ashley Ponsonby, Lord Taylor of Gryfe, the Earl of Gowrie.

**BENEFICIAL AREA:** National and East Africa

**INFORMATION:** Full accounts with schedule of grants is filed with the Charity Commission.

**GENERAL:** In 1992/93 the trust's grants were listed under the following categories:

Youth and Education (£535,800);

Conservation (£378,500);

General Welfare (£313,000);

Religion (£288,000);

Peace and Security (£118,000);

Industrial Understanding (£99.000);

Africa (£97,000);

Preservation (£59,000);

Minor appeals (£66,400);

With the remainder allocated to miscellaneous, local appeals, subscriptions and final donations.

The trust's secretary is assisted by the following consultants:

- H H Tucker, in the fields of Peace, Security and International Relations;
- Brigadier T R Jones in the fields of Youth, Education and General Welfare;
- Colonel R J A Hornby in the filed of Religious Education;
- G Foggon in the field of Industrial Relations.

During 1992/93, 273 grants were made. The annual report for 1992/93 notes: 'Peace and Security is limited to selected national bodies who specialise in the broader analysis of possible courses of action in the fields of international security, disarmament and defence ... the trust's activities ... have, in the main, been limited to those institutions who have more readily and effectively reacted to world events over the past year. These include the Royal Institute for International Affairs (£20,000) and the Royal United Services' Institute (£24,000). A final annual grant, for the time being, was made to the British Atlantic Committee after ten years of continuous funding. Funding has been provided to the Research Institute for the Study of Conflict and Terrorism (£16,000) towards the cost of an important study on the future of South African police and military forces.'

At a meeting in October 1993 trustees resolved that, for the future, Industrial Relations and Peace and Security would be regarded as Minor Categories of activity by the trust. Other grants noted in the annual report with some relevance to this scope of this guide were:

Under Conservation –

 CARE Britain (£20,000);

Under Youth and Education –

 VSO (£16,000);

 Project Trust (£19,000);

 Ditchley Foundation for overseas students' travel costs, endowment fund (£25,000);

 Northern Ireland Council of Integrated Education (£10,000);

Under Miscellaneous –

 Charity Know How (£10,000).

**EXCLUSIONS:** A full list is found in the annual report which includes Northern Ireland except for specific nominated charities, and overseas except for a reducing number of long established associations in East Africa.

**APPLICATIONS:** In writing to the correspondent. Trustees' meetings are held four times a year in January, May, July and October.

# Wilfred and Elsie Elkes Charity Fund

**GRANT TOTAL:** £113,000 (1992)

**MAIN AREAS OF WORK:** Overseas relief

**ADDRESS:** Royal Bank of Scotland, North of England Trustee & Taxation Department, P O Box 356, 45 Mosley Street, Manchester M60 2BE

**TELEPHONE:** 061-242 3134

**CORRESPONDENT:** Nigel Dibble

**BENEFICIAL AREA:** National and international

**INFORMATION:** Accounts are on file at the Charity Commission.

**GENERAL:** In 1992 the charity gave grants to the following:

 Save the Children Fund (£3,000);

 Observer/Save the Children Fund Somalia Appeal (£5,000);

 Crisis in Africa (£5,000).

In 1990 the Gulf Crisis Appeal received £3,000. The British Red Cross and the Albanian Children's Appeal have also received support.

**APPLICATIONS:** In writing to the correspondent.

*no individuals or operation charities in their right*

# The John Ellerman Foundation

(formerly the Moorgate Trust Fund and the New Moorgate Trust Fund)

**GRANT TOTAL:** £3,686,000 (1992/93)

**MAIN AREAS OF WORK:** Medicine, disability, the environment, the arts

**ADDRESS:** Suite 10, Aria House, 23 Craven Street, London WC2N 5NT

**TELEPHONE:** 071-930 8566

**CORRESPONDENT:** Peter C Pratt, Secretary

**TRUSTEES:** Angela Boschi, R Alastair Lloyd, David Martin-Jenkins, Dennis Parry, Peter C Pratt, Sir David Scott, Hon Peter Strutt

**BENEFICIAL AREA:** National and international

**INFORMATION:** Accounts are on file at the Charity Commission.

**GENERAL:** The accounts for 1992/93 show that grants with some relevance to the scope of this guide were given to:

 United World Colleges International (£10,000);

 Belfast Charitable Trust for Integrated Education, Ulster Defence Regiment Benevolent Fund (£5,000);

 Population Concern, Save the Children, Oxfam, Friends of Sephardi and other Jewish Refugees, Earthwatch Europe, Medical Foundation for the Care of Victims of Torture (£5,000 each)

 Marie Stopes International (£3,000);

 British Executive Service Overseas, Council of Christians and Jews, Refugee Action (£2,000 each);

 War on Want (£1,000).

The foundation is a supporter of Charity Know How (see separate entry).

**APPLICATIONS:** In writing to the correspondent.

# Miss M E Ellis 1985 Charitable Trust

**GRANT TOTAL:** £28,000 (1991/92)

**ADDRESS:** Messrs Field Fisher Waterhouse, 41 Vine Street, London EC3N 2AA

**TELEPHONE:** 071-481 4841

**CORRESPONDENT:** A P P Honigmann

**TRUSTEES:** A P P Honigmann, E H Milligan

**BENEFICIAL AREA:** National and international

**GENERAL:** Its objects are as follows: 'General charitable purposes including religious and educational projects and projects in the international field specially related to economic, social and humanitarian aid to developing countries. Ecumenical and Quaker interests are favoured.' Grants are 'Modest contributions towards launching new schemes or tiding over moments of shortfall in experiments within the general purposes outlined above.'

In 1991/92 grants relevant to this were given to:

Friends World Committee for Consultation (£3,250 and in the previous year);

Quaker Peace Studies Trust (£1,000 and in the previous year);

Quaker Council for European Affairs (£1,000 and in the previous year);

Gandhi Foundation (£1,000);

Belfast Trust for Integrated Education (£1,000 and in the previous year);

Hazelwood Integrated Primary School (£500 and in the previous year);

Oxford Project for Peace Studies (£500, and in the previous year);

European and Near East Young Friends (£700 in 2 grants);

Northern Friends Peace Board (£170).

**APPLICATIONS:** In writing to the correspondent.

# Enkalon Foundation

**GRANT TOTAL:** £123,000 (1992/93)

**ADDRESS:** 25 Randalstown Road, Antrim BT41 4LJ

**TELEPHONE:** 08494-6353

**CORRESPONDENT:** J W Wallace, Secretary

**TRUSTEES:** R L Schierbeek (Chairman), J A Freeman, D H Templeton

**BENEFICIAL AREA:** Northern Ireland

**INFORMATION:** Guidelines are available.

**GENERAL:** The foundation supports the work of groups in Northern Ireland only. It is interested in cross community groups, self-help, assistance to the unemployed and groups helping the disadvantaged. The priorities may vary from year to year. Grants are made up to a maximum of £6,000.

Grants have been given to: The Corrymeela Community; Community of the Peace People; Lagan College, Belfast; Children's Community Holidays; Ulster Peoples College; Harmony Community Trust; Community Technical Aid. In 1991 a grant was given to the Peace and Reconciliation Group, L'Derry.

**APPLICATIONS:** Applications should be in writing. Decisions are made at three monthly intervals.

# Ericson Trust

**GRANT TOTAL:** £39,000 (1992/93)

**MAIN AREAS OF WORK:** General

**ADDRESS:** Flat 2, 53 Carleton Road, London N7 OET

**CORRESPONDENT:** Mrs A M C Cotton.

**TRUSTEES:** Mrs A M C Cotton, A Weston, Mrs L Campbell.

**BENEFICIAL AREA:** National and international

**INFORMATION:** Accounts are filed at the Charity Commission.

**GENERAL:** The trust states that it is 'interested in smaller, unique undertakings, preferably in urban settings, especially any concerned with the care, shelter, reconciliation, re-education and improvement in the quality of life of disadvantaged or vulnerable groups such as immigrants and refugees, offenders, the mentally ill in the community, victims of aggression and people who find themselves isolated through changing patterns of the population of inner cities'. Concerning developing countries, 'preference is given to smaller scale, partly self-help projects rather than to disaster relief'.

Grants relevant to this guide were:

In 1992/93 –

Community of Reconciliation and Fellowship (£13,000 in 3 grants);

British Refugee Council,

Oxfam (£1,500 each);

Medical Foundation for the Care of Victims of Torture (£1,250);

Amnesty International, Anti Slavery

International, Christian Aid, Friends of the Earth, One World Action, Survival International, the Howard League (£1,000 each).

The trust has noted that most grants ore of £1,000 and that the allocation of £13,000 is 'very exceptional'.

**APPLICATIONS:** Applications may be made at any time but are not usually acknowledged. Grants are made in March and October.

# European Educational Research Trust

**GRANT TOTAL:** £102,000 (1993)

**ADDRESS:** 76 Alfriston Road, London SW11 6NW

**TELEPHONE:** 071-228 4157

**CORRESPONDENT:** Mrs Lynda Dawson, Secretary

**TRUSTEES:** Lord Aldington (Chairman), Professor Lord Briggs, Lord Lever, Lord Tordoff, Lord Rippon

**BENEFICIAL AREA:** Europe, particularly EEC countries.

**INFORMATION:** Accounts are on file at the Charity Commission.

**GENERAL:** The amount allocated for grants in 1993 was significantly higher than in the previous year – £103,000 compared with £19,500. This rise seems to be the result of a major donation received in 1993. The main aim of the trust is to promote education across a wide range of disciplines: history, geography, science, art, literature and the culture of the countries of Europe. Grants are given to individuals and study groups of young people preferably between 18–35 years of age.

Support is confined to western Europe, mainly though not exclusively to the 12 countries of the EEC.

**EXCLUSIONS:** No grants to individuals.

# Esmée Fairbairn Charitable Trust

**GRANT TOTAL:** £7,700,000 (1993)

**ADDRESS:** 5 Storey's Gate, London SW1P 3AT

**TELEPHONE:** 071-222 7041

**CORRESPONDENT:** Margaret Hyde, Director

**TRUSTEES:** J. S. Fairbairn (Chairman), A G Down, Sir Antony Acland, General Sir John Hackett, C J M.Hardie, Mrs P Hughes-Hallett, Martin Lane Fox, Mrs V Linklater, Lord Rees-Mogg, Andrew Tuckey.

**BENEFICIAL AREA:** National

**INFORMATION:** Information is available from the trust, and report and accounts are on file at the Charity Commission.

**GENERAL:** The following is taken from the trust's annual report for 1992: 'The trust was founded in 1961 by Ian Fairbairn, a prominent City figure and pioneer of the unit trust industry, who named it in the memory of his wife. A large part of its income is derived from M&G Group PLC, in which the trust is the largest shareholder. The trust's main areas of interest currently are: Education; the Arts and National Heritage; Social Welfare; The Environment; and Economic and Social Research. The trust is committed to the preservation and development of a free and stable society and to free market principles. It seeks to encourage the pursuit of excellence and innovation ... The trust continued to make grants for core-funding to a number of institutions concerned with economic and social research, including the Institute of Economic Affairs, the Adam Smith Institute, the Centre for Economic Performance at the LSE, the Centre for Economic Policy Research and the Policy Studies Institute. ... An interesting innovation was a donation of £100,000 over two years to the Marshall Plan of the Mind, which is concerned with spreading understanding of the free market in Russia, using imaginative methods, including broadcasting a soap opera. In view of the importance of helping the countries of Eastern Europe in this respect, the trustees decided to relax their normal 'UK-only' rule. On the same grounds a donation of £75,000 was made towards the establishment of the English College in Prague.'

The report for 1992 available from the trust itself does not give a full list of grants. The following list of grants relevant to this guide comes from a review of the trust's 1991 accounts at the Charity Commission.

King's College, London – Liddel Hart Centre for Military Archives (£25,000);

Intermediate Technology Development Group (£20,000);

Royal Institute of International Affairs, Ditchley Foundation (£15,000 each);

Ranfurly Library Service (£11,000);

Twenty-First Century Trust, Centre for Research into Communist Economies, Partnership Trust (£10,000 each);

United World College of the Atlantic (£8,750);

Institute for Strategic Studies (£8,000);

Research Institute for the Study of Conflict and Terrorism (£5,500);

Earthwatch Europe, Centre for Environmental and Economic Development (£5,000);

Council for Arms Control (£3,000);

Queen Elizabeth College, Oxford – Refugee Study, Institute of Development Studies, Mongolian Programme (£2,500 each);

Euroforum (Families for Defence) (£1,500);

Oxford University Strategic Studies Group, British Executive Service Overseas (£1,000 each).

**APPLICATIONS:** Applicants are advised to make preliminary enquiries, by telephone or letter, of the Organising Secretary, Miss Judith Dunworth, who will be able to advise on the desirability of making a formal application and on the particular points to be covered.

## Ferguson Benevolent Fund Limited

**GRANT TOTAL:** £31,000 (1991)

**MAIN AREAS OF WORK:** General with a particular interest in the Methodist Church

**ADDRESS:** Aldenham School, Elstree, Herts WD6 3AJ

**CORRESPONDENT:** Mrs E Higginbottom

**TRUSTEES:** Mrs E Higginbottom (Chairman), Mrs M W Ferguson, Mrs C M A Metcalfe, Ms S Ferguson

**BENEFICIAL AREA:** National and international

**INFORMATION:** Accounts are on file at the Charity Commission.

**GENERAL:** Grants with relevance to this guide were given in 1991 to:

Methodist Relief Fund (£2,000);

V S O (£1,000);

Intermediate Technology Development Group (£750);

Y Care International (£500);

Minority Rights Group (£250).

**APPLICATIONS:** In writing to the correspondent. Meetings are held in September and March to decide on grants. Applications are not acknowledged.

## Allan and Nesta Ferguson Charitable Trust

**GRANT TOTAL:** Between £8,000 and £10,000

**ADDRESS:** 102 Oakfield Road, Selly Oak, Birmingham, B29 7ED

**TELEPHONE:** 021-472 1922

**CORRESPONDENT:** See below

**TRUSTEES:** Mrs E Ferguson

**GENERAL:** The trust has general charitable objects and aims to assist in education, overseas development and world peace. There are no records on file at the Charity Commission since 1977 so it is not possible to indicate what allocations have been made which fall within the scope of this book.

**APPLICATIONS:** It is understood that funds are likely to be fully committed.

## Firbank Charitable Trust

**GRANT TOTAL:** £7,000 (1991/92)

**ADDRESS:** c/o Messrs Ambrose Appelbe, 7 New Square, Lincoln's Inn, London WC2A 3RA

**CORRESPONDENT:** See above.

**TRUSTEES:** A Appelbe, Felix Appelbe, V Thomas.

**BENEFICIAL AREA:** National

**INFORMATION:** Accounts are on file at the Charity Commission.

**GENERAL:** Its interests are Quaker, educational and social welfare oriented. In 1991/92 the Society of Friends received a grant of £1,500 with

£1,000 given in the previous year. It is believed this includes support to Quaker Peace and Service. In 1990/91 small grants were given to United World Colleges (£500) and International Young Quakers (£100).

**APPLICATIONS:** Applications are not welcomed.

## Fitton Trust

**GRANT TOTAL:** £71,500 (1992)

**MAIN AREAS OF WORK:** General

**ADDRESS:** Messrs Walker Martineau, 64 Queen Street, London EC4R 1AD

**TELEPHONE:** 071-236 4232

**CORRESPONDENT:** See above.

**TRUSTEES:** Dr R P A Rivers, D M Lumsden, D V Brand.

**BENEFICIAL AREA:** National

**INFORMATION:** There are no schedules of grants with the accounts at the Charity Commission.

**GENERAL:** The most recent accounts at the Charity Commission with a grants schedule were for 1980/81 which showed gifts to: Voluntary Services, Belfast; IVS; Corrymeela Community. It is known that a grant was made to the Belfast Integrated Education Charitable Trust (BELTIE) in 1986.

**APPLICATIONS:** Unsolicited applications cannot expect an acknowledgement.

## The Flow Foundation

**GRANT TOTAL:** £26,000 (1990/91)

**MAIN AREAS OF WORK:** General

**ADDRESS:** 30 Hyde Park Gate, London SW7

**CORRESPONDENT:** H Woolf

**TRUSTEES:** Michael Harris, Harry Woolf, Josiane Woolf, James Woolf, Nathalie Shashou, Eduward Woolf.

**BENEFICIAL AREA:** National and international

**INFORMATION:** Accounts are on file at the Charity Commission.

**GENERAL:** This young foundation was established in 1989. In 1990/91 it made 31 grants many of

which were to Jewish charities. Grants relevant to this guide were given to :

Save the Children (£10,000);

Support for Romanians (£100).

**APPLICATIONS:** In writing to the correspondent.

## Jill Franklin Trust

**GRANT TOTAL:** £55,000 (1992/93)

**MAIN AREAS OF WORK:** See below

**ADDRESS:** 78 Lawn Road, NW3 2XB

**TELEPHONE:** 071-722 4543

**CORRESPONDENT:** Norman Franklin

**TRUSTEES:** Norman Franklin, Sarah Franklin, Andrew Franklin, Samuel Franklin, T N Franklin

**BENEFICIAL AREA:** National and international

**INFORMATION:** Accounts are on file at the Charity Commission.

**GENERAL:** The trust operates in tandem with the Norman Franklin Trust (see separate entry). Its report with its accounts for 1991/92 is identical and states that its policy is to give to: Culture and environment; Overseas relief and development; relief of poverty, disablement and distress, particularly seed corn money and for development. 'Overseas our interests are in special projects with low overheads that will actually deliver, both in the Third World (particularly the Commonwealth) and in Eastern Europe'.

In 1991/92 the following grants with relevance to this guide were:

Medical Foundation for the Care of the Victims of Torture (£1,000);

Quaker Peace and Service, Prison Reform Trust, Canon Collins Educational Trust for South Africa, Nicaragua Health fund, LEPRA (£500 each).

**EXCLUSIONS:** Travel; students.

**APPLICATIONS:** In writing to the correspondent, Applications should be clear and succinct, contain accounts and a budget. No acknowledgement will be given to unsolicited applications.

# Norman Franklin Trust

**GRANT TOTAL:** £44,500 (1992/93)

**MAIN AREAS OF WORK:** See below

**ADDRESS:** 78 Lawn Road, NW3 2XB

**TELEPHONE:** 071-722 4543

**CORRESPONDENT:** Norman Franklin

**TRUSTEES:** Norman Franklin, Thomas Franklin, S A Franklin

**BENEFICIAL AREA:** National and international

**INFORMATION:** Accounts are on file at the Charity Commission.

**GENERAL:** See the Jill Franklin Trust entry for aims and objects. This trust supports similar organisations at the same level. Grants in 1993 relevant to this guide were also given to:

Oxfam (1,694);

Medical Foundation for the Victims of Torture (£1,000).

In 1991/92 support was also given to Book Aid (£1,000) and the Jan Hus Educational Foundation which assists education in Czechoslovakia.

**EXCLUSIONS:** Travel; students.

**APPLICATIONS:** In writing to the correspondent. Applications should be clear and succinct, contain accounts and a budget. No acknowledgement will be given to unsolicited applications.

# Fray's Charitable Trust

**GRANT TOTAL:** £18,000 (1991/92)

**MAIN AREAS OF WORK:** Overseas relief

**ADDRESS:** Currey & Co, 21 Buckingham Gate, London SW1E 6LS

**TELEPHONE:** 071-828 4091/8

**CORRESPONDENT:** E R H Perks

**TRUSTEES:** Mrs C N Withington, D B Withington, E R H Perks.

**BENEFICIAL AREA:** International, particularly Africa.

**INFORMATION:** Accounts are on file at the Charity Commission.

**GENERAL:** The trust has assets of some £226,000. In 1991/92 it gave nine grants all to development agencies. These included:

Oxfam (£9,292, also given £6,000 in the previous year);

Ranfurlay Library Service (£2,000);

ActionAid and Africa Now (£1,500 each);

Tree Aid (£1,250);

CARE (£1,000).

**APPLICATIONS:** In writing to the correspondent.

# Fulbright Commission

**ADDRESS:** United States – United Kingdom Educational Commission, Fulbright House, 62 Doughty Street, London WC1N 2LS

**TELEPHONE:** 071-404 6880; Fax 071-404 6834; Education Advisory Service: 071-404 6994; Fax 071-404 6874

**CORRESPONDENT:** Heather Robson, British Programme Administrator.

**INFORMATION:** Detailed guidelines of criteria and benefits are available and should be accompanied by a SAE.

**GENERAL:** The Origins of the Commission: Inspired by his early experience as a Rhodes Scholar at Oxford, Senator William Fulbright sponsored legislation in the United States after the Second World War to use funds from the sale of surplus war property for programmes of education and cultural exchange. The purpose of the Fulbright programme is to further mutual understanding between the United States and other nations. The programme operates in more than 100 countries, and in 43 of them bi-national commissions have been established to administer it. The British bi-national commission was set up in 1948. Since 1965 the United Kingdom Government has contributed to its funding, and at present provides one third of the Commission's annual budget. Under the provisions of the Fulbright-Hays programme, a number of grants are available to citizens of the United Kingdom and dependent territories for academic study or assistance for the travel costs of lecturing or research, in the United States of America. The awards are competitive and are made by the Commission in London in cooperation with the Board of Foreign Scholarships in Washington. Applicants must be citizens of, and ordinarily resident in the United Kingdom or its dependent territories. Some basic criteria are listed below; full details should be obtained from the Commission.

**Awards for Postgraduate Students:** These cover round-trip travel and full maintenance for one academic year. There are no strictures regarding the disciplines favoured and no age limits. Applicants must have at least an upper second class honours degree, or its equivalent. Some 25 awards are made each year. No list of awards is available from the Commission. (Travel only awards are also offered.)

**Travel Grants for Visiting Lecturers and Research Scholars:** Applicants must hold an appointment to undertake lecturing or research at an approved American institution of higher learning. Grants to Visiting Lecturers are confined to those who have been invited to lecture at a University or College or at some other approved institution of higher learning in the United States. Senior Research Scholars normally should have achieved professional standing in their chosen field and should be planning advanced work of a postdoctoral nature at an approved institution of higher learning in the United States. Junior Research Scholars normally should not be older than 30 years on the closing date for the competition, and should have a PhD or its equivalent, or be expecting to complete requirements for a PhD before departing for the United States. All scholars should have good reasons for pursuing their work in the United States.

Applicants must be planning a minimum stay of about four months at one academic institution in the United States. The Commission stresses that it is the objective of this programme that a maximum amount of time be spent in the United States. Preference is therefore given to those applicants who intend to spend a full academic year there. Of this time about two-thirds should be spent at one university or recognised research institution. Applications for the summer months only will not be considered. About 18 awards are made each year.

**APPLICATIONS:** Application forms for awards for postgraduate students are available from July each year and no requests for them can be made after late October. Applications have to be made by the first week in November and short listed candidates are interviewed in January. Application forms for Visiting Lecturers and Research Scholars should not be requested till their plans are complete so that details of the appointment and funding available to them can be given. Forms are available from the beginning of October. No requests for forms will be considered after late April. The closing dates: 4th March 1994 for those travelling between June and July; 1994 and 6th May 1994 for those travelling between August 1994 and May 1995. All enquiries must be accompanied by a large SAE with 38p stamp.

## Fund for Human Need

**GRANT TOTAL:** £16,000 (1991)

**MAIN AREAS OF WORK:** Overseas relief

**ADDRESS:** 1 Central Buildings, London SW1H 9NH

**TELEPHONE:** 071-222 8010

**CORRESPONDENT:** The Secretary

**TRUSTEES:** The Methodist Church, Division of Social Responsibility

**BENEFICIAL AREA:** Worldwide

**INFORMATION:** Accounts are on file at the Charity Commission.

**GENERAL:** In 1990 the fund give to Y Care International, China (£1,000). In 1989 grants included Ecuadorian Foundation for Popular Construction (£1,000), British Refugee Council (£500), Kurdish Refugees in Hackney (£500), Prisoners of Conscience Appeal Fund (£100).

**APPLICATIONS:** In writing to the correspondent at any time, Trustees meet twice a year.

## The Gatsby Charitable Foundation

*+ many charitable organisation only*

(see also entry for the Sainsbury Family Charitable Trusts)

**GRANT TOTAL:** £11,119,000 (1992/93)

**MAIN AREAS OF WORK:** General

**ADDRESS:** 9 Red Lion Court, London EC4A 3EB

**TELEPHONE:** 071-410 0330

**CORRESPONDENT:** Hugh L de Quetteville

**TRUSTEES:** C T S Stone, Miss J S Portrait

**BENEFICIAL AREA:** Unrestricted

**INFORMATION:** Report and accounts are on file at the Charity Commission, but without details of the amount given for each grant.

**GENERAL:** This foundation, regarded as the main charitable vehicle for David Sainsbury, is endowed primarily with shares in Sainsbury plc. It is noted that the trustees met nine times in the year 1992/93 to discuss disbursements.

The categories under which donations were made in 1992/93 were: Management Development; Technical Education; Health Care & Service Delivery; Disadvantaged Children; Plant Science; Third World Development; General.

Grants with relevance to this guide were made in 1991/92 in the following categories (it should be noted that the Economic Research category was discontinued in 1992/93):

**Economic Research** – total disbursement: £1,651,000

European Movement;

Royal Institute for International Affairs;

Federal Trust.

**Third World Development** – total disbursement: £623,000

ActionAid;

Cape Town University;

Tanzania Gatsby Charitable Trust.

**APPLICATIONS:** In writing to the correspondent at any time. An application to one of the Sainsbury family trusts (see separate entry) is an application to all.

# J Paul Getty Jr General Charitable Trust

**GRANT TOTAL:** £1.278 million

**MAIN AREAS OF WORK:** Social welfare

**ADDRESS:** 149 Harley Street, London W1N 2DH

**TELEPHONE:** 071-4861859

**CORRESPONDENT:** Bridget O'Brien Twohig, Administrator

**TRUSTEES:** J Paul Getty Jr, James Ramsden, Christopher Gibbs, Vanni Treves.

**BENEFICIAL AREA:** National

**INFORMATION:** Accounts are on file at the Charity Commission.

**GENERAL:** The trust was established in 1985 for 'all such legally charitable purposes in the UK or outside the UK as the trustees in their absolute discretion from time to time think fit'. In 1991 it divided its grant into the following categories: Conservation, heritage, environment; Drugs and alcohol; Mental health; Mental handicap; Youth (including counselling and training); Community groups; Offenders; Ethnic minorities; Homeless; AIDS; Women; Physically handicapped; Miscellaneous. In recent years grant relevant to this guide have been made:

In 1993 –

Committee on Administration of Justice (£12,000);

Independent Immigration Support Agency (£3,000);

In 1992 –

Immigrants Aid Trust (£7,500 x 3);

In 1991 –

Refugee Support Centre (£7,500);

In 1990 –

Prisoners Abroad (£5,000);

In 1989 –

Family Rights Group (£6,000);

**EXCLUSIONS:** These include research, education, children.

**APPLICATIONS:** Initially a letter of not more than two pages can be sent at any time. It should give details of the project and its needs, its existing sources of finance and what other applications, including those to statutory sources, have been made. Annual accounts are always seen before the trustees consider the application. The trustees meet quarterly but, because they usually like projects to be visited before grants are made there may be considerable delay between an application and its consideration. Both revenue and capital grants are made.

## Give Peace a Chance Trust

**GRANT TOTAL:** £4,000 (1987)

**ADDRESS:** 20 The Drive, Hertford SG14 3DF

**TELEPHONE:** 0992-586 943

**CORRESPONDENT:** Gerald Drewett, Secretary.

**TRUSTEES:** Alex Bryan, Eleanor Barden, Anne Brewer, John Endersby, Allen Jackson.

**GENERAL:** The trust was founded in 1986 by a group of Quakers who were seeking a legal way to divert taxes from military purposes to peace-building purposes. Its aim is to record the history and current activities of the peace movements, and it produces exhibitions and publications which will form the nucleus for locally-inspired and charitably-based Peace Education Centres. Its ultimate aim is a National Peace Museum, or a series of provincial museums. The Provincial Museum cum Peace Education Centre is seen as an integrated concept.

It is an active trust which seeks funds for projects it identifies from applications received. Applications can be for very small personal grants, e.g. for historical research which results in something tangible; or larger projects which are moderate in terms of their financial need. It is known for example that the Institute for Law and Peace has received £100 from this trust.

## GNC Trust

**GRANT TOTAL:** £104,000 (1990)

**ADDRESS:** c/o Messrs Price Waterhouse, Livery House, 161 Edmund Street, Birmingham, West Midlands

**CORRESPONDENT:** See above.

**TRUSTEES:** R N Cadbury, Mrs J E B Yelloly, G T E Cadbury.

**INFORMATION:** Accounts are on file at the Charity Commission but not with annual regularity.

**GENERAL:** The trust has general charitable objects, a national scope and a particular interest in the Midlands, Avon, Cornwall and Hampshire. A review of the most recent accounts on file at the Charity Commission showed the following grants with some relevance to this guide:

1990 –
   Society of Friends (£5,905);
   CARE (£500);
   ActionAid (£200);
1988 –
   Bangladesh Flood Appeal (£2,000);
   ActionAid (£1,000);
   Medical Aid for Poland (£500).

**APPLICATIONS:** In writing to the correspondent.

## Godinton Charitable Trust

**GRANT TOTAL:** £267,700 (1992)

**ADDRESS:** Godinton Park, Ashford, Kent TN23 3BW

**TELEPHONE:** 0233-20773

**CORRESPONDENT:** A W Green

**TRUSTEES:** R J Eddis, Moran Caplat, M F Jennings, W G Plumtre

**BENEFICIAL AREA:** National

**INFORMATION:** Accounts are on file at the Charity Commission.

**GENERAL:** This charity makes a very large number of small grants of £500 and less. In 1992 the following grants relevant to this guide were:

   Institute for Scientific Information, Moscow University (£567);

   Northern Ireland Council for Voluntary Action (£500);

   Turning Point, VSO, CARE, LEPRA (£500 each);

   UNICEF, Russian Immigrant Aid Fund (£250 each);

**APPLICATIONS:** In writing to the correspondent.

## The Goldsmiths' Company's Charities

**GRANT TOTAL:** Over £1 million

**ADDRESS:** Goldsmiths' Hall, Foster Lane, London EC2V 6BN

**TELEPHONE:** 071-606 7010

**CORRESPONDENT:** R D Buchanan-Dunlop, Clerk

**TRUSTEES:** The Goldsmiths' Company

BENEFICIAL AREA: National with a special interest in London charities.

INFORMATION: Accounts are on file at the Charity Commission.

GENERAL: The Goldsmiths' Company is a City Livery Company. It controls at least ten charities which have been inherited or given substantial charitable funds and endowments. Its three largest charities have around £17 million in assets. Substantial awards are given to certain educational institutions and colleges.

Only a few grants have been given in recent years to organisations which fall within the scope of this guide, for instance:

In 1992 –

Ditchley Foundation (£5,000);

Youth Action, NI (£1,500);

Cooperation Ireland (£1,000);

Grants have also been given earlier to Refugee Action (£2,000) and the Medical Foundation for the Care of Victims of Torture.

APPLICATIONS: In writing to the correspondent, including Charity Registration number, an annual report and audited accounts, two independent referees, the object of the appeal, the appeal target and the amount needed to meet it, organisations approached and results to date. Preference for a single grant or for annual grants for up to three years.

## S & F Goodman Trust Fund

GRANT TOTAL: £27,000 (1991/92)

ADDRESS: 42 Shirehall Lane, London NW4 2PS

CORRESPONDENT: Clive Goodman

TRUSTEES: Clive Goodman, Mrs Deborah Jalalay

GENERAL: Grants relevant to this guide in recent years included:

In 1991/92 –

Greenpeace Environmental Trust (£700 with £600 in the previous 2 years);

Friends of the Earth (£600 with grants also in the 2 previous years);

Refugee Council (£200 with grants also in the 2 previous years);

In 1989/90 –

War on Want (£600 with £700 in the previous year);

VSO (£100).

APPLICATIONS: In writing to the correspondent.

## The Grand Charity

GRANT TOTAL: £2.1 million (1989)

MAIN AREAS OF WORK: General

ADDRESS: 60 Great Queen Street, London WC2B 5AZ

TELEPHONE: 071-831 9811

CORRESPONDENT: Commander M B S Higham

TRUSTEES: Masonic Charity Trustee Ltd

BENEFICIAL AREA: England and Wales

INFORMATION: Accounts are on file at the Charity Commission.

GENERAL: The charity makes grants to freemasons in need or their dependants, to charities (both masonic and non-masonic) working in the fields of health, social welfare or disaster relief.

## The Great Britain-Sasakawa Foundation

GRANT TOTAL: £450,000 (1993)

MAIN AREAS OF WORK: Links between Great Britain and Japan

ADDRESS: 43 North Audley Street, London W1Y 1WH

TELEPHONE: 071-355 2229; Fax: 071-355 2230

CORRESPONDENT: Donald Warren-Knott

TRUSTEES: Lord Butterfield (Chairman), Kazuo Chiba, David Corsan, Sir Edward du Cann, Brandon Gough, Akira Iriyama, Professor Harumi Kimura, Professor Makoto Momoi, Sir Angus Ogilvy, Yoshio Sakurauchi, Yohei Sasakawa, Professor Shoichi Watanabe, Sir John Whitehead

INFORMATION: An annual report is available.

GENERAL: The foundation's aim is to improve Anglo-Japanese relations by bringing together the citizens of the United Kingdom and Japan in projects which contribute to their mutual education and understanding. Since its establishment in 1985 grants have been donated in the following categories: Cultural; Anglo-Japanese Relations: General; Science, Industry, Technology; Youth Exchange; Japanese Language Teaching; Medical Research; Japanese Studies; Sport; Religion, Conservation, Ecology.

Grants in 1992 with some relevance to the scope of this guide included:

Youth Exchange Centre for exchange programme with Japan (£56,000);

National Educational Resources Information Service (NERIS) for a database of resources in the UK for schools and education centres teaching Japanese (£20,000);

Experiment in International Living, exchanges of disadvantaged youth between Japan and the UK (£14,000).

EXCLUSIONS: Applications are not accepted from individuals but an organisation may apply on behalf of an individual. Only applicants who are citizens of Japan or the UK may benefit.

APPLICATIONS: The grants committee meets in Spring and Autumn and applicants are notified shortly after each meeting. There is no printed application form.

# Walter Guinness Charitable Trust

GRANT TOTAL: £118,000 (1991/92)

MAIN AREAS OF WORK: General

ADDRESS: Biddesden House, Andover, Hampshire SP11 9DN

TELEPHONE: 0264-790 237

CORRESPONDENT: The Secretary

TRUSTEES: Lord and Lady Moyne, F B Guinness, Rosaleen Mulji.

BENEFICIAL AREA: National and international

GENERAL: The following grants with relevance to this guide were given:

In 1991/92 –

Medical Aid for Palestinians (£1,000);

NACRO (£500);

Anti-Slavery Trust (£200);

Medical Foundation for the Care of Victims of Torture (£100);

Oxfam, SOS Sahel (£100 each);

LEPRA (£100, also given in the previous year);

In 1990/91-

The Gulf Trust (£5,000);

Intermediate Technology Development Group (£1,000).

APPLICATIONS: The following caution for new applicants was sent by the trust for the previous edition 'The trustees are not able to give individual students' grants. They have a long list of causes which they support and are actively seeking to reduce this by concentrating on long-standing commitments. They are not able to reply to appeals to which they are not able to respond'.

# Gunter Charitable Trust

GRANT TOTAL: £61,000 (1991/92)

MAIN AREAS OF WORK: General

ADDRESS: 4 John Carpenter Street, London EC4Y 0NH

CORRESPONDENT: H R D Billson

TRUSTEES: H R D Billson, J de C E Findlay

BENEFICIAL AREA: National and international

INFORMATION: Accounts are on file at the Charity Commission.

GENERAL: Grants with relevance to this guide were made:

In 1991/92 –

Save the Children Fund (£3,550);

Oxfam (£1,220, with £4,450 given in the previous year);

Marie Stopes International (£2,214);

Survival International (£550 within £450 given in the previous year);

VSO Belfast, Corrymeela Community, Friends of the Earth, Intermediate Technology Development Group (£500 each);

In 1990/91 –

Romanian Children AIDS Appeal (£8,000).

APPLICATIONS: Unsolicited applications are not welcomed.

# The Hadrian Trust

**GRANT TOTAL:** £158,000 (1992)

**MAIN AREAS OF WORK:** Social Welfare in the North East

**ADDRESS:** c/o Stanford & Lambert, Alliance House, Hood Street, Newcastle-upon-Tyne NE1 6LD

**TELEPHONE:** 091-232 6226

**CORRESPONDENT:** John Parker

**TRUSTEES:** Richard Harbottle, Brian J Gillespie, John B Parker

**INFORMATION:** Accounts are on file at the Charity Commission.

**GENERAL:** A review of the trust's grant making showed the following grants with relevance to this guide in 1991 (there being none in 1992):

North East Refugee Service (£1,000 and in the previous year);

Cleveland Family Conciliation Service (£1,000);

Help International Relief Development Agency (Romania).

**APPLICATIONS:** In writing to the correspondent. Meetings are held four times a year to consider applications.

# The Hambland and Lankelly Foundations

**GRANT TOTAL:** £1,630,300 (Hambland 1992/93) £1,850,200 (Lankelly 1992/93)

**MAIN AREAS OF WORK:** See below

**ADDRESS:** 2 The Court, High Street, Harwell, Didcot, Oxon OX11 OEY

**TELEPHONE:** 0235-820044

**CORRESPONDENT:** Peter Kilgarriff

**TRUSTEES:** A Ramsay Hack, C Heather, W J Mackenzie, Shirley Turner.

**BENEFICIAL AREA:** National

**INFORMATION:** Accounts are on file at the Charity Commission.

**GENERAL:** The two foundations were established by the same anonymous benefactor and share common trustees.

A policy has been formulated which centres on social welfare, disability, heritage and conservation. The foundations have particular interest in Northern Ireland where the following sums were disbursed: in 1990/91 £135,000; in 1991/92 £72,000; in 1992/93 £214,000.

Grants agreed included:

In 1992/93 –

Voluntary Service Belfast (£52,000);

123 House Belfast (£33,900);

Northern Ireland Women's Aid Federation Belfast (£20,000);

NICOD (£18,000);

Knocks Community Association, Presbyterian Church in Ireland Board of Social Witness, Richmond Fellowship Kinnahalla Project, Roslea Heritage and Visitor Centre (£15,000 each);

Dunlewey Substance Advice Centre, Karen Mortlake Trust (£10,000 each);

Northern Ireland Council for Voluntary Action (£7,500).

In 1991/92 –

Voluntary Service Lisburn (£20,000);

Simon Community (£19,000);

Belfast Centre for the Unemployed, East Belfast Mission (£15,000 each);

In 1990/91-

Belfast Women's Aid, Lower Falls Association for Handicapped, Belfast (£20,000 each);

Belcoo and District Development Group, NICOD, Cathedral Community Services, Belfast (£15,000 each);

Ulster Quaker Service Community Belfast, Share Centre Lisnakea, Foreglen Community Association, Northern Ireland Association for Mental Health (£10,000 each);

Playboard Northern Ireland (£2,000 and in the next 2 years);

Voluntary Service Belfast for play scheme (£1,000 and in the next 2 years).

**APPLICATIONS:** All applicants should first obtain the foundations' guidelines. All the assets of the Hambland Foundation have now been transferred to the Lankelly Foundation and applications should *only* be made to the Lankelly Foundation. Applications cannot simply be transferred to the Chase Charity or vice versa.

# Harbour Foundation Ltd

**GRANT TOTAL:** £125,000 (1991/92)

**ADDRESS:** 8–10 Half Moon Court, Bartholomew Close, London EC1A 7HE.

**CORRESPONDENT:** S A Simmonds.

**TRUSTEES:** Council of Management

**BENEFICIAL AREA:** National and international

**INFORMATION:** Accounts are on file at the Charity Commission but without a schedule of grants since 1982.

**GENERAL:** The foundation's objects are: The relief of poverty, suffering and distress amongst refugees, homeless and displaced persons throughout the world; The advancement of education, learning and research of persons and students of all ages and nationalities throughout the world and to disseminate the results of this research; General charitable purposes.

# The Mrs J S Harcus Charitable Trust

**GRANT TOTAL:** £47,000 (1990/91)

**MAIN AREAS OF WORK:** Christian and general

**ADDRESS:** 4 The Paddock, North Ferriby, North Humberside HU14 3JU

**CORRESPONDENT:** Mrs J S Harcus

**TRUSTEES:** Jeanetta Harcus, Alfred Harcus

**BENEFICIAL AREA:** National and international

**INFORMATION:** Accounts are on file at the Charity Commission.

**GENERAL:** The trust's assets of £420,000 are largely in shares in the confectioners, Thorntons. Grants of relevance to this guide were given to:

Amnesty International (£1,000);

Red Cross (£1,000);

Oxfam (£750);

Refugee Year, Tear Fund, UNICEF (£250 each).

**APPLICATIONS:** The trust has written that it is not their policy to reply to, or support, unsolicited applications

# L G Harris & Co Ltd Charitable Trust

**GRANT TOTAL:** £8,000 (1992/93)

**MAIN AREAS OF WORK:** General

**ADDRESS:** Stoke Prior, Bromsgrove, Hereford and Worcester B60 4AE

**TELEPHONE:** 0527-31441

**CORRESPONDENT:** The Secretary.

**TRUSTEES:** L G Harris, B Middleton.

**BENEFICIAL AREA:** National and local

**INFORMATION:** Accounts are on file at the Charity Commission.

**GENERAL:** In 1992/93 the following grants with relevance to this guide were given:

One World Trust (£3,000);

UNA Trust (£1,000);

Community for Reconciliation (£100).

**APPLICATIONS:** New applications are not welcomed.

# The Hayward Foundation

**GRANT TOTAL:** £1,005,000 (1992)

**MAIN AREAS OF WORK:** See below

**ADDRESS:** 45 Harrington Gardens, London SW7 4JU

**TELEPHONE:** 071-370 7063

**CORRESPONDENT:** Mark Schnebli, Administrator

**TRUSTEES:** I F Donald (Chairman), E G Sykes, Sir Jack Hayward, Dr J C Houston, Mrs S J Heath, G J Hearne, C W Taylor, J N van Leuven.

**BENEFICIAL AREA:** National

**INFORMATION:** Accounts are on file at the Charity Commission.

**GENERAL:** In 1992 the following grants with some relevance to this guide were given to:

Greenpeace (£50,000);

Howard League (£14,800);

Northern Ireland Council for Integrated Education (£10,000);

CARE (£5,000).

**APPLICATIONS:** Applications should contain a brief outline of the benefits a grant would make, how many people will benefit or what saving would be achieved. A full set of the latest accounts must be included and the application signed by a trustee.

## The Charles Hayward Trust

**GRANT TOTAL:** £609,000 (1992/93)

**MAIN AREAS OF WORK:** General with a particular interest in the poor and the aged.

**ADDRESS:** 45 Harrington Gardens, London SW7 4JU

**TELEPHONE:** 071-370 7067

**CORRESPONDENT:** M T Schnebli, Administrator

**TRUSTEES:** I F Donald (Chairman), M R Cowper, A D Owen, Miss A T Rogers, A H McIlreath

**BENEFICIAL AREA:** National

**INFORMATION:** Accounts are on file at the Charity Commission.

**GENERAL:** In 1991/92 the trust made the following grants with relevance to this guide:

Northern Ireland Voluntary Trust (£30,000 with £15,000 and £12,000 in the two previous years); Ulster Quaker Service, Belfast (£7,800).

**EXCLUSIONS:** Registered charities in the UK only.

**APPLICATIONS:** In writing to the correspondent.

## The Headley Trust

**GRANT TOTAL:** £1,347,500 (1992)

**MAIN AREAS OF WORK:** General

**ADDRESS:** 9 Red Lion Court, London EC4A 3EB

**TELEPHONE:** 071-410 0330

**TRUSTEES:** Rt Hon T A D Sainsbury MP, Mrs S M Sainsbury, J Sainsbury, J R Benson, Miss J Portrait

**BENEFICIAL AREA:** National

**INFORMATION:** Accounts are filed at the Charity Commission with a report and categories of grant making but without scale of individual grants.

**GENERAL:** See the entry for the Sainsbury Family Trusts. In 1992 grants were given in the following categories:

Arts and Environment (Home and Overseas); Medical; Developing Countries; Social Work and Research (Children/Young People, Old People and Work for the Community); Education; Museums, Galleries and Libraries.

In 1991 grants relevant to the scope of this guide were given:

**Under 'Developing Countries' –**

Schools Partnership Worldwide; WaterAid; Medical Electives; Health Unlimited; Friends of Conservation; Sandy Gall's Afghanistan Appeal;

**Under 'Children and Young People' –**

Voluntary Service Belfast.

**APPLICATIONS:** Ann application to one of the Sainsbury Family Trusts is an application to all.

## Hickinbotham Charitable Trust

**GRANT TOTAL:** £30,000 (1992)

**MAIN AREAS OF WORK:** General with a particular interest in local and Quaker charities.

**ADDRESS:** 69 Main Street, Bushby, Leicester LE7 9PL

**CORRESPONDENT:** Mrs C R Hickinbotham.

**TRUSTEES:** Mrs C R Hickinbotham, P F J Hickinbotham, R P Hickinbotham.

**GENERAL:** In 1992 the trust gave a small grant of £50 to the Prisoners of Conscience Relief Fund. In 1991 when a larger disbursement of £51,000 was made grants were given to:

Friends World Committee for consultation (£100 with £600 given in the previous year); Christian Aid (£110).

**APPLICATIONS:** In writing to the correspondent. Unsuccessful applicants cannot expect a reply.

## Walter Higgs Charitable Trust

**GRANT TOTAL:** £20,000 (1992)

**MAIN AREAS OF WORK:** General with a particular interest in the West Midlands

**ADDRESS:** 12 Heaton Drive, Edgbaston, Birmingham B15 3LW

**TELEPHONE:** 021-454 0322

**CORRESPONDENT:** D C Y Higgs.

**TRUSTEES:** D C Y Higgs, Mrs A J Higgs, Lady E P Higgs.

**BENEFICIAL AREA:** National and particularly the West Midlands

**GENERAL:** Small grants relevant to this guide were given in 1991 to the Oxfam Gulf Fund and the Relief of Ethiopia and Somalia Appeal.

**APPLICATIONS:** There is little leeway for new applications.

# Hilden Charitable Fund

**GRANT TOTAL:** £455,000 (1992/93)

**MAIN AREAS OF WORK:** Homelessness, minorities, penal affairs, race relations, Third World countries

**ADDRESS:** 34 North End Road, West Kensington, London W14 OSH

**TELEPHONE:** 071-603 1525

**CORRESPONDENT:** Rodney Hedley, secretary to the trustees

**TRUSTEES:** Mrs G J S Rampton, J R A Rampton, Dr D S Rampton, Mrs H M Rampton, Dr M D H Rampton, Mrs A M A Rampton, Mrs M G Duncan, Professor C H Rodeck, Mrs E K Rodeck, Calton Younger

**BENEFICIAL AREA:** UK and the Third World

**INFORMATION:** Accounts are on file at the Charity Commission.

**GENERAL:** In their short report with their accounts for 1991/92 the trustees expressed 'a continuing interest in the third world and in minorities, however defined, in the UK ... overseas grants concentrate on development aid in preference to disaster relief'.

Grants with relevance to this guide were made in 1991/92 to:

Intermediate Technology Development Group (£30,000 in 2 grants);

Christian Aid Bangladesh appeal (£20,000);

Runnymede Trust (£20,000 in 2 grants);

Northern Refugee Centre (£10,000 in 2 grants);

INTERIGHTS (£7,000);

Immigrants Aid Trust (£6,500);

Tools for Self Reliance (£5,000);

Minority Rights Group (£4,000);

Africa Now, United World Colleges, Barinas, Venezuela (£2,000 each);

East European Advice Centre, Prisoners of Conscience Appeal Fund, Medical Foundation for the Care of Victims of Torture (£1,000);

United Nations Association (£850);

Tamil Refugee Action Group (£750).

In 1990/91 grants were also given to:

Northern Ireland Voluntary Trust (£15,000);

British Refugee Council (£3,500).

**APPLICATIONS:** Applicants should write to the secretary describing the need, including full details of cost, on no more than two side of A4. A copy of the latest report and accounts should also be sent, together with the names of other trust which may have been approached.

# Hillcote Trust

**GRANT TOTAL:** £3,650 (1991/92)

**MAIN AREAS OF WORK:** See below

**ADDRESS:** 29 Galton Road, Westcliffe-on-Sea, Essex SSO 8TE

**TELEPHONE:** 0702-45860

**CORRESPONDENT:** J S Coe

**TRUSTEES:** J S Coe, Mrs D J Coe, G S Hemingway.

**BENEFICIAL AREA:** National and international

**INFORMATION:** Accounts are on file at the Charity Commission.

**GENERAL:** The trust has general charitable objects and its deed states clearly that it gives not only to registered charities but also to 'such other charitable purposes as recognised as such by law'. It gives small grants to organisations concerned with peace, reconciliation, conservation and social and therapeutic aid.

In 1991/92 the following grants with relevance to this guide were made:

Refugee Council (£500);

Ulster Quaker Peace Centre, Canon Collins Educational Trust for Southern Africa (£250 each);

Northern Ireland Council for Integrated Education, Capetown Quaker Peace Centre (£200 each);

Northern Friends Peace Board, Give Peace a Chance (£100 each);

National Peace Council , Responding to Conflict (£50 each).

**APPLICATIONS:** In writing to the correspondent. Applications are considered in January each year.

## P H Holt Charitable Trust

**GRANT TOTAL:** £310,000 (1989/90)

**ADDRESS:** c/o Ocean Transport and Trading plc, India Buildings, Liverpool, Merseyside L2 0RB

**TELEPHONE:** 051-236 9292

**CORRESPONDENT:** The Secretary.

**TRUSTEES:** Not disclosed.

**BENEFICIAL AREA:** National and international

**INFORMATION:** Accounts have not been filed at the Charity Commission since 1989/90.

**GENERAL:** Grants are made for charitable purposes in Great Britain, particularly in the Merseyside area also where 'original work or work of special excellence is being undertaken'. The trust made grants under the following headings in 1989/90: Community; Education; Visual arts, music, theatre; Health; Marine. The following grants with some relevance to the scope of this book were then made:

VSO, European Educational Trust (£1,000 each);

Royal Institute of International Affairs (£620);

All Children Together, Belfast Education Trust, Grangetown Primary School (£500 each);

Runnymede Trust (£400);

British Atlantic Committee (£250);

British Executive Service Overseas, Overseas Development Institute, Parliamentary Democracy Trust (£200 each);

International Voluntary service, NW branch (£150);

Returned Volunteer Action (£100).

**APPLICATIONS:** In writing to the correspondent.

## Housing Associations Charitable Trust (HACT)

**GRANT TOTAL:** About £1.2 million annually in over 250 grants

**ADDRESS:** Yeoman House, 168-172 Old Street, London EC1V 9BP

**TELEPHONE:** 071-336 7774

**CORRESPONDENT:** Reena Mukherji, Adviser, Black, Ethic Minority & Refugee Housing (071-336 7877)

**TRUSTEES:** Sir Hugh Cubitt (Chair), Victoria Stark, David Wolverson, Basil Bollers, Severt Cox, Arvinda Gohil, Christine Hunt, Vivienne Sugar

**BENEFICIAL AREA:** National

**INFORMATION:** Annual report and Housing for Black, Ethnic Minority and Refugee Groups information sheet and others.

**GENERAL:** HACT is a 'specialist national charity which aims to help voluntary housing organisations provide good quality housing and related services for homeless people, people with special care and support needs and people living in bad housing conditions. HACT is particularly keen to support projects involving elderly people, people with special needs, and people from black, ethnic and minority and refugee communities.'

**APPLICATIONS:** The relevant information sheet should be obtained and the special adviser contacted (both are noted above).

## Inchcape Charitable Trust Fund

**GRANT TOTAL:** £231,00 (1991/92)

**MAIN AREAS OF WORK:** General

**ADDRESS:** St James's House, 23 King Street, London SW1Y 6QY

**TELEPHONE:** 071-321 0110

**CORRESPONDENT:** The Secretaries.

**TRUSTEES:** The Earl of Inchcape; Sir David Plastow, Viscount Glenapp, M E St Q Wall, C D Mackay, R C O'Donoghue, R C Williams.

**BENEFICIAL AREA:** National and international

**INFORMATION:** Accounts are on file at the Charity Commission.

**GENERAL:** The trust supports the work of national and international charities especially those in the

Commonwealth. Over 200 grants a year are made, with the largest amount by value going to benevolent organisations with military connections, to medical research and to educational and youth charities. The following grants relevant to this guide were given :

In 1991/92 –

United World Colleges (£4,000, also in the previous year);

British Executive Service Overseas (£3,000);

ActionAid (£2,000);

Save the Children Fund (£1,500);

Ranfurly Library Service (£1,200. also given in the previous year);

O D I , Royal Air Force Benevolent Fund (£1,000 each);

Cooperation Ireland, Commonwealth Youth Exchange Council, VSO (£500 each);

LEPRA (£300);

Northern Ireland Voluntary Trust (£250).

In 1990/91 –

Y Care (£5,000);

Oxfam Gulf Appeal (£5,000);

Oxfam, Ethiopia Appeal (£2,000);

Centre for World Development Education (£1,000).

**APPLICATIONS:** In writing to the correspondent including report and accounts. Applications are considered quarterly.


# Inter-Church Emergency Fund for Ireland

**GRANT TOTAL:** £40,000 (1993)

**ADDRESS:** Inter-Church Centre, 48 Elmwood Avenue, Belfast BT9 6AZ

**TELEPHONE:** 0232-663145

**CORRESPONDENT:** Rob Fairmichael, Projects Officer

**TRUSTEES:** The Fund Committee of 12 members is jointly appointed by the Roman Catholic Church and the Irish Council of Churches. Its two co-chairpersons are currently Mrs Olive Marshall and the Very Rev Canon P J Early.

**BENEFICIAL AREA:** Northern Ireland

**INFORMATION:** Information and guidelines sheet or phone-line assistance available Wednesday mornings.

**GENERAL:** The fund supports reconciliation, community development and youth work in, or in relation to, Northern Ireland. It administers gifts given by the Conference of European Churches Emergency Fund for Ireland and the European Catholic Bishops' Fund for Ireland, as well as contributions from other churches and individuals. Applications are normally visited prior to the committee deciding on an application.

Grants awarded in 1993 included:

Rathcoole Self Help Group (£3,000);

Speedwell schools environmental education project, Dungannon (£1,500);

Alliance-Ardoyne Playscheme, Belfast (£886);

Creggan Community Care, Derry (£650);

Brookeborough and District Community Development Association, Boulevard Drop-In Centre Bangor, Glenstar Boys' Club Poleglass (£500 each).

The highest grant given is usually £3,000.

**EXCLUSIONS:** There are a number of exclusions operating (which are more fully listed on the Guidelines sheet) including; no retrospective grants and salaries are funded; no grants are made to the arts, sport, advice work, work with disabled people, work with elderly people, pre-school play groups, uniformed organisations, or events taking place outside Ireland.

**APPLICATIONS:** An application form is provided when it is known that the applicant potentially fits the criteria of the fund. The deadline is usually three weeks before committee meetings which take place in February, June and October.


# Irish Ecumenical Church Loan Fund Committee

**GRANT TOTAL:** £160,000 (current capital in 1993)

**ADDRESS:** Inter-Church Centre, 48 Elmwood Avenue, Belfast BT9 6AZ

**TELEPHONE:** 0232-663145.

**CORRESPONDENT:** Rob Fairmichael, Secretary

**BENEFICIAL AREA:** Northern Ireland and the Republic of Ireland

**INFORMATION:** An information sheet is available.

**GENERAL:** The fund exists to promote the spiritual, physical, moral and social welfare of all the people of Ireland, North and South, by making low interest loans to Christian communions and other bodies e.g. community and reconciliation organisations and co-operatives.

Loans of up to £15,000 are made (currently under review) with an interest rate currently of 5%. They are usually repayable within 3-7 years. Some form of security is required and not more than 60% of total costs of a project are covered.

Loans made in 1993 include:

Bridge Community Trust Belfast (£12,000);

Share Centre, Co Fermanagh (£10,000);

Cornerstone Community Belfast (£5,000).

Other current loans in 1993 include Ulster People's College, Lamb of God Community, Belfast Centre for the Unemployed, Dismas House, and the Irish School of Ecumenics.

**APPLICATIONS:** There is an application form. The fund committee meets twice a year in September and March.

## The Jerusalem Trust

(see also Sainsbury Family Trusts)

**GRANT TOTAL:** £1,655,000 (1992)

**MAIN AREAS OF WORK:** The advancement of Christianity

**ADDRESS:** 9 Red Lion Court, London EC4A 3EB

**TELEPHONE:** 071-410 0330

**CORRESPONDENT:** Hugh de Quetteville

**TRUSTEES:** Tim Sainsbury MP, Mrs S M Sainsbury, V E H Booth MP, Rev T Dudley-Smith, Mrs D Wainman

**BENEFICIAL AREA:** Unrestricted

**INFORMATION:** Accounts are on file at the Charity Commission but without details of the amounts made for each grant.

**GENERAL:** This is one of the Sainsbury trusts which share a common administration. Grants are categorised as follows:

- Christian evangelism at home;
- Christian evangelism overseas;
- Christians in the media;
- Christian education;
- Christian social responsibility (home);
- Christian relief work overseas;
- Christian art.

It is known that in 1990 a grant was given under the social responsibility category to the Council on Christian Approaches to Defence and Disarmament.

**APPLICATIONS:** See proviso under the Sainsbury Family Trusts entry.

## The Jessel, Toynbee and Gillett Charitable Trust

**GRANT TOTAL:** £2,225 (1991)

**MAIN AREAS OF WORK:** Quaker, peace and reconciliation

**ADDRESS:** c/o Alexanders Discount plc, Broadwalk House, 5 Appold Street, London EC2A 2DA

**CORRESPONDENT:** The Secretary

**TRUSTEES:** R A S Moser, G L Blacktop.

**BENEFICIAL AREA:** National

**INFORMATION:** Accounts are on file at the Charity Commission but with not schedule of grants since 1979.

**GENERAL:** The trust (known as the Gillett Charitable Trust until 1991) has been allocating about £3,000 a year in grants since the late 1970s. The most recent indication of its grantmaking is from 1979 when the following grants relevant to this guide were made:

Quaker Peace and Service Council (£1,710);

Council for Education in World Citizenship (£346);

Bristol Resources and rights Centre (£300);

Conflict Education Library Trust (£200);

Conflict Research Society and Fellowship of Reconciliation (£120 each );

Lansbury House Trust Fund (£100).

# J G Joffe Charitable Trust

**GRANT TOTAL:** £287,000 (1991/92)

**ADDRESS:** Liddington Manor, The Street, Liddington, Swindon SN4 OHD

**CORRESPONDENT:** Joel Joffe

**TRUSTEES:** V L Joffe, J G Joffe

**BENEFICIAL AREA:** National and international

**INFORMATION:** Accounts are on file at the Charity Commission.

**GENERAL:** The trust has general charitable objects. There is a strong policy in favour of projects in or working on behalf of Third World development. A review of the trust's accounts lodged at the Charity Commission has shown the following grants with relevance to the scope of this book:

In 1991/92 –

Saferworld Foundation (£27,000);

One World Action, Canon Collins Educational Trust for Southern Africa (£12,500 each);

Oxford Research Group, Survival International, International Health Exchange (£10,000 each);

In 1990/91 –

Marie Stopes International (£20,000);

Minority Rights Groups, Tools for Self Reliance, Foundation for International Security (£10,000);

United Nations Association, Cambodia Trust (£5,000);

In 1989/90 –

UNA Trust (£10,000);

British Pugwash, (£5,000).

**APPLICATIONS:** Funds are fully committed to charities of special interest to the trustees and there will be no consideration or acknowledgement of unsolicited applications.

# The Ian Karten Charitable Trust

**GRANT TOTAL:** £110,000 (1991/92)

**MAIN AREAS OF WORK:** General

**ADDRESS:** The Mill House, Newark Lane, Ripley, Surrey GU23 6DP

**CORRESPONDENT:** I H Karten

**TRUSTEES:** I H Karten, Mrs M Karten, T M Simon

**BENEFICIAL AREA:** National and international

**INFORMATION:** Accounts are on file at the Charity Commission.

**GENERAL:** In 1991/92 this trust which has assets of some £5 million, gave £39,425 in 107 donations to charities and £70,230 in scholarships and bursaries to 141 students.

The grants to charities include many to Jewish organisations. Grants in recent years with relevance to this guide have been given :

In 1991/92 –

Group Relations Educational Trust (£750);

Save the Children Fund (£150);

Northern Refugee Centre (£100 also in 1989/90);

In 1989/90 –

Enniskillen Community Development Project (£100);

In 1988/89 –

Refugee Studies Programme, Queen Elizabeth House, Oxford (£150);

Intermediate Technology Development Group (£100).

**APPLICATIONS:** In writing to the correspondent. It is understood that the trustees prefer to take their own direct initiatives in support of charities.

# Kleinwort Benson Charitable Trust

**GRANT TOTAL:** £272,000 (1992).

**MAIN AREAS OF WORK:** General

**ADDRESS:** PO Box 560, 20 Fenchurch Street, London EC3P 3DB

**TELEPHONE:** 071-623 8000

**CORRESPONDENT:** Philip Prain.

**TRUSTEES:** Kleinwort Benson Trustees Limited, Philip Prain.

**BENEFICIAL AREA:** National

**INFORMATION:** Accounts are on file at the Charity Commission.

**GENERAL:** The trust's accounts for 1992 showed the following grants with some relevance to the scope of this guide:

Atlantic College (£9,250 with £8,250 in the previous year);

British Red Cross, Bosnia and Somalia appeals (£6,000);

WaterAid (£3,780 with £300 in the previous year);

Ditchley Foundation £2,000 with £500 in the previous year);

Women Caring Trust (£600);

English Speaking Union (£500 with £3,500 in the previous year);

Save the Children (£500 with £1,000 in the previous year);

Christian Aid (£100).

**APPLICATIONS:** In writing to the correspondent.

## Sir Cyril Kleinwort Charitable Settlement

**GRANT TOTAL:** £500,000 (1991/92)

**ADDRESS:** c/o Kleinwort Benson Trustees Limited, P O Box 191, 10 Fenchurch Street, London EC3M 3LB

**TELEPHONE:** 071-956 6600

**CORRESPONDENT:** The Secretary

**TRUSTEES:** Kleinwort Benson Trustees Ltd

**BENEFICIAL AREA:** National with interest in Gloucestershire

**INFORMATION:** Full accounts are on file at the Charity Commission.

**GENERAL:** The following grants given by the trust in the past few years are relevant to the scope of this guide:

In 1991/92 –

Population Concern (£10,000, a regular grant);
Ross McWhirter Foundation (£5,000);

In 1990/91 –

Royal Institute of International Affairs (£5,000);
University of Oxford, Centre for Modern Chinese Studies (£3,000);

In 1989/90 –

Trust for Education in International Living re Eskdalamuir Training Scheme (£13,600 in 2 grants).

**APPLICATIONS:** In writing to the correspondent. The trustees generally meet in May and September. They prefer to 'contribute to the start-up expenses of specific projects, rather than towards running expenses'.

## Ernest Kleinwort Charitable Trust

**GRANT TOTAL:** £1,138,000 (1991/92)

**ADDRESS:** PO Box 191, 10 Fenchurch Street, London EC3M 3LB

**TELEPHONE:** 071-956 6000

**CORRESPONDENT:** The Secretary.

**TRUSTEES:** Kleinwort Benson Trustees Ltd, Mrs J N Kleinwort, Sir Kenneth Kleinwort, Lady Kleinwort, The Earl of Limerick, R D Kleinwort, F A James.

**BENEFICIAL AREA:** National and international, with a particular interest in Sussex

**INFORMATION:** Accounts are on file at the Charity Commission.

**GENERAL:** The trust's objects are for 'general charitable purposes in restricted fields'. It makes grants on a national basis and on a worldwide basis for conservation and planned parenthood. It makes the following types of grant: Donations towards specific projects; Annual subscriptions (mostly confined to Sussex); Temporary loans for short periods to launch specific projects. Grants with some relevance to this guide have been made:

In 1991/92 –

UK Centre for Economic & Environmental Development (£5,000, with £10,000 in 1989/90);
Panos Institute (£1,000);
Prison Fellowship (£750 and in the 2 previous years);

In 1990/91 –

International Institute for Environment and Development (£25,000 and in the previous year. Large grants were also made in earlier years);
Youth for Understanding (£2,000);

In 1989/90 –

International Planned Parenthood Federation (£10,000);
Population Concern (£3,000).

It is also known that a grant was given to Survival International during 1992.

**APPLICATIONS:** In writing to the correspondent.

# Neil Kreitman Foundation

**GRANT TOTAL:** £442,500 (1992/93)

**MAIN AREAS OF WORK:** General

**ADDRESS:** 6 Balcombe House, Taunton Place, London SW1

**CORRESPONDENT:** N R Kreitman

**TRUSTEES:** H Kreitman, Mrs S I Kreitman, R A Kreitman, E A Charles.

**BENEFICIAL AREA:** National and with a particular interest in Israel

**INFORMATION:** Accounts are on file at the Charity Commission.

**GENERAL:** This trust was originally called The Evergreen Charitable Trust and changed its name in 1987. The following grants with relevance to this guide have been made:

In 1992/93 –

Onaway Trust (£10,690, with grants of £6,119 and £9,505 in the 2 previous years);

Lansbury House Trust Fund (£5,000);

Minority Rights Group (£5,000 with £3,000 in the 3 previous years);

Save the Children Fund (£2,000 and in many previous years);

In 1990/91 –

Survival International (£10,000 and in the previous year);

Oxfam (£5,066 with £6,250 in the previous year).

**APPLICATIONS:** In writing to the correspondent.

# The Kulika Trust

**GRANT TOTAL:** £428,000 (1992)

**MAIN AREAS OF WORK:** Education, religious, general

**ADDRESS:** Hesketh House, Portman Square, London W1A 4SU

**TELEPHONE:** 071-224 2696

**CORRESPONDENT:** Andrew Jones, Director

**TRUSTEES:** J H Elvin, W R Middleton, M C Webb

**BENEFICIAL AREA:** Unrestricted, but mainly East Africa

**INFORMATION:** Accounts are on file at the Charity but without a schedule of grants.

**GENERAL:** In 1992 the trust had assets of £3.2 million with an excess of income over expenditure of £2.3 million. Grantmaking was categorised in the 1992 accounts as follows:

General religious and charitable purposes (£50,000);

Advancement of education: General (£367,000);

Youth and child welfare (£11,000).

The major part of its grantmaking under the heading the advancement of education is given through universities for students from East Africa. It is known that in 1992/93 the trust gave a grant of over £1,000 to the Catholic Institute for International Relations.

**APPLICATIONS:** in writing to the correspondent.

# Beatrice Laing Trust

**GRANT TOTAL:** £592,000

**ADDRESS:** Box 1, 133 Page Street, Mill Hill, London NW7 2ER

**TELEPHONE:** 081-906 5200

**CORRESPONDENT:** R M Harley

**TRUSTEES:** Sir Kirby Laing, Sir Maurice Laing, John Laing, David Laing, Christopher Laing, John Laing.

**BENEFICIAL AREA:** Unrestricted

**INFORMATION:** Accounts are on file at the Charity Commission.

**GENERAL:** This trust is administered alongside the Maurice and Kirby Laing Foundations and an application to one will be treated as an application to all.

The charity is primarily concerned with the relief of poverty. The following grants relevant to the scope of this guide have been given:

In 1991/92 –

Oxfam (£20,000);

British-Yugoslav Society, Cambodia Trust (£5,000 each);

Medical Foundation for the Care of Victims of Torture (£2,500 and in the previous year);

WaterAid (£2,000 with £1,800 in the previous year);

Tools for Self Reliance (£1,350, with £1,250 in the previous year);

Africa Now (£1,250);

Population Concern, Prisoners Abroad (£1,100 each with £1,000 in the previous year);

ActionAid (£1,000 and in the previous year);

Gaia Foundation, Marie Stopes International (£1,000 each);

Refugee Support Centre (£1,000);

Voluntary Service Belfast (£1.000 with £550 in the previous year);

Youth Action Northern Ireland, Northern Ireland Voluntary Trust (£600 each);

Anti-Slavery Society, Afghanaid, Anglo-Thai Foundation (£500 each);

Other grants in 1990/91 –

Commonwealth Human Ecology Foundation (£3,000);

UNA Trust, Nicaragua Health Fund (£2,000 each);

Eritrean Relief Association (UK) (£1,000).

**APPLICATIONS:** In writing to the correspondent. The trust does not encourage exploratory telephone calls on 'how best to approach the trust'. Each application should contain all the information needed to allow a decision to be reached, in as short and straightforward a way as possible. Each application should say what the money is for; how much is needed; how much has already been found; where the rest is to come from. Unless there is reasonable assurance on this last point the grant is unlikely to be recommended.

## The Kirby Laing Foundation

**GRANT TOTAL:** £1,140,000 (1992)

**MAIN AREAS OF WORK:** General

**ADDRESS:** Box 1, 133 Page Street, Mill Hill, London NW7 2ER

**TELEPHONE:** 081-906 5200

**CORRESPONDENT:** R M Harley

**TRUSTEES:** Sir Kirby Laing, Lady Isobel Laing, David E Laing, Simon Webley

**BENEFICIAL AREA:** Unrestricted

**INFORMATION:** Accounts are on file at the Charity Commission.

**GENERAL:** The trust is administered alongside the Maurice and Beatrice Laing Foundations, and an application to one will be treated as an application to all.

The charity is primarily concerned with the relief of poverty. The charity altered its financial year for accounting purposes and a nine month period in 1991 is not covered in this note.

In 1990/91 a total of £40,500 was given in seven grants in its Overseas Aid category. There was an increase in 1992 to nine grants totalling £106,500.

Grants in 1990/91 of particular relevance to this guide were:

ActionAid (£10,000);

Commonwealth Human Ecology Council, Intermediate Technology Development Group, Find Your Feet, (£5,000 each).

**APPLICATIONS:** In writing to the correspondent (see Beatrice Laing Trust).

## Maurice Laing Foundation

**GRANT TOTAL:** £1,476,000

**MAIN AREAS OF WORK:** Social welfare, general

**ADDRESS:** Box 1,133 Page Street, Mill Hill, London NW7 2ER

**TELEPHONE:** 081-906 5200

**CORRESPONDENT:** R M Harley

**TRUSTEES:** Sir Maurice Laing, David Edwards, Thomas D Parr, John H Laing, Mrs Sheila Saad.

**BENEFICIAL AREA:** Unrestricted

**INFORMATION:** Accounts are on file at the Charity Commission.

**GENERAL:** This trust is administered alongside the Kirby and Beatrice Laing Foundations, and an application to one will be treated as an application to all. The charity is primarily concerned with the relief of poverty. Grants relevant to this guide were made in 1991/92 to:

United World College of the Atlantic (£50,000 with £25,000 in the 2 previous years);

ActionAid (£20,000);

Global Care (£10,000);

International Institute for Environment and Development (£5,000 also given in the 2 previous years).

It is also understood that grants have been given in recent years to Survival International.

**APPLICATIONS:**

In writing (see Beatrice Laing Trust).


# The Allen Lane Foundation

**GRANT TOTAL:** £325,000 (1991/92)

**ADDRESS:** 32 Chestnut Road, London SE27 9LF

**TELEPHONE:** 081-761 4835

**CORRESPONDENT:** Gillian Davies, Secretary

**TRUSTEES:** Christine Teale, Zoe Teale, Charles Medawar, Clare Morpurgo, Sebastian Morpurgo, Ben Whitaker.

**BENEFICIAL AREA:** National and Ireland.

**INFORMATION:** An information leaflet is available from the foundation. Accounts are on file at the Charity Commission.

**GENERAL:** It is worth quoting from the foundation's helpful leaflet: 'The Allen Lane Foundation was started in 1966 by the late Sir Allen Lane, founder of Penguin Books, to support general causes .

'The trustees support charitable organisations working in areas of social disadvantage within the United Kingdom (with the exception of their programme for Women's Groups in Ireland). Their grants are generally made to groups which the trustees feel are undeservedly unpopular, such as those working with disadvantaged children, refugees, victims of violence, ex-offenders, young people at risk, women's groups, members of minority groups, community projects and travellers, among others.

'Grants are divided into major and minor categories. The former might be of a national and/or strategic nature, looking at issues underlying some of the problems in society, while minor grants might go to local groups encouraging self help and using volunteers, where a small grant will have a significant impact on the project...'

The trustees have embarked on a second three-year funding programme for women's groups in the Republic of Ireland. Starting in June 1992 they awarded 74 grants totalling £40,000 to groups throughout Ireland, The programme will continue in 1993 and 1994 with the help of an advisory committee set up through the Combat Poverty Agency in Dublin.

The following list of grants relevant to this guide has been extracted from the trust's accounts for 1991/92 (the most recent available):

Refugee Arrivals Project, Heathrow (£10,000);

Immigrants Aid Trust (£5,000);

Council for the Homeless, Gaia Trust (£3,000 each);

UNICEF UK Children's Rights (£2,500);

Ballybeen Women's Centre, NI (£2,300);

Northern Refugee Centre, Somali Counselling Project SE1, Prison Reform Trust, Voluntary Service Belfast, Windmill Integrated Primary School NI (£2,000);

Minority Rights Group (£1,500);

UNA Trust, Ulster Quaker Service Committee Belfast, Centre Care Project Enniskillen, Kurdish Information Centre Islington (£1,000);

Community of Reconciliation and Friendship (£750).

**EXCLUSIONS:** Travel overseas, publications, university or similar research. See information leaflet for full list.

**APPLICATIONS:** In writing to the correspondent. All applicants are advised to obtain the information leaflet for more details.


# Lansbury House Trust Fund

**GRANT TOTAL:** £40,000 (1991/92)

**ADDRESS:** 5 Caledonian Road, London N1 9DX

**CORRESPONDENT:** John Hyatt, Secretary

**TRUSTEES:** Trefor Rendall Davies (Chairman), Godric Bader, Howard Clark, Alec Davison, Anne Feltham, Harry Mister, Tony Smythe. Consultants: April Carter, Adam Curle, Jan Melichar, Margaret Melicharova, Michael Randle.

**INFORMATION:** Accounts are filed at the Charity Commission.

**GENERAL:** The trust fund was set up in 1968 to promote research into the peaceful resolution of conflict and to disseminate knowledge about this, about the social, economic and legal aspects of compulsory military service and about other related matters. It has no capital fund and provides support in three ways. It initiates a project and appoints a co-ordinator who is responsible for raising funds from other sources. If approached by an existing body with a project which matches the fund's educational brief it will channel money raised for that project through the fund. Where some funds have accrued from investment and commissions small grants are made for educational work.

Projects supported in 1991/92 include:

Verification Technology Information Centre (VERTIC) (£26,074 with £46,480 in the previous year);

Myrtle Solomon Research Project on Conscription and Conscientious Objection (£14,300 annually);

Commonweal Collection, University of Bradford (£682 with £814 in the previous year);

Housman's Peace Resource Project (£1,500 with £1,000 in the previous year);

Peace Education Project, Peace Pledge Union (£1,551).

**EXCLUSIONS:** Campaigns or party political activities, general appeals, deficit funding and large well-established organisations.

**APPLICATIONS:** In writing to the correspondent. There is no application form.

## The Lawlor Foundation

**GRANT TOTAL:** £308,000 (1990/91)

**MAIN AREAS OF WORK:** Northern Ireland and the Republic of Ireland, general charitable purposes, poverty and education in particular

**ADDRESS:** 2 Prince Albert Road, Regent's Park, London NW1 7SN

**CORRESPONDENT:** Mrs Carly Brown, Secretary.

**TRUSTEES:** Edward Lawlor, Virginia Lawlor, Kelly Lawlor, Stephen Morris, Martin Spiro.

**BENEFICIAL AREA:** Mainly Northern Ireland also with Republic of Ireland and Britain

**INFORMATION:** Accounts are on file at the Charity Commission.

**GENERAL:** The main areas of interest (see above) are currently focused in a policy of support for designated schools and education for individuals in deprived areas of Northern Ireland, women's groups in Ireland, needy Irish people in Britain.

The foundation has assets of over £2 million. In 1991/92 the following donations with relevance to this guide were given:

Co-operation Ireland (£25,000 with £50,000 given in the previous year);

Corrymeela Community (£20,000, with £20,000 also given in the previous year);

Ulster Quaker Service Committee (£5,000);

Shankil Community Education Centre (£5,000);

Shankill Community Council (£2,500).

In 1989/90 grants were also given to the Cornerstone Community, Belfast (£2,000) and the Anglo-Irish Association (£1,000).

It is also known that the Foundation has supported a reconciliation project at the Centre for the Study of Conflict, University of Ulster.

**APPLICATIONS:** The trustees give to causes known to them and are unlikely to support unsolicited applications.

## Edgar Lee Foundation

**GRANT TOTAL:** £26,600 (1992/93)

**MAIN AREAS OF WORK:** General

**ADDRESS:** The Old House, Blandford Road, Iwerne Minster, Blandford Forum, Dorset DT11 8QN

**CORRESPONDENT:** Mr and Mrs B M Lee

**TRUSTEES:** B M Lee, E E Lee, C M Lee, Snow Hill Trustees Ltd

**BENEFICIAL AREA:** National

**INFORMATION:** Accounts are on file at the Charity Commission.

**GENERAL:** About 85 charities were supported in 1992/93. Grants relevant to this guide have been given to:

In 1992/93 –

Intermediate Technology Development Group (£300, with £500 in the 2 previous years);

Pestalozzi (£250, with £300 in the previous year);

In 1991/92 –

Enniskillen Together (£450 with £400 in the previous year).

**APPLICATIONS:** In writing to the correspondent.

# The Leigh Trust

**GRANT TOTAL:** £230,000 (1991/92)

**ADDRESS:** Clive Marks & Company, 44a New Cavendish Street, London W1M 7LG

**TELEPHONE:** 071-486 4663

**CORRESPONDENT:** Clive Marks

**TRUSTEES:** David Bernstein, Dr R M E Stone, H B Levin

**BENEFICIAL AREA:** National

**INFORMATION:** Accounts are on file at the Charity Commission.

**GENERAL:** The trust has general charitable objects. The trustees decided in the early 1990s to concentrate donations over a three year period in the field of addiction and criminal justice.

Applicants should note that the trust gives assistance towards projects concerned with the immediate quality of life of people rather than the broader aspects of work for peace and international understanding. Grants with some relevance to this guide have been made to:

In 1991/92 –

Tools for Self Reliance, Prison Reform Trust (£5,000 each with grant also given in the previous year);

In 1990/91 –

National Association for Prisoners Abroad (£20,000);

Medical Foundation for the Care of Victims of Torture (£16,000).

**APPLICATIONS:** Initial applications should be made in writing to the registered office of the trust, enclosing most recent annual accounts and a self-addressed envelope. Applicants should state clearly what their charity does and what their funding request covers. They should provide a detailed budget and show other sources of funding for the project. It is likely that one or more trustees or officers of the trust will wish to visit the project before any grant is made. Grants can only be made to registered charities.

# Lester Trust Fund

**GRANT TOTAL:** £15,000 (1990/91)

**MAIN AREAS OF WORK:** Religious, educational, social work in Bow and elsewhere

**ADDRESS:** c/o Messrs Midgley, Snelling & Co, Ibex House, Baker Street, Weybridge, Surrey KT13 8AHC

**CORRESPONDENT:** C W Snelling

**TRUSTEES:** C W Snelling, H Faulkener, J Johnson

**BENEFICIAL AREA:** National and international

**INFORMATION:** Accounts are on file at the Charity Commission.

**GENERAL:** The trust which has assets of £139,000, gives its largest grants annually to Kingsley Hall in Dagenham and Kerala Ballagram (£2,500 each). Other grants with relevance to this guide, all but one of which were recurrent, were given to:

Victims Support Group (£800);

Quaker Peace and Service (£600);

International Voluntary Service (£550);

International Fellowship of Reconciliation (£500);

Gandhi Foundation (£500);

Women's International League (£250).

# The Leverhulme Trust

**GRANT TOTAL:** £11,220,000 (1993)

**ADDRESS:** 15–19 New Fetter Lane, London EC4A 1NR

**TELEPHONE:** 071-822 6938

**CORRESPONDENT:** Professor Barry Supple

**TRUSTEES:** Sir Kenneth Durham (Chairman), Viscount Leverhulme, C F Sedcole, Sir Michael Angus, Sir Michael Perry.

**INFORMATION:** For applicants: A booklet on policies and application procedures is available. The trust now publishes an annual report.

**GENERAL:** The trust is restricted to purposes of research and education and the trustees may not make grants for any other kind of charitable purpose. The terms of the trust, on the other hand, impose no restriction as to the fields of study for which grants may be made and set no geographical limits to eligibility. These are matters within the discretion of the trustees. They are open to applications from any eligible quarter which show originality and imagination and which promise to contribute to knowledge or cultural life.

Grants made by the trustees are currently classified under four heads:

- Grants to institutions for research;
- Grants to institutions for academic exchange;
- Grants to institutions for education;
- Grants to individuals under schemes administered by the Research Awards Advisory Committee.

Grants to institutions for research are made under the following headings: Business Studies; Industrial Relations and Economics; Government, Law and International Relations; Medicine and Health; Education; Basic Sciences; Applied Sciences; Humanities; Fine Arts; Libraries, Archives and Museums; Environmental Resources; Regional and Period Studies.

The report for 1991 and 1992 showed the following grants to institutions:

Royal Institute of International Affairs, re Turkish foreign policy (£100,000 over 2 years);

LSE, for study of security and co-operation in the Balkans (£21,500 for 1 year).

Grants to individuals included the following Fellowships:

D A Pinder, Professor of Economic Geography, Polytechnic South west, for study of oil-based energy in the new Eastern Europe;

E M Spiers, Reader in Strategic Studies, Leeds University, for study of chemical weapons in the Third World.

Grants to institutions for academic interchange are normally for a limited period of up to five years. Current schemes include: postdoctoral fellowships from universities in the Commonwealth and the USA to universities in the UK; and post-doctoral fellowships to universities in the UK for scholars in pure and applied science from Bulgaria, Czech Republic, Slovakia, Hungary, Poland and countries of the ex-Soviet Union.

The selection of visitors is delegated by the trustees to an appropriate agency. The trustees do not entertain applications by, or on behalf of, individual scholars.

**EXCLUSIONS:** The trustees are precluded from making capital grants for endowments, sites or buildings, or from giving grants for equipment. They cannot make block grants or grants for such purposes as administration and running costs or to meet deficits. They cannot contribute to appeals.

**APPLICATIONS:** The trust has detailed and specific requirements and procedures which applicants must meet, both as to timing and content. All applicants should first ask for the trust's current Policies and Procedures brochure before attempting to submit an application.

# Livingstone Trust

**GRANT TOTAL:** £7,700 (1991/92)

**ADDRESS:** c/o Wilde & Partners, 10 John Street, London WC1N 2EB

**CORRESPONDENT:** E Wilde

**TRUSTEES:** E Wilde, Brenda Bailey

**BENEFICIAL AREA:** Unrestricted

**INFORMATION:** Accounts are on file at the Charity Commission.

**GENERAL:** Grants relevant to the scope of this guide have been donated in 1991/92 to:

Ulster Quakers (£1,000, with £750 in the previous guide);

British Refugee Council (£1,000);

Medical Foundation for the Care of the Victims of Torture (£500 with £100 in the previous year).

**APPLICATIONS:** In writing to the correspondent.

*no longer doing an [appeal]*

# Lloyd's Charities Trust

**GRANT TOTAL:** £340,450 (1992)

**MAIN AREAS OF WORK:** General

**ADDRESS:** Lloyd's, Lime Street, London EC3M 7HA

**TELEPHONE:** 071-327 5925

**CORRESPONDENT:** Mrs Linda Harper

**TRUSTEES:** H R Dobinson (Chairman), D J Barham, P Barnes, David Beck, Lady Delves Broughton, A W Drysdale, J Wade, A P Bartleet.

**BENEFICIAL AREA:** National and international

**INFORMATION:** Accounts are on file at the Charity Commission and available from the trust.

**GENERAL:** The report with the accounts available from the trust analyses donations under a wide range of headings including moral welfare and reform, environmental resources and international, commonwealth and foreign. This last heading is subdivided into general, disasters, relations and education. Grants relevant to this guide were given in 1992 to:

UNICEF (£2,000);

GAP, Save the Children Fund, Northern Ireland Council for Voluntary Action, International Christian Relief (£1,000 each);

Turning Point (£750);

Commonwealth Youth Exchange Council, WaterAid (£500 each);

Tools for Self Reliance (£350);

Northern Ireland Voluntary Trust (£300);

Women Caring Trust, Hope Romania, Prisoners Abroad, Project Orbis International (£250 each);

**APPLICATIONS:** In writing to the correspondent, including a copy of the latest annual report and accounts.

# The Lyndhurst Settlement

**GRANT TOTAL:** £140,000 (1992/93)

**MAIN AREAS OF WORK:** Social problems, civil liberties, the environment.

**ADDRESS:** Bowker Orford & Co, Chartered Accountants, 15–19 Cavendish Place, London W1M ODD

**CORRESPONDENT:** See above.

**TRUSTEES:** Michael Isaacs, Anthony Skyrme, Peter Schofield.

**BENEFICIAL AREA:** Usually national, but local or foreign applications considered if there is a strong civil liberty component.

**INFORMATION:** Full accounts are on file at the Charity Commission.

**GENERAL:** The objects of the Lyndhurst Settlement are to encourage research into social problems, with specific emphasis on safeguarding civil liberties, maintaining the rights of minorities, and protecting the environment. The trustees prefer to support charities (both innovatory and long-established) that seek to prevent as well as ameliorate hardship and regard protection of the environment as an important civil liberty.

Grants in 1992/93 with a particular relevance to the scope of this guide were:

Marie Stopes International (£5,000);

Immigrants Aid Trust (£4,000);

Medical Foundation for the Care of Victims of Torture, Survival International, Northern Refugee Centre, Civil Liberties Trust (£3,000 each);

Minority Rights Group, Population Concern, Prison Reform Group, Tibet Foundation, Howard League, 21st Century Trust, Shared Earth Trust, Greenpeace, Prisoners Abroad, Leaveners (£2,000 each);

Gaia Foundation (£1,000);

Leed DEC (£500).

The great majority of these organisations also received support in the previous year.

**EXCLUSIONS:** Grants are only made to registered charities. Grants to individuals are not given. The trustees do not normally support medical or religious charities.

**APPLICATIONS:** Requests for grants or further information must be in writing and include a brief description of the aims and objects of the charity.

# The Mackintosh Foundation

**GRANT TOTAL:** £1,903,000 (1992/93)

**MAIN AREAS OF WORK:** Arts, Children, Medical, Refugees

**ADDRESS:** For Appeals: 1 Bedford Square, London WC1B 3RA; For Administration: Watchmaker Court, 33 St John's Lane, London EC1M 4DB

**TELEPHONE:** For Appeals: 071-637 8866; For Administration: 071-405 2000

**CORRESPONDENT:** Appeals Secretary, or the Administration department

**TRUSTEES:** Cameron A Mackintosh, Martin J MacCallum, Nicholas D Allot, D Michael Rose, Patricia MacNaughton, Alain Boubil.

**BENEFICIAL AREA:** Unrestricted

**INFORMATION:** Full accounts are on file at the Charity Commission but with no list of donations. Information leaflet about the foundation and the Bui-Doi Fund.

**GENERAL:** This foundation was set up in 1988 by the highly successful musical producer, Cameron Mackintosh. £8 million has been injected and a further £2.5 million covenanted with assurances of more to follow. The foundation has wide general objects but is particularly concerned with: promotion of theatrical, musical and dramatic art; relief of people with HIV/AIDS and research into the syndrome; children and education; relief of refugees.

In 1990 a special 'Bui-Doi Fund' ('Bui-Doi' meaning 'dust of life') for the relief of Vietnamese refugees. The scope of this fund was enlarge in late 1993 to embrace the poor, the deprived the homeless and the sick in and refugees from Vietnam and other territories of S E Asia.

**EXCLUSIONS:** Religious and political objects.

**APPLICATIONS:** To the correspondent in writing.

# Linda Marcus Charitable Trust

**GRANT TOTAL:** £94,000 (1990/91)

**MAIN AREAS OF WORK:** Jewish

**ADDRESS:** Personal Financial Management, 22 Mount Sion, Tunbridge Wells, Kent TN1 1UN

**TELEPHONE:** 0892-510510

**CORRESPONDENT:** Secretary to the trustees

**TRUSTEES:** Sir Leslie Porter; Dame Shirley Porter; Linda Marcus.

**BENEFICIAL AREA:** National and international

**INFORMATION:** Accounts are on file at the Charity Commission.

**GENERAL:** The major part of the trust's investment (it has assets totalling some £3.5 million) is in Tesco shares. A large number of the 21 grants given in 1991/92 were to organisations based in Israel, many of which had received grants in previous years. Grants were particular relevance to this guide were:

Israel Agency for Nuclear Information (£20,000);

Jaffe Centre for Strategic Studies (£10,000).

**APPLICATIONS:** To the correspondent in writing.

# The Marsden Charitable Trust

**GRANT TOTAL:** £21,000 (1991/92)

**ADDRESS:** 4 The Chestnuts, Winscombe, Avon BS25 1LD

**CORRESPONDENT:** Mrs Hazel Marsden

**TRUSTEES:** Mrs Hazel Marsden, Mrs June Mossop

**BENEFICIAL AREA:** National and international

**GENERAL:** Grants with some relevance to the scope of this guide were given:

In 1991/92 –

Howard League (£1,000);

In 1989/90 –

Oxfam (£5,000);

Prisoners of Conscience Appeal Fund (£3,400);

Woodbrook College, Matthew Trust (£2,500 each);

Friends of the Earth Trust (£2,000);

UNA Trust, Howard League, Quaker Peace Studies Trust (£1,000 each);

Anti-Slavery Society, IVS, Save the Children (£500 each).

**APPLICATIONS:** Unsolicited applications will not be acknowledged. Appeals should be sent to: South Plain, Whitton Park, Milfield, Wooler, Northumberland NE71 6JB.

# The Marsh Christian Trust

**GRANT TOTAL:** £55,000 (1991)

**MAIN AREAS OF WORK:** General

**ADDRESS:** Flat 7, 30 Onslow Gardens, London SW7 3AH

**CORRESPONDENT:** The Secretary

**TRUSTEES:** B P Marsh, Mrs M Litchfield, Mrs A B Marsh.

**BENEFICIAL AREA:** National

**INFORMATION:** Accounts are on file at the Charity Commission.

**GENERAL:** In 1991 the trust had assets of £960,000 and gave grants of £55,000, less than its usual disbursement which is around £100,000. During the year the following grants relevant to this guide were given:

Council for Arms Control (£1,000 with £500 given in the previous year);

Oxfam (£500);

Save the Children Fund (£350);

V S O (£250);

Y Care International (£250);

Intermediate Technology Development Group (£200).

**APPLICATIONS:** In writing to the correspondent.

# The Maxco Trust

**GRANT TOTAL:** Over £1 million

**MAIN AREAS OF WORK:** Christian causes

**ADDRESS:** 62 The Drive, Rickmansworth, Herts WD3 4EB

**TELEPHONE:** 0923-710862

**CORRESPONDENT:** See above

**TRUSTEES:** N W H Sylvester (Managing Trustee), M D Birchall, P A Lovegrove, Colonel P Harvey, W R Frampton, B R C Sells, Sir Eric Richardson.

**BENEFICIAL AREA:** National and international

**INFORMATION:** Accounts are on file at the Charity Commission. Maxco can provide a full list of grants given.

**GENERAL:** The trust's name comes from its guiding aim of: 'Maximising Resources for Christian Outreach'. Grants with relevance to the scope of this guide were:

In 1992/93 –

Tear Fund (£43,035 with £31,100 in the previous year);

Far Eastern Broadcasting Association ( £26,415 with £8,735 in the previous year);

Christian Aid (£2,905 with £3,735 in the previous year);

All Nations Christian College (£300 with £1,600 in the previous year);

Corrymeela Community (£400 and in the previous year).

**APPLICATIONS:** The trust cannot respond to applicants. It distributes income and capital to Christian causes as requested by those who have provided capital in the first place.

# Maypole Fund

**GRANT TOTAL:** Not known (£4,000 in 1988)

**ADDRESS:** 32 Therfield Court, Brownswood Road, London N4 2XL

**CORRESPONDENT:** The Maypole Fund Committee.

**INFORMATION:** A useful leaflet is available from the fund with policy outline and guidelines for applicants.

**GENERAL:** The Maypole Fund was set up in 1986 by a group of women active in the peace movement. It gives grants to women and women's groups for the furtherance of peace with justice and environmental safety. Applications are welcomed from women with projects concerned with any of the following:

• disarmament and action against male violence;

• anti-militarism and action against male violence;

• nuclear and environmental issues;

• promoting women's economic and political autonomy in countries of the Third World;

• international links between women for these purposes.

Grants of up to £500 are given. Maypole has helped with printing leaflets, mounting exhibitions and making videos, travel costs, equipment etc.

**APPLICATIONS:** In writing shortly before on the submission dates: January 31 or June 30. Applicants are usually informed within three weeks of the outcome of their submission. Successful applicants are expected to spend the grant on the agreed activity and sometime in the following six months to write a short report of the activity and attach receipts for expenditure.

## The Mercers' Charitable Foundation

**GRANT TOTAL:** £2,235,000 (1991)

**MAIN AREAS OF WORK:** Education, general

**ADDRESS:** Mercers' Hall, Ironmonger Lane, London EC2V 8ME

**TELEPHONE:** 071-726 4991

**CORRESPONDENT:** The Charities Administrator

**TRUSTEES:** The Mercers' Company.

**BENEFICIAL AREA:** National

**INFORMATION:** Accounts are on file a the Charity Commission.

**GENERAL:** The schedule of grants with the accounts for 1991 show the following grants with some relevance to the scope of this guide:

Police Foundation (£15,000);

Ranfurly Trust (£6,000);

English Speaking Union (£5,000);

All Children Together, Belfast (£2,500);

Prison Reform Trust (£2,000);

Medical Foundation for the Care of Victims of Torture (£1,500);

Co-operation Ireland, Voluntary Service Belfast, Lagan (£1,000 each).

**APPLICATIONS:** In writing to the correspondent. The charitable trustees meet every month. Unsolicited general appeals are considered but not encouraged.

## Mercury Provident plc

**ADDRESS:** Orlingbury House, Lewes Road, Forest Row, East Sussex RH18 5AA

**TELEPHONE:** 034282-3739

**CORRESPONDENT:** Company Secretary, Matthew Robinson

**TRUSTEES:** Directors: Peter Blom, Ray Mitchell, Christian Nunhofer, Duncan Power, Matthew Robinson, Glen Saunders

**INFORMATION:** Annual report, various leaflets and list of projects assisted.

**GENERAL:** Status: Mercury started in 1974 as a Provident Society and converted to a plc in 1986 to be able to offer shares to the public. It takes its philosophical base from Rudolf Steiner, founder of anthroposophy.

**Deposits:** £6.3 million (1992) Mercury Provident is an authorised banking institution which finances socially beneficial enterprises; these may be products or services, or projects which are socially creative in their working structures. A central aim is the promotion of fuller consciousness in money matters. Mercury depositors can make several choices that are normally made for them by conventional banks. Depositors can choose what interest rate they need (not want); they can choose the projects in which their money is to be used; they can choose the term and notice of their deposit. And in all of this they are asked to consider the effect of their choices on the projects they wish to encourage. The rate at which money is lent is chosen by depositors plus a small percentage to cover operational costs. Low-interest deposits can be passed on as low-interest loans. Depositors' money must be secure when lent, but some projects do not have conventional property security to back a loan. In such cases Mercury is innovative in arranging human support-group security in various forms.

More conventional deposit accounts are also offered, including TESSAs. In these cases too the money will be used to fund social and environmental projects. A variety of ethical financial services are available, including pensions. Mercury has helped to finance over three hundred enterprises. These were all small-scale. Mercury has lent to organic growing, curative and medical work, housing associations, employment initiatives, education, publishing, toy and instrument making, and wholefood shops. It encourages projects to develop socially creative organisational structures: cooperatives, charities, and other schemes in which ownership, control and rewards are as widely distributed as possible.

Three types of Mercury shares are on offer to enlarge Mercury's capital base:

- Membership Shares bear no return but entitle owners to a vote at shareholders' meetings.
- Ordinary shares with no voting rights but with the probability of dividends. Buyers select the rate of return they need from those offered: three, five or seven percent.
- Variable rate shares with no voting rights but intended to give a return approximating to the interest payable on the Variable Rate Deposit Accounts.

## The Millfield Trust

**GRANT TOTAL:** £18,000 (1988/89)

**MAIN AREAS OF WORK:** Religious and relief work

**ADDRESS:** Millfield House, Ham Road, Liddington, Swindon, Wiltshire SN4 OHH

**CORRESPONDENT:** D Bunce

**TRUSTEES:** D Bunce, Mrs R W Bunce, P W Bunce, S D Bunce, A C Bunce

**BENEFICIAL AREA:** National and international

**INFORMATION:** Accounts are only on file at the Charity Commission up to 1988/89.

**GENERAL:** In 1988/89 the trust gave £16,000 in donations to charitable and religious organisations and £2,000 in donations to individual evangelists and missionaries. It made two grants with relevance to the scope of this guide:

Tear Fund (£1,110);

Trans World Radio (£1,000).

**APPLICATIONS:** It is understood that funds are committed.

## The Millicope Foundation

**GRANT TOTAL:** £123,000 (1991/92)

**MAIN AREAS OF WORK:** General

**ADDRESS:** c/o SUMIT Equity Ventures Ltd, Edmund House, 12 Newhall Street, Birmingham F3 3EJ

**CORRESPONDENT:** Mrs L J Collins

**TRUSTEES:** M L Ingall, L C N Bury, Mrs S A Bury, Mrs B Marshall

**BENEFICIAL AREA:** National and international

**INFORMATION:** Accounts are on file at the Charity Commission.

**GENERAL:** Grants with some relevance to the scope of this guide were given in 1991/92 to:

Marie Stopes International (£3,000);

Save the Children Fund (£2,000);

VSO (£1,000);

English Speaking Union (£250).

**EXCLUSIONS:** No grants for individuals.

**APPLICATIONS:** In writing to the correspondent with a SAE.

## Victor Mishcon Trust

**GRANT TOTAL:** £60,000 (1991/92)

**ADDRESS:** Messrs Mishcon DeReya & Co, 21 Southampton Row, London WC1B 5HA

**CORRESPONDENT:** See above

**TRUSTEES:** Lord Mischcon, Lady Mischcon, P A Cohen.

**BENEFICIAL AREA:** National and international

**INFORMATION:** Accounts are on file at the Chartity Commission.

**GENERAL:** In 1991/92 the following grants with some relevance to the scope of this book were given to:

Group Relations Educational Trust (£500 and in the previous year);

Public Law Project (£500);

Howard League (£200);

Medical Aid for Palestinians, Save the Children Fund, Federation of Hungarian Jews, Parliamentary Appeal for Romanian Children (£100 each).

**APPLICATIONS:** In writing to the correspondent.

## Esmé Mitchell Trust

**GRANT TOTAL:** £90,000 (1992/93)

**ADDRESS:** PO Box 800, Donegall Square West, Belfast BT2 7EB

**TELEPHONE:** 0232-245 277

**CORRESPONDENT:** Northern Bank Executor and Trustee Co Ltd.

**TRUSTEES:** Trust advisors: P J Rankin, Commander D J Maxwell, R P Blakiston-Houston

**BENEFICIAL AREA:** Northern Ireland

**GENERAL:** This Northern Ireland trust has general charitable objects. It gives principally in Northern Ireland and has a particular interest in cultural and artistic objects. A third of its funding is only available to a limited number of heritage bodies. The trust has given support to a joint project of the Irish Commission for Justice and Peace and the Irish Council of Churches, the Peace Education Resources Centre, Belfast.

**APPLICATIONS:** There is no formal application form but applicants are expected to submit a copy of their accounts, most recent annual report, tax and legal or charitable status and information about other sources of finance along with a description of the proposed project and list of officers.

# The Moores Family Charity Foundation

**GRANT TOTAL:** £542,000 (1990)

**MAIN AREAS OF WORK:** General, especially in Merseyside

**ADDRESS:** P O Box 28, Liverpool L23 OXJ

**TELEPHONE:** 051-949 0117

**CORRESPONDENT:** Mrs Patricia Caton

**TRUSTEES:** John Moores, Peter Moores, Lady Granchester.

**BENEFICIAL AREA:** National with a preference for Merseyside.

**INFORMATION:** Accounts are on file at the Charity Commission.

**GENERAL:** Each year the trust, which gets all its income from the Littlewoods Organisation, makes substantial grants to the five Littlewoods family trusts. Whilst the schedule of grants in 1990 did not show many grants relevant to this guide there have been a number of small grants in earlier years:

In 1990 –
  Royal Ulster Rifles Benevolent Fund (£250, an annual grant);
  Ballywater Youth Club (£100);
In 1989 –
  Somali Anglo British Association of Manchester (£350);
  Clogher Care Fermanagh (£160);
  Forces Help Society, Belfast (£110);
  Enniskillen Community Project (£160);
In 1988 –
  Sudan Emergency Appeal (£5,000);
  Bangladesh Emergency Appeal (£5,000);
  Fermanagh Unemployed Action Group (£250);
  Belfast Charitable Trust for Integrated Education (£150).

**APPLICATIONS:** In writing to the correspondent. Applications are considered quarterly.

# John Moores Foundation

**GRANT TOTAL:** £424,000 (1991/92)

**MAIN AREAS OF WORK:** Social welfare in Merseyside and Northern Ireland

**ADDRESS:** 21 Brancote Road, Oxton, Birkenhead L43 6TL

**TELEPHONE:** 051-653 6364

**CORRESPONDENT:** Ms Linda Lazenby.

**TRUSTEES:** Dr M Cole, G A Slater, Mrs J Moores.

**BENEFICIAL AREA:** National and with a particular interest in Merseyside and Northern Ireland.

**INFORMATION:** Accounts are on file at the Charity Commission but without a list of grants.

**GENERAL:** The foundation makes grants to charitable voluntary organisations who work in the more disadvantaged areas of Merseyside and Northern Ireland. The foundation is currently targeting its giving towards:
- Women's groups;
- Black or ethnic minority organisations;
- Second chance learning;
- Welfare rights advice;
- Work with people with HIV or AIDS, their partners and families;

- Work with tranquilliser users;
- Grass roots community organisations and, in Merseyside only;
- Carers;
- Unemployed people;
- Homeless people;
- Groups controlled by disabled people.

The foundation prefers to help small and new organisations, and those who find it more than usually difficult to raise money from other sources.

The foundation no longer funds cross community work in Northern Ireland, although it expects organisations funded to have cross community links.

In 1991/92 grants were made in Merseyside in the following categories:

Advice £110,600 (10 grants);

Black/anti-racist £42,000 (13 grants);

Women £167,000 (18 grants);

Social Welfare £6,200 (9 grants);

Community organisations £14,000 (5 grants);

Youth £21,400 (4 grants);

Second chance/training £29,700 (6 grants);

Homeless £900 (3 grants);

In Northern Ireland:

Advice £2,000 (1 grant);

Women £25,600 (19 grants);

Social welfare £700 (1 grant);

Community organisations £2,000 (1 grant);

Second chance/Training £200 (1 grant);

Black organisations/anti-racist £800 (1 grant).

**EXCLUSIONS:** The foundation does not make grants to national charities, for academic research, or for buildings.

**APPLICATIONS:** Applications may be made at any time. The trust does not have an application form, but requires a letter, on one or two pages, and the most recent audited accounts.

# Morel Charitable Trust

**GRANT TOTAL:** £18,000 (1991)

**ADDRESS:** 34 Durand Gardens, London SW9 OPP

**CORRESPONDENT:** S E.Gibbs

**TRUSTEES:** J M Gibbs, W M Gibbs, S E Gibbs.

**BENEFICIAL AREA:** National and international

**INFORMATION:** Accounts are on file at the Charity Commission up to 1989/90.

**GENERAL:** The trust's policy is to support the arts, organisations working for improved race relations, inner city projects and Third World projects. The most recent accounts on file at the Charity Commission included the following grants with some relevance to the scope of this book:

In 1989/90 –

Child to Child (£2,000 and in the previous year);

International African Institute (£1,850 and £1,450 in the previous year);

UK Foundation for the People of the Pacific (£750);

In 1988/89 –

Africa Centre (£1,400);

Christian Aid, Traidcraft Exchange (£1,000 each);

VSO (£500);

National Association of Development Education Centres (£150).

Africa Centre

# S C and M E Morland's Charitable Trust

**GRANT TOTAL:** £10,500 (1990/91)

**ADDRESS:** 88 Roman Way, Glastonbury, Somerset BA6 8AD

**TELEPHONE:** 04588-32162

**CORRESPONDENT:** M E Morland.

**TRUSTEES:** Mrs M E Morland, J C Morland, J E Morland

**BENEFICIAL AREA:** National and international.

**INFORMATION:** Accounts are on file for 1990/91. Prior to that no accounts had been filed since 1974.

**GENERAL:** The trust has general charitable purposes and supports Quaker charities and others in which the trustees have special interest. Mr Morland wrote for the previous edition of this guide 'most grants continue year after year, there is little surplus to support new applicants so we disappoint most of them'.

In 1990/91 the following grants with relevance to this guide were given:

Oxfam (£500);

Christian Action (£250);

Belfast Voluntary Service, Quaker Council for Europe (£100 each);

UNICEF, Quaker United Nations Office, Ulster Quaker Peace Committee (£50 each).

**EXCLUSIONS:** Grants are rarely given to individuals.

**APPLICATIONS:** It is preferable that applications include a reply paid envelope.

## Network Foundation

**GRANT TOTAL:** £165,000 (1991/92)

**MAIN AREAS OF WORK:** Environment, human rights, peace, arts

**ADDRESS:** BM Box 2063, London WC1N 3XX

**CORRESPONDENT:** Vanessa Adams, Administrator

**TRUSTEES:** Patrick Boase, John S Broad, Samuel P Clark, Manning Goodwin; Ingrid Broad, Andy Hunter, Sara Robin, Hugh MacPherson, Oliver Gillie

**BENEFICIAL AREA:** National and international

**INFORMATION:** Accounts are on file at the Charity Commission but without a list of grants.

**GENERAL:** In 1990/91 the trust had an income of £191,000 and gave grants totalling £165,000. The income comes from members of the company, the Network for Social Change Ltd. The members themselves select the projects to be considered for support. These are then assessed by other members. This selection process is initiated solely by the members and outside applications are not considered.

The following list of grants covers 1989/90 since in that year the foundation included a grants list with its accounts (a list did not accompany the 1990/91 accounts). Twenty grants were given including the following with particular relevance to this guide:

Gaia Foundation (£17,000);

New Economics Foundation (£11,000);

Centre for Alternative Technology (£9,829);

Institute for Development Studies, Living Earth Foundation (£7,000 each);

Oxford Research Group (£6.000);

Medical Foundation for the Care of Victims of Torture (£5,000).

**EXCLUSIONS:** Unsolicited applications are not accepted.

**APPLICATIONS:** The Network chooses the projects it wishes to support so unsolicited applications are not welcomed and do not receive an acknowledgement.

*[handwritten: W PGMT p.454]*

## Noel Buxton Trust

*[handwritten: new address → Cawless Cottage Winderton Rd Lower Brailes Nr Banbury OX15 5BG]*

**GRANT TOTAL:** £112,500 (1992)

**MAIN AREAS OF WORK:** See below

**ADDRESS:** 27-28 Russell Square, London WC1B 5DS

**TELEPHONE:** ~~071-580 5876~~ *[handwritten: 0207 8628844]*

**CORRESPONDENT:** Margaret Beard, Secretary.

**TRUSTEES:** Mrs E R Wallace (Chairman), Simon Buxton, Paul Buxton, Angelica Mitchell, Joyce Morton, Jo Tunnard. *[handwritten: Institute of Commonwealth Studies]*

**BENEFICIAL AREA:** National and international.

**INFORMATION:** Accounts are on file at the Charity Commission. A brief policy statement can be obtained.

**GENERAL:** The trust has assets of £1.3 million. In 1992 it gave grants in the following categories:

Child & Family Welfare (24%);

Education & Development in Africa (12%);

Penal Matters (16%);

Reconciliation & Human Rights (29%);

Youth (5%);

Other Social Welfare (14%).

The following grants in 1992 were relevant to this guide:

**Under Education and Development in Africa –**

Co-operation for Development (£4,000);

UNESCO Coordinating Committee for IVS (for Namibia) (£500);

Cape Town Quaker Peace Centre (£250);

**Under Reconciliation and Human Rights –**

Northern Ireland Council for Integrated Education (£3,500);

Northern Ireland Voluntary Trust (£3,500);

Mediation UK (£2,000);

Minority Rights Groups (£5,500);

North East Refugee Service (£2,000);

Scottish Refugee Council (£1,500);

St Andrew's and All Saints Refugee Ministry, Cairo (£1,000);

Dudley One World (£1,000);

Leeds Development Education Centre (£500).

In 1990 grants were given to the Oxford Research Group (£1,985) and the Sheffield Somalian Refugee Trust (£1,000).

**APPLICATIONS:** In writing to the correspondent.

## Northern Ireland Voluntary Trust

**GRANT TOTAL:** £443,500 (1993)

**MAIN AREAS OF WORK:** Social change in Northern Ireland

**ADDRESS:** 22 Mount Charles, Belfast BT7 1NZ

**TELEPHONE:** 0232-245927; Fax: 0232-329839

**CORRESPONDENT:** Paul Sweeney, Director

**TRUSTEES:** David Cook (Chairman), Eamonn Deane, Mary Black, Sheelagh Flanagan, Mark Conway, Jim Flynn, Avila Kilmurray, Sam McCready, Philip McDonagh, Aideen McGinley, Dr Mari Fitzduff, Dr Ben Wilson

**INFORMATION:** Annual report.

**GENERAL:** The trust works in partnership with community leaders to effect positive social change and improve the life opportunities for people in the most disadvantaged areas of Northern Ireland. In addition the trust acts as a resource to local groups and based on this experience seeks to influence public policy by way of analysis, commentary and advocacy.

The trust is particularly committed to the support of small scale community based projects. Its assistance was categorised in its 1992/93 annual report as follows: Neighbourhood and Rural Development; Women's Groups; Community care, Children and Young People; Community Arts and Education; Pluralism, Tolerance and Social Justice; Local Economic Development.

Examples of grants relevant to this guide were:

Initiative '92, to help maximise community input to the Opsahl Commission an

independent enquiry into ways forward for Northern Ireland (£25,000 over 2 years);

Charity Know How Fund, to facilitate involvement of projects from Northern Ireland (£4,000 over 2 Years).

In 1991 the trust launched its New Routes grant scheme, a partnership with the Joseph Rowntree Charitable Trust. This scheme provides the opportunity for individuals engaged in various areas of work, whether paid or voluntary, to benefit from a programme of visits to agencies in Europe or further afield.

**APPLICATIONS:** In writing to the correspondent.

## Nuffield Foundation

**GRANT TOTAL:** £5,845,000 (budgeted for 1993)

**MAIN AREAS OF WORK:** National and Commonwealth; Eastern Europe

**ADDRESS:** 28 Bedford Square, London WC1B 3EG

**TELEPHONE:** 071-631 0566; Fax: 071-323 4877

**CORRESPONDENT:** Robert Hazell, Director.

**TRUSTEES:** Lord Flowers, (Chairman), Sir John Banham, Professor Brenda Hoggett, Professor Robin Matthews, Professor Robert May, Mrs Anne Sofer, Professor Sir Michael Rutter.

**INFORMATION:** Detailed annual report and guidelines for applicants.

**GENERAL:** The objects of the foundation, as laid down in the trust deed, are:

**a)** The advancement of health and the prevention and relief of sickness, particularly by medical research and teaching;

**b)** The advancement of social well being, particularly by scientific research;

**c)** The care and comfort of the aged poor;

**d)** The advancement of education.

The foundation makes grants of three kinds:

**Project Grants**

These are given for experimental or development projects which advance health, education or social welfare. (These grants are distinguished from those made under academic schemes.) Projects usually involve the development of new ideas and methods. The trustees do not as a rule support research through project grants save in areas in which they have declared an interest. The foundation's main current areas of interest are:

- Human rights;
- Access to justice;
- Family justice system;
- Child protection;
- Research which looks critically at statutory arrangements;
- The voluntary sector;
- Public understanding of science;
- Science and mathematics education;
- Medical education;
- Bioethics;
- Health care.

Whilst there are no financial limits to the size of grants they are usually between £5,000 and £75,000, with the larger grants spread over a two or three year period.

The trustees are keen that project findings should be disseminated as widely as possible. The foundation hosts seminars for this purpose and applicants are encouraged to budget for dissemination costs as part of their grant.

Applicants are also encouraged to learn from experience overseas, and to budget for secondments of overseas experts or visits overseas where this is appropriate.

The foundation also makes a small number of grants to support health and self-help projects in Third World countries. These grants are often for projects involving education or training, and are rarely for sums greater than £10,000.

**Schemes for Support of Academic Research**
There are five schemes for supporting scientific and medical research; and two schemes of small grants and fellowships for social scientists.

**Individual Grants for Education and Training**
There are four schemes of educational bursaries and travelling fellowships. These include a long-standing scheme offering training for professional people from the Commonwealth, (this includes the work of the Commonwealth Relations Trust, see separate entry). There is also a small Eastern Europe Programme started in 1990 whereby Travelling Fellowships are offered for people from Eastern Europe to visit the United Kingdom for three month's professional training. These awards

are made on the nomination of the host institution and candidates should not apply to the foundation direct. Fellowships are awarded currently to agricultural experts, commercial and human rights lawyers and to journalists.

**EXCLUSIONS:** Capital grants for buildings, attendance at conferences. Grants for the following purposes are normally only made when the activity constitutes part of a project which is otherwise acceptable, or as a grant under a special scheme: work for degrees and other qualifications; organisation of conferences; publications or film productions; equipment purchase; day to day running expenses or accommodation needs.

**APPLICATIONS:** Applicants must send a one or two page outline of the project, with a rough budget, at least two weeks before the closing date. A response will be sent by one of the directors. If the project is suitable for consideration a formal application can be prepared. Requirements for the formal application are set out in the Guide for Applicants leaflet which all applicants should obtain before considering any request for assistance. This also lists the various closing dates for applications e.g. for Project Grants 1994 closing dates: 10 December, 4 March, 13 May, 30 September for meetings on 4 February, 29 April, 8 July, 25 November.

# Oakdale Trust

**GRANT TOTAL:** £110,000 (1992/93)

**MAIN AREAS OF WORK:** Priority is now given to applications from Wales

**ADDRESS:** Tan y Coed, Pantydwr, Rhayader, Powys LD6 5LR

**CORRESPONDENT:** Brandon Cadbury.

**TRUSTEES:** B Cadbury, Mrs F F Cadbury, R A Cadbury, F B Cadbury, Mrs 0 H TattonBrown, Dr R C Cadbury.

**BENEFICIAL AREA:** National and international

**INFORMATION:** Accounts are on file at the Charity Commission.

**GENERAL:** The trust has general charitable objects, a national and international scope with a particular interest in activities in the Wales. Categories of grants are given with the accounts:

Penal reform (£15,500);

Education (£11,500);

Medical (£18,325);

Care of old people (£10,700);

Art (£725);

Children & Youth Work (£32,250);

Church and Quaker work (£1,950);

Conservation (£6,500);

Social work and miscellaneous (£18,250).

The trust is known to support, or have supported, the following organisations: Quaker Peace and Service, Quaker Peace Studies Trust, Prisoners of Conscience, Medical Foundation for the Care of Victims of Torture, Howard League, Anti-Slavery Society.

**APPLICATIONS:** Applications may be sent at any time. Only successful approaches are acknowledged.

# Oakmoor Trust

**GRANT TOTAL:** £52,000 (1991/92)

**MAIN AREAS OF WORK:** General

**ADDRESS:** Trustee Department, Kleinwort Benson Trustees Ltd, PO Box 191, 10 Fenchurch Street, London EC3M 3LB

**CORRESPONDENT:** Kleinwort Benson Limited

**BENEFICIAL AREA:** National

**INFORMATION:** Full accounts are on file at the Charity Commission.

**GENERAL:** The trust, was established in 1969 and now has assets of £639,000 and receives regular donations from the settlor, Peter Andreae. In 1991/92 its 13 grants included the following with relevance to this guide:

CAFOD (£10,000);

Red Cross Gulf Appeal (£5,000).

# Onaway Trust

**GRANT TOTAL:** £160,000 (1990)

**MAIN AREAS OF WORK:** See below

**ADDRESS:** 275 Main Street, Shadwell, Leeds, West Yorks LSI7 8LH

**TELEPHONE:** 0532-659611

**CORRESPONDENT:** James Bradley

**TRUSTEES:** James Bradley, Eve Bury, Barbara Pilkington.

**BENEFICIAL AREA:** National and international

**INFORMATION:** Accounts are on file at the Charity Commission.

**GENERAL:** Whilst it has general charitable objects, the trust targets 'assistance and relief of poor and needy persons in any country'. However it is clear from the list of grants that this trust has a specific interest in the future of indigenous peoples particularly those in North America. Grants relevant to this guide were given in 1990 to:

Gaia Foundation (£10,500);

Survival International (£7,000);

Anti-Slavery Society, Oxfam (£5,000 each);

Friends of the Earth, Intermediate Technology Development Group (£3,500 each);

Minority Rights Group (£3,000);

Partners for Democracy (£2,632);

Nuclear Free Pacific (£1,100);

Y Care International (£1,000).

**APPLICATIONS:** The trust has written that it does not wish an entry in this guide 'as the trust's resources are fully committed to ongoing projects and new ones are researched and decided upon by themselves'.

# Oppenheimer Charitable Trust

*no individuals*

**GRANT TOTAL:** £119,000 (1992)

**ADDRESS:** 17 Charterhouse Street, London EC1N 6RA

**TELEPHONE:** 071-404 4444

**CORRESPONDENT:** J J I Hawkins

**TRUSTEES:** E G J Dawe, S P Shoesmith, T W H Capon, N Casselton Elliott, J J I Hawkins.

**BENEFICIAL AREA:** National and international

**INFORMATION:** Accounts are on file at the Charity Commission.

**GENERAL:** The trust gives grants only in areas where companies of the De Beers group operate. It has a particular interest in medicine and health, the young and the aged, and general welfare. A review of the trust's 1992 accounts lodged with the Charity Commission has shown the following grants with some bearing on the scope of this book:

English Speaking Union (£1,100);

Anti Slavery International, Federation of Jewish Relief Organisations, Airey Neave Trust, Police Foundation, VSO (£250 each);

Overseas Development Institute (£150).

**APPLICATIONS:** Applications are considered at meetings in January, April, July and October each year.

# Oxfam
(grants in the UK)

**GRANT TOTAL:** £260,000 for development education; £72,000 for PACE grants fund (1993/94)

**ADDRESS:** 274 Banbury Road, Oxford OX2 7DZ

**TELEPHONE:** 0865-311311 x 3162

**CORRESPONDENT:** Peter Davis, Educational Campaigns Executive, for development education grants; Martin Knops, Marketing Directorate for PACE grants;

**TRUSTEES:** Development Education Committee: Ten members including one Oxfam trustee

**INFORMATION:** Further information for applicants: The terms of reference; list of priorities for grant making; guidelines about how applications should be prepared and detailed notes on the information required for both major and small grants.

**GENERAL:** In its support and promotion of development education programmes Oxfam is guided by three principles.

The first is that these programmes are essentially concerned with the ways in which society is changing today and should lead people to a critical understanding of these changes and towards constructive involvement in them.

The second is that these development education programmes should help to reflect the aspirations of people in the countries of Asia, Africa and Latin America who are working to bring about beneficial changes to their own lives.

The third is that they should at the same time contribute to the education of our own people: in knowledge, in responsibility, and in the skills and attitudes needed to shape a multicultural and interdependent society.

The committee has agreed the following constituent groups, areas of work and regions in development education grant-aid as priorities:

1) Projects and programmes with primary school age children;

2) Projects and programmes with secondary school age students;

3) Programmes in the voluntary and statutory youth sector;

4) Programmes associated with Oxfam's education programme and campaign themes;

5) Projects and programmes that raise Southern perspectives in education for sustainability:

6) Programmes in Scotland, Wales and Northern Ireland;

7) Small grants (up to £500 per application).

Core budget support is provided for organisations within these priority areas. Applicants are asked to note the following factors:

- Project specifications should include information on proposed evaluatory methods;

- Notice will be taken of groups and projects developing innovatory work;

- Projects will be expected to incorporate procedures for good reporting, publicity and dissemination of their work.

Within the main grants scheme, a discretionary small grant scheme also operates. Its total fund is £5,000 a year for grants between £25 and £500 for local school and community education projects.

Grants in 1992/93 included:

National Association of Development Education Centres (now the Development Education Association) (£42,846);

International Broadcasting Trust (£36,724);

Hull DEC (£30,604);

DEED, Bournemouth (£27,544);

Bangor DEED/World Education Project (£24,483);

World Studies 8-13 Project (£24,483);

Third World First (£18,998);

Returned Volunteer Action (£10,555);

National Curriculum Monitoring Project (£2,480).

A separately administered PACE Grants Fund (Public Affairs, Campaigning and Adult Education grants) provides funds for adult education and campaigning work in the UK and Ireland. This fund is currently (November 1993) under review.

A small **Director's Discretionary fund** also operates. Contact Oxfam Directorate, ext 312244. These funds are very limited.

APPLICATIONS: Applications should be made in writing and guidelines for both the development education grants scheme and the small grants fund are available upon request. The Development Education Advisory Group meets twice a year in May and October. The heavy demands on its resources mean that the majority of funding decisions are made at the May meeting (except for the small grants). The small grants scheme is discretionary, and applications can be made to the secretariat throughout the year.

## P F Charitable Trust

GRANT TOTAL: £671,000 (1990/91)

ADDRESS: 25 Copthall Avenue, London EC2R 7DR

TELEPHONE: 071-638 5858

CORRESPONDENT: The Secretary.

TRUSTEES: R Fleming, V P Fleming, P Fleming, G A Jamieson.

BENEFICIAL AREA: National

INFORMATION: Accounts are on file at the Charity Commission.

GENERAL: The trust's policy is to make contributions to medical research, hospitals, religious and educational bodies and other legal charities.

The accounts on file at the Charity Commission show the following grants with relevance to this guide:

Northern Ireland Voluntary Trust, Help Poland Fund, ActionAid, Oxfam (£1,000 each);

Co-operation Ireland, Belfast Charitable Trust for Integrated Education, Kathmandu Environmental Education Project, Survival International, Voluntary Service Belfast, VSO (£500 each);

Polish Air Force Association (£300);

Harmony Community Trust, Howard League, IVS (£250 each).

APPLICATIONS: In writing to the correspondent. Replies will be sent to unsuccessful applications when a SAE is enclosed. The trustees meet monthly.

## Paget Charitable Trust

GRANT TOTAL: £68,000 (1991/92)

ADDRESS: 41 Priory Gardens, London N6 5QU

CORRESPONDENT: Joanna Herbert-Stepney

TRUSTEES: Joanna Herbert-Stepney, Joy Pollard, Lesley Mary Rolling

BENEFICIAL AREA: National and international

INFORMATION: Accounts are on file at the Charity Commission.

GENERAL: Grants in recent years with some relevance to the scope of this guide were donated to:

In 1991/92 –

Oxfam (£4,000 with £12,000 in the previous year);

Intermediate Technology Development Group (£2,000 with £10,000 in the previous year);

Survival International (£1,000 with £2,000 in the previous year);

Tibet Society (£1,325);

ActionAid, Afghan Relief, Africa Now, Marie Stopes International, UNA International Service (£1,000 each);

UNICEF UK, Cambodia Trust (£750 each);

Greenpeace, Friends of the Earth (£500 each with £1,000 each in the previous year);

Calcutta Rescue Fund (£500 with £3,000 in the previous year);

Calcutta Research Fund (£500).

The Medical Foundation for the Care of Victims of Torture was given a grant of £6,000 in 1990/91.

The trust prefers to support projects with practical, rather than theoretical outcomes.

APPLICATIONS: In writing to the correspondent.

# Partners in Europe

ADDRESS: The Prince's Trust, 8 Bedford Row, London WC1R 4BA

TELEPHONE: 071-405 5799

CORRESPONDENT: Anne Engel, Project Director

BENEFICIAL AREA: UK and Europe

INFORMATION: An annual report and guidelines for applicants.

GENERAL: This scheme is run by the Prince's Trust and the Prince's Youth Business Trust with support from Severn Trent.

Young people of 25 and under (29 for people with disabilities) can receive a grant to assist them in developing a project of mutual benefit with another European partner. They must be no longer in full-time education, but either unemployed, employed or self-employed.

There are several types of grants: **Go and See Grants** up to a maximum of £500, help fund visits to potential partners in Europe to discuss how a collaborative project may work (sports projects are excluded). The money can be used for travel, accommodation and preparation costs of the UK participant (part of the grant may be a free airline ticket). **Go Ahead Grants** support the most promising projects resulting from Go and See visits.

Another scheme **the British Hungarian Grants** is supported by the Prince's Trust in London and the European House in Budapest. Partnership projects for young artists, designers and crafts people between the ages of 18 and 25 who are no longer in full-time education may be helped with a **Setting Up Grant** (maximum £500) which enables British applicants who have not yet found a Hungarian partner to make a first visit and establish the basis of a joint project. A **Project Grant** enables a well-planned project with a firm partner to take place. A maximum of £1,500 is available to cover activity in UK or Hungary. It can be used for travel, accommodation and expenses only. Study visits, attendance at conferences/festivals will not be funded.

**Richard Mills Travel Fellowships,** funded by the Gulbenkian Foundation, the Paul S Cadbury Trust and the Prince's Trust in association with the Community Development Foundation, enable three community artists per year to travel to another European country in order to meet artists, visit projects and for any purpose that will help them learn more about the arts in local communities. The fellowships are not available to researchers, academics and full-time students. Three fellowships of £1,000 each are offered for use from 1st April 1994 for people under the age of 35.

APPLICATIONS: Application forms are available for all schemes except the Richard Mills Travel Fellowships for which the closing date is 14th January, 1994.

# Harry Payne Trust

*Geographically Birmingham*

GRANT TOTAL: £44,000 (1993)

MAIN AREAS OF WORK: General

ADDRESS: 25 Bury Green, Wheathampstead, St Albans, Herts AL4 8DB

TELEPHONE: 0582-832876 ?

CORRESPONDENT: R C King, Secretary

TRUSTEES: Mrs A K Burnett, D J Cadbury, J E Payne, R King (Chairman), D F Dodd, R C King (Secretary), R I Payne, Mrs B J Major.

BENEFICIAL AREA: Birmingham and West Midlands

INFORMATION: Accounts are on file at the Charity Commission.

GENERAL: The following grants with relevance to this guide were made:

In 1993 –
   Woodbrooke College (£750 with £1,000 in the previous year);
   Northern Friends Peace Board (£250);
   Warwick Quaker Centre (£100);

In 1992 –
   Quaker Peace Studies Trust (£200);
   Cornerstone (3250).

Several grants have been given to Quaker schools.

APPLICATIONS: Application forms are available. These should be sent to the secretary and accompanied by up-to-date audited accounts. Trustees meet in June and December each year and applications should reach the secretary by the beginning of May or the beginning of November.

# Hugh Pilkington Charitable Trust

**GRANT TOTAL:** £565,000 (1993)

**MAIN AREAS OF WORK:** Refugees in East Africa

**ADDRESS:** 27 Northmoor Road, Oxford OX2 6UR

**TELEPHONE:** 0865-56947

**CORRESPONDENT:** Robin Shawyer, Executive Officer

**TRUSTEES:** Roger Northcott, James Richardson, Cynthia Rumboll.

**BENEFICIAL AREA:** International

**INFORMATION:** Accounts are on file at the Charity Commission but without a schedule of grants.

**GENERAL:** The trust has assets of £8.5 million which generated an income of £818,243 in 1993. The trust aims to give assistance for 1) Refugees; 2) Education; 3) Research into human rights and refugees in particular.

The following account is taken from the Third World Directory (1993): 'The trust provides educational support, mainly at tertiary level to refugees with asylum in East Africa, studying in Africa and elsewhere. The trust supports the Refugee Studies Programme at Oxford University and one or two charitable bodies in East Africa addressing the needs of refugees.'

**EXCLUSIONS:** Applications from refugees with, or seeking, asylum in Britain.

**APPLICATIONS:** In writing to the correspondent. Applicants should note that most of the trust's work is based on existing contacts in East Africa.

# G S Plaut Charitable Trust Limited

**GRANT TOTAL:** £34,000 (1991/92)

**MAIN AREAS OF WORK:** General

**ADDRESS:** Flat 25B, Lees Rest Houses, Anlaby High Road, Hull HU4 6XZ

**TELEPHONE:** 0482-505475

**CORRESPONDENT:** Mrs D G Coupland

**TRUSTEES:** The Directors.

**BENEFICIAL AREA:** National

**INFORMATION:** Accounts are on file at the Charity Commission.

**GENERAL:** This trust makes several hundred small grants under £1,000, and many of these are less than £500. Grants with some relevance to this guide were made in
1991/92 to:

Oxfam (£500);

Save the Children Fund (£400);

UNICEF (£300);

VSO (£200);

Ranfurly Library Service, Miriam Dean Refugee Trust Fund, Jewish Refugees in GB (£100 each);

**APPLICATIONS:** In writing to the correspondent.

# The Polden-Puckham Charitable Foundation

**GRANT TOTAL:** £223,300 (1991/92)

**MAIN AREAS OF WORK:** Peace, spiritual and ecological values

**ADDRESS:** P O Box 951, Bristol BS99 5QH

**CORRESPONDENT:** The Secretary

**TRUSTEES:** Nicholas Gillettt, Candia Gillett, David Gillett, Harriet Gillett, Jean Barlow, Rachel Fruchter, Jenepher Gordon.

**BENEFICIAL AREA:** National and international

**INFORMATION:** Accounts are on file at the Charity Commission.

**GENERAL:** The foundation has assets of over £4 million. In 1991/92 the following grants were given:

Quaker Peace and Service (£25,000);

UNA Trust (for Safer World £22,000, for John Bright appeal £11,000, for Emergency Preparedness Fund £2,000);

Oxford Research Group (£11,500);

Network Foundation (£10,200);

New Economics Foundation (£7,000);

Foundation for International Security (£6,000);

Prisoners of Conscience Appeal Fund (£5,000);

British American Security Information Council (£5,000);

Caroline Gourlay Trust/Centre for International Peacebuilding (£5,000);

Friends World Committee for Consultation (£5,000);

Oxfam (£5,000);

Minority Rights Group (£4,000);

Survival International (£6,000);

Capetown University, Centre for Inter Group Studies (£4,000);

Natural Justice (£3,000);

Manchester Development Education Project (£3,000);

International Broadcasting Trust (£3,000);

Anti-Slavery Society (£2,000);

Gandhi Foundation (£2,000);

Quaker Peace Studies Trust (£2,000);

Fellowship of Reconciliation (£1,600);

Womankind (£1,500);

Institute for Law and Peace (£1,000);

United World Education & Research Trust, Gulf Crisis Working Group (£1,000).

**EXCLUSIONS:** Grants to individuals; travel bursaries; study, academic research; capital projects; community or local projects (except innovative prototypes for widespread application); general appeals.

**APPLICATIONS:** The trustees meet twice a year in late March/early April, and October. The foundation will not send replies to applications outside its area of interest. Applications should be no longer than two pages and should include the following:

- A short outline of the project, its aims and methods to be used.
- The amount requested (normally between £500 and £5,000 for one to three years), the names of other funders and possible funders, and expected sources of funding after termination of PPCF funding.
- Information on how the project is to be monitored, evaluated, and publicised.
- Background details of the key persons in the organisation.

Please also supply: latest set of audited accounts; a detailed budget of the project; annual report if available; list of trustees or board of management; names of two referees not involved in the organisation; charity registration number, or name and number of a charity which can accept funds on your behalf.

# Simone Prendergast Charitable Trust

**GRANT TOTAL:** £24,600 (1992)

**MAIN AREAS OF WORK:** General with a particular interest in medicine, old people and children

**ADDRESS:** Flat C, 52 Warwick Square, London SW1V 2AJ

**CORRESPONDENT:** Dame Simone Prendergast

**TRUSTEES:** Dame Simone Prendergast, C A Prendergast

**BENEFICIAL AREA:** Great Britain, Northern Ireland, Israel

**INFORMATION:** Accounts are on file at the Charity Commission.

**GENERAL:** In 1992/93 the largest grant was given to the Central British Fund for Worldwide Jewish Relief (£7,040). Other grants with some relevance to this guide were:

Anglo Israel Association (£1,750);

Police Foundation (£500);

Airey Neave Trust, Council for Christians and Jews (£250 each);

Women Caring Trust (£100).

**APPLICATIONS:** In writing to the correspondent.

# Quaker Peace & Service, Peace Committee

**GRANT TOTAL:** £8,500 (1994)

**MAIN AREAS OF WORK:** Local peace work

**ADDRESS:** Religious Society of Friends, Friends House, Euston Road, London NW1 2BJ

**TELEPHONE:** 071-387 3601: Fax 071-388 1977

**CORRESPONDENT:** Peace Section

**GENERAL:** The purpose of QPS local peace work grants is to enable work arising from our peace testimony to be carried out at a local level. This work may be:

- directed towards Friends, to enhance our understanding of, and action arising from the peace testimony, and to challenge Friends to see the relevance for the peace testimony to all aspects of life; or

• work outside Friends which strengthens our contribution, based on our historical peace witness and particular insights, to the community and/or the peace movement.

Grants are given for three main types of need:

• pump-priming for long-term projects where there is evidence (not just hope) of financial viability;

• specific finite pieces of work or projects by individuals or groups;

• Friends acting under concern.

The maximum grant has been £3,000 pa but the budget for this fund seems is steadily diminishing in scale (in 1993 the fund was £13,500) and it is highly unlikely that this normal maximum can be maintained.

All applicants must have endorsement from a Quaker meeting.

**APPLICATIONS:** Detailed guidelines are available from QPS after a brief statement of proposed work has been sent and considered appropriate. Applications are due in the beginning of May and the beginning of November. Applications are considered by a subgroup of the committee and final decisions are taken at meetings in June and December.


# Radley Charitable Trust

**GRANT TOTAL:** £14,000 (1993)

**MAIN AREAS OF WORK:** See below

**ADDRESS:** 12 Jesus Lane, Cambridge CB5 8BA

**CORRESPONDENT:** P F Radley

**TRUSTEES:** P F Radley, I R Menzies, Jane Wheatley, C F Doubleday.

**BENEFICIAL AREA:** National and international

**INFORMATION:** Accounts are on file at the Charity Commission up to 1989.

**GENERAL:** The trust supports social and international causes and education in these areas. It makes grants to Quaker bodies, international and peace work, for racial equality, community projects, education and conservation. It is a policy of the trustees to support applicants unlikely to have general public support or appeal.

The trust has noted that its grants are normally between £250 and £500. It wished the following information to be excluded whilst not giving up-to-date information. Since it has been obtained from public records it is included.

In 1987/88 the trust disbursed £28,000 and the following grants relevant to the scope of this guide were given to:

Quaker Service South Africa (£10,000);

Friends World Committee (£500);

SOAS (£250);

Anti-Slavery Society (£50);

British Refugee Council, IVS (£25 each).

**APPLICATIONS:** In writing to the correspondent enclosing a SAE.


# Rank Foundation Ltd

**GRANT TOTAL:** £5,370,000 (1992)

**MAIN AREAS OF WORK:** Christian communication, the elderly, the handicapped, youth

**ADDRESS:** Unit 2, SES House, Butchers Row, Banbury, Oxon OX16 8JH

**TELEPHONE:** 0295-272337

**CORRESPONDENT:** S J B Langdale

**TRUSTEES:** R F H Cowen (Chairman), M D Abrahams, Lord Charteris, Mrs S M Cowen, M E T Davies, Mrs L G Fox, J D Hutchison, J R Newton, F A R Packard, D R Peppiatt, V A L Powell, Sir Michael Richardson, Lord Shuttleworth, D R W Silk, M J M Thompson.

**INFORMATION:** Information available for applicants: a brochure; report for 1990/92.

**GENERAL:** The foundation describes its policy as: The promotion, by means of the exhibition of religious films, of the Christian religion, Christian principles, Christian religious education and the study of the history of the Christian faith. Also the promotion of the Christian religion by an other lawful means. The promotion of education. The promotion of any other objects or purposes which are exclusively charitable according to the laws of England in force from time to time.

The foundation's report, 1990/92, shows that the following groups with some relevance to the scope of this guide received support of £5,000 and more:

Belfast Charitable Trust for Integrated Education;

Corrymeela Community;

Imperial War Museum;

YMCA Belfast;

Youth Action Northern Ireland.

**APPLICATIONS:** Audited accounts should be sent with the application. Preliminary enquiries are welcomed.

## The Eleanor Rathbone Charitable Trust

**GRANT TOTAL:** £158,000 (1992/93)

**ADDRESS:** Rathbone Bros & Co, Port of Liverpool Building, 4th Floor, Pier Head, Liverpool L3 lNW

**TELEPHONE:** 051-236 8674

**CORRESPONDENT:** Rathbone Bros & Co

**TRUSTEES:** Dr B L Rathbone, P W Rathbone, W Rathbone Jnr, Miss J A Rathbone, R H Hobhouse

**BENEFICIAL AREA:** National

**INFORMATION:** Accounts are on file at the Charity Commission but without a schedule of grants.

**GENERAL:** The trust has general charitable objects, with a special interest in women's causes, and whilst having the ability to give support nationally, has a particular interest in work in Merseyside and a preference for charities known to the trust or in which they take a special interest. Only occasional donations are made for overseas work.

Recent grants have included: a substantial grant to Womankind Worldwide for projects in India in 1992/93 and an earlier grant to the Women Caring Trust (see separate entry).

**APPLICATIONS:** In writing to the correspondent.

## Albert Reckitt Charitable Trust

**GRANT TOTAL:** £51,000 (1993)

**ADDRESS:** Southwark Towers, 32 London Bridge Street, London SE1 9SY.

**TELEPHONE:** 071-939 2360

**CORRESPONDENT:** J Barrett, Secretary.

**TRUSTEES:** Sir Michael Colman, B N Reckitt, Mrs M Reckitt, H C Shaw, Mrs G M Atherton, Mrs s Bradley, D F Reckitt, J Hughes-Reckitt.

**BENEFICIAL AREA:** Great Britain

**INFORMATION:** Accounts have not been filed at the Charity Commission since 1974.

**GENERAL:** The trust has general charitable objects and in 1993 grants totalling £51,000 were given to about 100 charities. Little is known about the trust's beneficiaries as accounts have not been filed with the Charity Commission since the early 1970s. Then a particular interest was shown in the Society of Friends with some grants also to organisations working in overseas relief and development.

**EXCLUSIONS:** Political and sectarian organisations except non-political charities connected with the Society of Friends.

**APPLICATIONS:** In writing to the correspondent. Submissions should be made before the end of March.

## Eva Reckitt Trust Fund

*would not consider*

**GRANT TOTAL:** £44,000 (1991)

**MAIN AREAS OF WORK:** Overseas relief, housing, prisoners

**ADDRESS:** 21 Mitchell Walk, Amersham, Bucks HP6 6NW

**TELEPHONE:** 0494-725146

**CORRESPONDENT:** George Bunney.

**TRUSTEES:** A R H Birch, G Bunney, Mrs D Holliday, C Whittaker.

**BENEFICIAL AREA:** National and international

**INFORMATION:** Accounts are on file at the Charity Commission

**GENERAL:** The trust's objects are the 'relief of hardship caused by civil unrest, political or legal injustice or war; betterment and education of the poor'. The following grants relevant to this guide have been made in 1991:

**Under Education –**

Society for Cultural Relations with USSR (£1,500 with £1,00 in the previous year);

Civil Liberties Trust (£1,000 and in the previous year);

Gandhi Foundation (£500 and in the previous year);

**Under Environment –**

Friends of the Earth, Greenpeace (£1,500 each and in the previous year);

**Under Ireland –**

Voluntary Service Belfast, Northern Ireland Children's Holiday Scheme, Drumquin Youth Centre (£500 each);

**Under Overseas –**

Amnesty International, Canon Collins Educational Trust for Southern Africa (£1,000 each);

Quaker Council for European Affairs, Nicaragua Health Fund (£500 each);

Save the Children Fund (£411);

Tools for Self Reliance (£300).

In the previous year grants had also been given to:
UNICEF (£1,000):

Baluchistan Development Resource Centre (£603);

Peace and Reconciliation Group, NI (£200).

**APPLICATIONS:** Meetings are held regularly about every two months. Applications should be in writing and should indicate the level of support asked for and, if possible, other sources of income and applications made.

# The Sir James Reckitt Charity

**GRANT TOTAL:** £352,000 (1992)

**MAIN AREAS OF WORK:** General

**ADDRESS:** 14 Seacroft Road, Withernsea, North Humberside HU19 2NY

**TELEPHONE:** 0964-212023

**CORRESPONDENT:** J R Clayton

**TRUSTEES:** Descendants of the founder

**BENEFICIAL AREA:** National with a particular interest in the area around Hull.

**INFORMATION:** Accounts are on file at the Charity Commission.

**GENERAL:** Grants with relevance to this guide were given in 1992 to:

Quaker Council for European Affairs (£1,260 with £1,150 in the previous year);

Intermediate Technology Development Group (£860 with £780 in the previous year);

Northern Friends Peace Board (£520 with £475 in the previous year);

Ulster Quaker Peace Committee, Give Peace a Chance Trust (£500 each);

Oxford Project for Peace Studies (£500 with £150 in the previous year);

Saferworld, Africa Now (£300 each).

**APPLICATIONS:** In writing to the correspondent. The trustees meet in Spring and Autumn.

# Rest-Harrow Trust

**GRANT TOTAL:** £16,000 (1993)

**ADDRESS:** Clark Whitehill, Chartered Accountants, 25 New Street Square, London EC4A 3LN

**TELEPHONE:** 071-3531577

**CORRESPONDENT:** Clark Whitehill.

**TRUSTEES:** Miss E. R. Wix, First CB Trustee Ltd.

**BENEFICIAL AREA:** National and international

**INFORMATION:** Accounts are on file at the Charity Commission.

**GENERAL:** The trust has general charitable objects with a particular interest in innovatory projects to assist disadvantaged groups. The accounts for 1993 showed the following grants with some relevance to the scope of this book:

In 1993 –

Anglo-Israel Association, CBF World Jewish Relief (£250 each);

Cannon Collins Educational Trust for Southern Africa, Council for Christians and Jews, Intermediate Technology, Oxfam, Prison Reform Trust, Ranfurly Library Service, Refugee Council, Save the Children, UNICEF UK, VSO, WaterAid (£100 each, and most received a similar grant in the previous year).

In 1992 –

International Centre for Peace in the Middle East, British Section (£1,000);

Belfast Charitable Trust for Integrated Education (£100);

Civil Liberties Trust, IVS (£100 each).

**APPLICATIONS:** In writing to the correspondent. Appeals are considered quarterly.

*all funds allocated future??*

# Ripple Effect Foundation

**GRANT TOTAL:** £75,000 (1993)

**MAIN AREAS OF WORK:** General, with a particular interest in human rights

**ADDRESS:** Messrs Farrer & Co, 6 Lincoln's Inn fields, London WC2A 3LH

**TELEPHONE:** 071-242 2022

**CORRESPONDENT:** See above

**TRUSTEES:** Caroline Marks; Ian Roy Marks; Mary Falk; Ian Wesley.

**BENEFICIAL AREA:** National and overseas.

**GENERAL:** The foundation was formerly known as the CDM Charitable Trust. Organisations relevant to this guide which received support in 1993 included:

Network Foundation (£28,000 with £25,000 given in the previous year);

Gaia Foundation (£10,000);

ITDG (£10,000);

Ashoka (UK) Trust (£9,300 in 2 grants);

Opportunity Trust (£5,000);

British Red Cross (£5,000):

Ian Roy Marks is also a trustee of the Aim Foundation (see separate entry)

# Mr C A Rodewald's Charitable Settlement

**GRANT TOTAL:** £7,000 (1992/93)

**ADDRESS:** Kleinwort Benson Trustees Limited, PO Box 191, 10 Fenchurch Street, London EC3M 3LB

**CORRESPONDENT:** The Secretary.

**TRUSTEES:** Kleinwort Benson Trustees Limited.

**BENEFICIAL AREA:** National and international

**INFORMATION:** Accounts are on file at the Charity Commission.

**GENERAL:** The policy of the trustees is 'not limited but their main aims are to enhance; (i) the protection of Humane Freedom, (ii) the promotion of the study of Greek Civilisation, (iii) support for arts, civic amenities and social welfare in the Manchester area'. A review of the trust's accounts showed the following grants relevant to this guide:

In 1993 –

Minority Rights Group (£600 and in the previous year);

Prisoners of Conscience Fund (£480 and in the previous year);

Civil Liberties Trust (£240);

Northern Refugee Centre, Prison Reform Trust (£120 each);

Latin America Information Centre (£60);

In 1992 –

Anti-Slavery International, Prisoners Abroad, Penal Reform Group (£120 each);

Survival International (£200).

**APPLICATIONS:** Applications should be made in writing and are considered quarterly.

# Mrs L D Rope's Third Charitable Settlement

**GRANT TOTAL:** £499,000 (1992/93)

**MAIN AREAS OF WORK:** Religion, education, relief of poverty, general

**ADDRESS:** Crag Farm, Boyton, Near Woodbridge, Suffolk IPI2 3LH

**TELEPHONE:** 0394-411387

**CORRESPONDENT:** Crispin M Rope

**TRUSTEES:** Mrs Lucy D Rope, Jeremy P W Heal, Crispin M Rope

**BENEFICIAL AREA:** National and international with a particular interest in south east Suffolk.

**INFORMATION:** Accounts are on file at the Charity Commission.

**GENERAL:** Recent grants with relevance to the scope of this guide:

In 1992/93 –

CAFOD ( £23,000 with £25,000 in the previous year);

Oxfam (£6,000 with £16,500 in the previous year);

In 1991/92 –

Intermediate Technology Development Group (£3,750 with £2,000 given in the previous year);

Friends of Peru (£1,250);

Corrymeela Community (£1,250).

**APPLICATIONS:** In writing to the correspondent, however major commitments by the trust mean that only a very limited sum is available to meet new requests.

# Rotary International in Great Britain and Ireland

**ADDRESS:** Kinwarton Road, Alcester, Warwickshire B49 6AV

**TELEPHONE:** (0789-765 411)

**CORRESPONDENT:** Mrs S Smith

**INFORMATION:** Published information on the scholarships is available from the address above.

**GENERAL:** The purpose of the Rotary Foundation scholarships is to further international understanding and friendly relations among peoples of different countries, rather than to enable beneficiaries to achieve any particular qualification. Both women and men are eligible.

For 1995/96 the Rotary Foundation offers the following scholarships:

**Academic-Year Ambassadorial Scholarships** – awarded for one academic year of study abroad. The round-trip airfare, plus a scholarship of up to US$21,500 or its equivalent to be used for tuition and fees, living expenses and one month of intensive language training.

**Multi-Year Ambassadorial Scholarships** – a flat grant of US$10,000 a year of its equivalent awarded for two or three years of specific degree-oriented study abroad.

**Cultural Ambassadorial Scholarships** – awarded for three of six months of intensive language study and cultural immersion in another country. Funding will provide for the round-trip airfare, tuition and fees, and reasonable living expenses.

**APPLICATIONS:** Each scholar is assigned both a sponsor and host Rotarian counsellor. Study or training must be undertaken in another country or territory in which there are Rotary clubs, but not in the sponsoring Rotary country or district. Applications need to be made through a Rotary club in the district where the applicant lives, studies or works. Applicants are advised to contact the address above for full details and advice.

# The Rothley Trust

**GRANT TOTAL:** £120,000 (1991/92)

**ADDRESS:** Mea House, Ellison Place, Newcastle-upon-Tyne NE1 8XS

**TELEPHONE:** 091-232 7783

**CORRESPONDENT:** Peter L Tennant, Secretary.

**TRUSTEES:** I H Clegg, Dr H A Armstrong, Mrs R Barkes R R V Nicholson, J R Barrett, R P Gordon (Chairman).

**BENEFICIAL AREA:** The North East of England (Northumberland to North Yorkshire) exclusively. Third World arising from this area only will be considered.

**INFORMATION:** Full accounts are on file at the Charity Commission.

**GENERAL:** In 1990/91 £90,000 was distributed in grants to organisations and £30,000 in educational grants (school fees for individuals up to GCSE level). Whilst the great majority of grants are given in the North East of England the following grants with relevance to the scope of this guide were given:

Corrymeela Community (£1,050);

Northern Ireland Voluntary Trust (£1,300); (Longstanding recipients of Rothley support, the Ulster list is unlikely to be extended.)

Children's International Summer villages for Newcastle branch only (£525);

Prison Reform Trust (£150);

**APPLICATIONS:** In writing to the correspondent.

# Rowan Charitable Trust

**GRANT TOTAL:** £213,000 (1991)

**ADDRESS:** c/o Coopers and Lybrand, 9 Greyfriars Road, Reading, Berks RG1 1JG

**TELEPHONE:** 0734-597111

**CORRESPONDENT:** The Trustees

**TRUSTEES:** D D Mason, J M McKenzie, Mrs H Russell

**BENEFICIAL AREA:** National and international

**INFORMATION:** Accounts are on file at the Charity Commission.

**GENERAL:** The trust aims to further humanitarian

causes. It particularly considers agencies working for development and human rights overseas as well as those working in deprived areas in Britain. The most recent accounts at the Charity Commission were for 1991 and showed the following grants with some relevance to the scope of this book:

Christian Aid (£35,000);

Intermediate Technology Development Group (£24,000);

Medical Aid for Palestinians, UNICEF (£10,000 each);

Nicaragua Health Fund (£6,000);

Tools for Self Reliance (£5,000);

Refugee Support Centre (£3,500);

Canon Collins Educational Trust for Southern Africa (£3,000);

Relief Society for Tigray (£2,500);

VSO, World Development Movement (£1,500 each).

It is also known that Co-operation Ireland received support in 1992.

**APPLICATIONS:**  In writing to the correspondent.

*Juliette Prague – spoke with before.*

# Joseph Rowntree Charitable Trust

**GRANT TOTAL:**  £3,360,000 (1993)

**MAIN AREAS OF WORK:**  Security & Disarmament; Racial Justice; South Africa; Democratic Process; Poverty; Corporate Responsibility; Mediation & Nonviolence

**ADDRESS:**  The Garden House, Water End, York YO3 6LP

**TELEPHONE:**  0904-627810; Fax: 0904-651990

**CORRESPONDENT:**  Steven Burkeman, Secretary

**TRUSTEES:**  Gillian Hopkins (Chair), Christopher Holdsworth (Vice-Chair), Andrew Gunn, Geoffrey Hubbard, Ruth McCarthy, Roger Morton, Marion McNaughton, Derek Guiton, Margaret Bryan, David Shutt, Hilary Southall.

**BENEFICIAL AREA:**  Mainly UK, with some work in Southern Africa, the Republic of Ireland, and also in a European context.

**INFORMATION:**  Information leaflets and Triennial Report for 1991/93.

**GENERAL:**  The trust information leaflet for 1992/93 stated that it then 'supported work aimed at:

- developing ways of resolving interpersonal, inter-community and international conflicts peacefully. This includes work in the field of security and disarmament, nonviolence and mediation.

- enhancing democratic values and the democratic process in the United Kingdom; encouraging corporate responsibility in both the private and public sectors; and strengthening the position of individual citizens or associations of individuals.

- contributing to peace, justice and reconciliation in Northern Ireland.

- contributing to the development of just, peaceful and non-racial societies in Southern Africa.

- securing fairness and justice for all citizens in the United Kingdom regardless of ethnic origin, colour, religion, disability, gender or sexual orientation. Special emphasis is given to race relations and immigration.

- understanding and eliminating the causes of poverty in the United Kingdom, and creating an economically just society.

- facilitating work linked closely with the Religious Society of Friends (Quakers), if it seems appropriate that such work should be funded from sources outside the society itself.

- witnessing to spiritual or non-material values in an increasingly secular and materialistic culture.'

The trust's accounts for 1993 listed grants given in the following categories:

African Affairs £578,915

Corporate Responsibility £208,414

Democratic Process £282,408

Peace and Development Education £56,736

Mediation & Nonviolence £191,751

Northern Ireland £351,063

Racial Justice £405,937

Religious Studies & Quaker Service £330,535

Security & Disarmament £513,557

Poverty & Economic Justice £267,737

Miscellaneous £174,036

The following extracts are taken from the trust's draft Triennial Report for 1991/93.

**Security and Disarmament**

'The trust seeks to support policy-oriented research, dissemination and advocacy, directed at decision-makers and opinion-leaders, developing and promoting credible alternative strategies for achieving peace and disarmament with security.'

'The trust has funded work by independent experts on stocks and flows of fissile material, on chemical weapons and on the verification of arms control agreements – work which is officially accepted as 'indispensable' and is closely related to critical steps towards a peaceful world, such as implementation of the Chemical Weapons Convention (opened for signature in January 1993) and the review and extension of the Nuclear Non-Proliferation Treaty in 1995 ... One theme of trust grant-making has been the use of extensive databases and expert opinion to provide reliable and easily assimilated briefings for MPs, editors and others, as well as officials in Whitehall, NATO, Washington and elsewhere.'

Grants given between 1991/93 included:

British American Security Information Council (BASIC) (£199,838);

Verification Technology Information Centre (VERTIC) (£169,045);

Farndon House Information Trust (Dfax) (£160,845);

Saferworld (£134,999);

NATO Alerts Network (NAN) (£126,017);

Bradford University, Department of Peace Studies (£110,789);

Science Policy Research Unit, Sussex University (£95,567);

International Security Information Service (£57,168);

Trust for Research & Education on the Arms Trade (£52,760);

European Public Policy Institute, Warwick University (£48,061).

**Mediation and Nonviolence**

'The trust is particularly interested in those aspects of mediation which stress the potential for people to resolve their own conflicts, and the possibility of equipping people to find community solutions to community problems ... The trust is willing to consider applications from innovative mediation projects working at international, national or local levels to resolve inter and intra community conflicts. Priority will be given to umbrella schemes which offer assistance and support to those operating at a local level'.

'The trust is willing to consider applications which address the problems of both personal and structural violence, and which seek to promote the application of a nonviolent approach to the restoration of justice and unity in society.'

Grants have been given to:

Association to Protect All Children (APPROACH) (£114,432);

Responding to Conflict, Woodbrooke College (£86,858);

Michael Randle, study of nonviolent defence (£50,920);

Mediation UK (£41,534);

Gil Fell, reducing violence in the playground (£38,075);

International Fellowship of Reconciliation, education and training project (£32,489);

Conflict Mediation Network (Northern Ireland) (£22,500);

Leeds Inter Agency Project (Women and Violence ) (£8,777).

**Northern Ireland**

'The trust seeks to support programmes which aim to contribute towards peace, justice and reconciliation in Northern Ireland. It does this through core and project funding for organisations and individuals working in the following fields:

- Community Development and Education: promoting a sense of self-confidence in communities experiencing deprivation and helping to build new community structures independent of traditional power bases; tackling the issues of poverty.

- Community Relations: challenging sectarianism; promoting dialogue; and increasing understanding and co-operation across the political and religious divide.

- Women: addressing disadvantages faced by women in Northern Ireland; developing the leadership potential of women; experimenting with new learning processes and patterns of organisation for women's groups.
- Rights and Justice: upholding the freedom and rights of the individual citizen; informing and educating about misuses of power and miscarriages of justice whether perpetrated by state agencies or others; promoting new ideas to sustain the democratic process.'

'The trust also welcomes applications from the Republic of Ireland and from Great Britain which directly or indirectly have a bearing on the situation in Northern Ireland.'

Examples of grants included:

Initiative 92/The Opsahl Commission (£120,000);

The Integrated Education Fund (£125,000);

Committee on the Administration of Justice (CAJ) (£61,060);

Centre for the Study of Conflict, Ulster University (£32,688);

Counteract (£13,000).

### South Africa

'The trust seeks to support programmes which aim to contribute towards peace, justice and reconciliation in Southern Africa. It does this through the provision of core and project funding for the legally charitable endeavours or organisations and individuals:

- working on the use of nonviolence and mediation, the legal system or other peaceful means of resolving conflict and achieving change;
- providing skills and support for those working for peaceful social change;
- helping to develop the skills necessary to bring about and sustain a democratic society in South Africa. The trust seeks to support work which cannot raise support from sources within the region or from mainstream funders such as statutory organisations, business and aid agencies.'

The trust is an associate member of Interfund which serves international donors working in South Africa who do not wish to set up their own offices there, but are keen to ensure that their grant-making is authoritative and soundly based.

Grants have included:

Centre for Inter Group Studies, University of Cape Town, for research aiming to influence policy on the restructuring of the police and military (£210,754);

Community Dispute Resolution Trust, Centre for Applied Legal Studies, University of Witwatersrand., which aims to help communities establish local community dispute resolution centres (£80,000);

Quaker Peace Centre, Cape Town, for two peace workers based in the townships (£36,726).

### Refugees

Within a programme on racial justice the trust allocates a small proportion of its resources to support work with refugees. Grants are confined to organisations in the North of England and in Scotland offering advice and advocacy or working to influence policy. Emphasis is given to work relating to the legal status of refugees – the trust is unable to support direct service provision.

Grants given under the racial justice programme have included:

Joint Council for the Welfare of Immigrants (£140,384);

The Runnymede Trust (£68,750);

The Society of Black Lawyers (£57,685);

Scottish Refugee Council (£20,984).

**EXCLUSIONS:** General appeals and large, well established national charities, buildings, purely academic research, educational bursaries and travel. See also the trust's leaflet for applicants.

**APPLICATIONS:** There is no application form. All applicants should obtain the trust leaflet giving guidance to applicants. Trustee meetings are held four times a year. Applications may take as long as five months to process but may be completed in about two months, rarely less. The trust has specialist sub-committees for Northern Ireland, Southern Africa, Racial Justice and Democracy.

# Joseph Rowntree Reform Trust

**GRANT TOTAL:**  About £500,000 annually

**MAIN AREAS OF WORK:**  Radical and reforming work which is not eligible for charitable status

**ADDRESS:**  The Garden House, Water End, York YO3 6LP

**TELEPHONE:**  0904-625744; Fax: 0904- 651502

**CORRESPONDENT:**  Lois Jefferson, Secretary.

**TRUSTEES:**  Professor Trevor Smith (Chairman), David Currie, Christine Day, Christopher Greenfield, Archy Kirkwood, Richard Rowntree, David Shutt

**BENEFICIAL AREA:**  Mainly UK

**INFORMATION:**  Information leaflet

**GENERAL:**  This trust is not a charitable trust but a limited company. Because it is not a charitable trust it can give grants for political and propagandist activities outside the scope of charitable law. The trust particularly reserves its help for organisations, groups or individuals not eligible for charitable funding because of their lobbying, campaigning or other 'political' work, and which are unable to raise funds from other sources.

The trust did not want an entry although an extensive one was given in the previous guide. An extract from a letter in January 1994 by the secretary follows: 'This trust does not have a specific interest in peace, security and international relations and in contrast to the period covered by the first edition of the directory, has made only a tiny number of grants in these areas in the past two or three years. My trustees are in fact very much more likely to reject than to grant any applications in the fields covered by your directory.

'We also feel that our inclusion would, in an important sense, fail those we seek to support. This is because, being (most unusually) a company rather than a charity, we have been able to develop a special remit to help plug the funding gap for political reform created by charity law. That is to say, our specific role is to consider support for any individual or organisation which a charitable trust could not support because of the political nature of the work in question.

'In practice, and of necessity, choices are made – but not according to a fixed menu of issues. Our interests are, by definition, inclusive of any political action that our trustees judge to be efficient and appropriate in righting wrongs. Hence, we have certainly funded people and organisations working on peace and security matters, but not exclusively so. We think, therefore, to be listed as an organisation which has a particular interest in this area – or in any other specific subject – would send the wrong message to all those bodies we seek to support who are involved in any other aspect of political reform.'

# A & B Sainsbury Charitable Trust

**GRANT TOTAL:**  £387,550 (1992/93)

**MAIN AREAS OF WORK:**  General

**ADDRESS:**  Clark Whitehill, 25 New Street Square, London EC4A 3LN

**CORRESPONDENT:**  D J Walker, Trustees Accountant

**TRUSTEES:**  Lord Sainsbury, Simon Sainsbury, Miss J S Portrait

**BENEFICIAL AREA:**  National

**INFORMATION:**  Accounts are on file at the Charity Commission.

**GENERAL:**  The trust gave grants under the following categories in 1992/93:

Education £22,000;

Health and Social Welfare £141,800;

Overseas £129,000;

Scientific and Medical Research £50,000;

The Arts £19,000;

Religion £12,000;

The Environment £13,750.

The trust does not give information about the specific sums donated with its list of grants given under each category. Donations with relevance to the scope of this guide were given:

**Under Education –**

Holocaust Educational Trust;

**Under Overseas –**

Anglo-Israel Association; Canon Collins Educational Trust for Southern Africa;  International Committee for Andean Aid;  IVS; VSO; Pestalozzi Children's Village Trust;

**Under Religion –**

Council of Christians and Jews.

**APPLICATIONS:** In writing to the correspondent.

## Sainsbury Family Charitable Trusts

*[handwritten: umbrella Parcel Sainsbury Trusts. Only pays to Charitable organisations]*

**ADDRESS:** 9 Red Lion Court, London EC4A 3EB

**TELEPHONE:** 071-410 0330

**CORRESPONDENT:** Hugh L de Quetteville

**GENERAL:** The nine Sainsbury Family Charitable Trusts include: the Elizabeth Clark Charitable Trust, the Gatsby Charitable Foundation, the Headley Trust, the Jerusalem Trust, the Kay Kendall Leukaemia Fund, the Linbury Trust, the Lisa Sainsbury Foundation, the Monument Trust, the Monument Historic Buildings Trust. One letter to the above office will ensure that an appeal is considered by whichever of the trusts is the most appropriate. The Gatsby, Headley and Jerusalem Trusts are those which have supported work within the scope of interest of this guide. See separate entries for these three trusts.

## Peter Samuel Charitable Trust

**GRANT TOTAL:** £125,000 (1991/92)

**MAIN AREAS OF WORK:** General

**ADDRESS:** Farley Hall, Farley Hill, Reading, Berks RG7 1UL

**CORRESPONDENT:** Viscount Bearsted

**TRUSTEES:** Viscount Bearsted, Hon Nicholas Samuel, Hon Michael Samuel

**BENEFICIAL AREA:** National with a particular interest in Berkshire and Hampshire

**INFORMATION:** Accounts are on file at the Charity Commission.

**GENERAL:** In 1991/92 the following grants with some relevance to this guide were given:

Save the Children (£5,000 with £2,000 in the 2 previous years);

Groups Relations Educational Trust (£1,500 with £1,000 in the 2 previous years);

Council for Christians and Jews (£1,000 also in the 2 previous years).

**APPLICATIONS:** In writing to the correspondent.

## Save & Prosper Foundation

*[handwritten: Mr Alister MacIntosh writing letter from charities no individuals]*

**GRANT TOTAL:** £158,000 (1992)

**ADDRESS:** 1 Finsbury Avenue, London EC2M 2QY

**TELEPHONE:** 071-588 1717

**CORRESPONDENT:** Duncan Grant, Director

**TRUSTEES:** Managing Committee for the Save & Prosper Group Ltd

**BENEFICIAL AREA:** National and international

**INFORMATION:** Accounts are on file at the Charity Commission.

**GENERAL:** The foundation gave the following grants with relevance to this guide:

In 1991/92 –

Friends of the Earth (£10,000 with £12,750 in the previous year);

Centre for World Development Education (£2,000);

Ulster Sports and Recreation (£686 with £1,000 in the previous year);

In 1990/91 –

Living Earth Ltd (£2,500);

Help Romania Ltd (£2,000);

Romania Orphanage Trust (£100).

**APPLICATIONS:** In writing to the correspondent.

## Schroder Charitable Trust

**GRANT TOTAL:** £440,500 (1992)

**ADDRESS:** 120 Cheapside, London EC2V 6DS

**TELEPHONE:** 071-382 6000

**CORRESPONDENT:** The Secretary.

**TRUSTEES:** The trust is also an unlimited company.

**BENEFICIAL AREA:** National

**INFORMATION:** Accounts are on file at the Charity Commission.

**GENERAL:** The stated preference is for national, registered charities. The range of giving is broad with beneficiaries in the fields of health, social welfare, refugees, education and the arts. A review of the most recent accounts for 1992 showed the following with some relevance to the scope of this book:

British Executive Service Overseas (£3,000);

CAFOD (£2,000);

Disasters Emergency Committee, African famine (£1,000);

Northern Ireland Voluntary Trust, Runnymede Trust, VSO (£750 each);

Ditchley Foundation, British Southern Slav Society, Ethiopia Aid, Romania Project UK, Save the Children, Royal Institute of International Affairs (£500 each);

ActionAid (£470);

Intermediate Technology Development Group (£370);

Oxfam (£350);

Christian Aid (£250);

Amnesty International (£200);

Afghan Relief (£190).

The great majority of these organisations had also received support in the previous year. In 1991 grants had also been given to:

British Institute of International and Comparative Law (£300);

British Atlantic Committee (£100).

**APPLICATIONS:** In writing to the correspondent. Applications are considered on a monthly basis.

*no individuals*   *once in schools*

# Scott Bader Commonwealth Ltd

**GRANT TOTAL:** £125,000 (1991)

**ADDRESS:** Wollaston, Wellingborough, Northants

**TELEPHONE:** 0933-663100

**CORRESPONDENT:** Michael Jones, Secretary.

**TRUSTEES:** The Board of Management.

**INFORMATION:** Accounts are on file at the Charity Commission.

**GENERAL:** The primary objective of the charity is to contribute to the development of a genuinely just and peaceful industrial and social order. It has four main areas of concern:

- 'Sharing the fruits of our labours with those less fortunate' – projects which respond to the needs of those who are most underprivileged, disadvantaged, poor or excluded;

- 'To question to what extent violence resides in the demands we make upon the earth's resources' – projects which encourage the careful use and protection of the earth's resources;

- 'To foster a movement towards a new peaceful industrial and social order – peace-building projects through education, conflict resolution, reconciliation of citizen diplomacy;

- 'Far reaching reconstruction' and change through the 'principle of common ownership' – projects which encompass these principles of co-operation and democratic participation.

Grants with relevance to this guide were given:

In 1991 –

ActionAid (£4,280);

Tools for Self Reliance (£5,000 2nd of 3);

Gandhi Foundation (£2,000);

Windmill Integrated Nursery School, Dungannon (£2,000);

Help Tibet (£1,010);

Christian Aid (£500);

Save the Children (£400);

Amnesty International (£250)

Medical Aid for Poland, Tear Fund (£150 each);

CAFOD (£100);

Fourth World Educational Research Assistance Trust (£75);

In 1990 –

Peace Child (£3,000);

Intermediate Technology Development Group (£2,000);

Quaker Peace and Service (£1,000);

Pugwash Conference (£500);

UNICEF UK (£120);

Peace Education Project (£50).

**APPLICATIONS:** There is no application form. There is no special time frame, appeals are considered throughout the year on a monthly basis.

*[handwritten: future? DGMT p.574]*

# Scouloudi Foundation

(formerly known as the Twenty-Seven Foundation)

**GRANT TOTAL:** £152,000 (1991/92)

**ADDRESS:** c/o Hays Allan, Southampton House, 317 High Holborn, London WC1V 7NL

**TELEPHONE:** 071-831 6233

**CORRESPONDENT:** The Administrator

**TRUSTEES:** J M Carr, A J Parr, M E Demetriadi, Miss B R Masters, J D Marnham, Miss S E Stowell

**BENEFICIAL AREA:** National

**INFORMATION:** Accounts are on file at the Charity Commission and guidance notes are available.

**GENERAL:** The foundation is particularly interested in funding historical awards, social welfare and the environment. Donations other than historical awards are split into 'regular' and 'special'.

'Regular' grants with relevance to this guide were made in 1991/92 to:

WaterAid (£800);

IVS, Oxfam, Pestolozzi Children, VSO, Y Care International (£400 each);

Voluntary Service Belfast (£400).

A 'Special' grant was given in 91/92 to:

Save the Children Kurdish Refugees Appeal (£1,000).

**APPLICATIONS:** Only some 22% of funds is uncommitted. Applications are considered three times a year, in March, September and December.

# Henry Smith's (Kensington Estates) Charity

**GRANT TOTAL:** £12 million (1992)

**MAIN AREAS OF WORK:** Health, Social Welfare

**ADDRESS:** 5 Chancery Lane, Clifford's Inn, London EC4A 1BU

**TELEPHONE:** 071-242 1212

**CORRESPONDENT:** Brian McGeough, Treasurer. The Chief Visitor is Virginia Graham. Other Visitors are responsible for county allocations.

**TRUSTEES:** Lord Kindersley (Chairman), Lord Abergavenny, Mrs Anne Allen, Lord Ashcombe, Lord Crashaw, T E Egerton, Lord Egremont, Lady Euston, H N Cage, J D Hambro, J O Hambro, Lord Hamilton of Dalzell, T D Holland-Martin, Lord Kingsdown, Major E J de Lisle, J N C James, Lord Lloyd of Berwick, R S Norman, Major B Shand, J J Sheffield, J F Smith, G E Lee-Steere. Members of the Distribution Committee are Lord Kindersley (Chairman), J O Hambro, J F E Smith, J J Sheffield, Sir Anthony Lloyd, T D Holland-Martin.

**BENEFICIAL AREA:** National, but with special allocations for certain counties (see list below).

**INFORMATION:** Full accounts with a comprehensive report are on file at the Charity Commission and available direct from the charity itself. These are for 1991/92. Information about the charity's activities in the years before then has been minimal.

**GENERAL:** This massive charity has been included since the last of its nine specific objects is of direct relevance to this guide. This refers to donations to 'Organisations, bodies, or persons engaged in the restoration of slaves or serfs to their freedom and certain related activities". Whilst the scale of its actual giving is small the potential remains.

In practice the trustees classify their donations into the following categories: Medical, Disability, Social Service and Moral Welfare. The trustees do not set rigid budgetary targets for the categories in order to maintain flexibility.

The charity makes three kinds of donations: one-off grants in response to applications received; annual grants to a list of charities to help them with their running costs; and grants from a separate budget to organisations in particular counties where the charity has a traditional connection – Gloucestershire, Hampshire, Kent, Leicestershire, Suffolk, Surrey, East Sussex, West Sussex.

Each county list is the responsibility of a particular trustee who is normally resident in the county.

In addition the trustees have decided to select a specific area which will be the subject of a major donation over a period of three years, in order to make a significant impact in each chosen field. To date these have been drug and alcohol abuse, mental health and the geographic area of the North East.

Grants given in 1992 with relevance to this guide were:

Anti-Slavery Society (£5,000);

Prisoners Abroad (£20,000);

World University Service (UK) (£35,650);

Development Education Project and Worker, Leicestershire (£1,300);

Committee for the Welfare of Migrants, Kent (£750);

**APPLICATIONS:** Applications should be made in writing to the correspondent. Before this the general guidelines should be obtained.

# W F Southall Trust

**GRANT TOTAL:** £168,000 (1991/92)

**ADDRESS:** Rutters Solicitors, 2 Bimport, Shaftesbury, Dorset SP7 8AY.

**CORRESPONDENT:** Stephen T Rutter.

**TRUSTEES:** Mrs Daphne Maw, C M Southall, D H D Southall, Mrs Annette Wallis, M Holtom.

**BENEFICIAL AREA:** National and international

**INFORMATION:** Accounts are on file at the Charity Commission.

**GENERAL:** The trust makes grants mainly within the UK though it can give internationally. Its objects cover the Society of Friends, peace education, alcohol and drug addiction and related charities. In 1991/92 the following grants were made:

**Central Committees of Society of Friends – £48,700**

Friends World Committee for Consultation (£6,000);

Quaker Council for European Affairs (£1,000);

Other Quaker Charities £45,450 Woodbrooke (responding to conflict (£5,000); Ulster Quaker Service Committee (£2,450);

West Midlands Quakers Peace Education Project (£2,000);

Quaker Peace Studies Trust (£1,000);

Bradford Peace Studies Department (£100);

**Others – £69,700**

Intermediate Technology Development Group, UNICEF (£1,500 each);

Tools for Self Reliance, Gandhi Foundation, Lansbury House Trust Fund (£1,000 each);

Give Peace a Chance Trust (£850);

Marie Stopes International, IVS Northern Ireland (£750 each);

Save the Children (£600);

UNA Trust, University of Ulster (£600);

Christian Aid, Gulf Crisis Working Group, VSO, Medical Foundation for the Care of Victims of Torture (£500 each);

CARE (£350);

Amnesty International (£300);

British Refugee Council, Peace and Reconciliation Group, UNAIS (£250).

**EXCLUSIONS:** No applications for individuals are considered e.g. Operation Raleigh.

**APPLICATIONS:** Trustees meet twice a year but most of the grants are made in the Autumn. These applications should be sent by September. All should include a reply paid envelope. The trust is not in a position to correspond with all applicants. Applicants are asked to remember that this is principally a Quaker Trust.

# Sir Sigmund Sternberg Charitable Foundation

**GRANT TOTAL:** £73,000 (1991/92)

**MAIN AREAS OF WORK:** General

**ADDRESS:** Star House, Grafton Road, London NW5 4BD

**CORRESPONDENT:** Sir Sigmund Sternberg

**TRUSTEES:** Sir Sigmund Sternberg, Lady Hazel Sternberg, M V Sternberg

**BENEFICIAL AREA:** National and international

**INFORMATION:** Accounts are on file at the Charity Commission

**GENERAL:** The grantmaking by the foundation fluctuates considerably, for instance £73,000 was disbursed in 1991/92 compared with £207,000 in 1990/91.

Grants with some relevance to scope of this guide were given in 1991/92 to:

Council for Christians and Jews (£1,500 with £1,000 in the previous year);

Israel Diaspora Trust (£1,250 also in the previous year);

OXFAM (£1,000 also in the previous year);

Ditchley Foundation (£500 with £250 in the previous year);

Group Relations Educational Trust (£500);

Federation of Jewish Relief Organisations (£100);

World Congress of Faiths (£50);

Council for Arms Control (£30).

**APPLICATIONS:** It is understood that funds are already allocated and unsolicited applications are unlikely to be considered.

## Sir Halley Stewart Trust

*[handwritten: possibility of funding when I go into schools as long as fund through a charity]*

**GRANT TOTAL:** £589,000 (1992/93)

**ADDRESS:** ~~88 Long Lane~~, Willingham, Cambridge CB4 5L~~B~~ *[handwritten: 22 Earith Rd CB4 5LS]*

**TELEPHONE:** 0954-260707

**CORRESPONDENT:** ~~Mrs Polly Fawcitt, Secretary~~ *[handwritten: Mrs Sue West, Secretary]*

**TRUSTEES:** Sir Charles Carter (Chairman), Professor Harold C. Stewart, Dr Duncan Stewart, Sir Ronald C Stewart, Dr Joan Haram, William P. Kirkman, Lord Stewartby, Professor John Lennard-Jones, Professor Phyllida Parsloe, Michael S R Collins, George Russell, Barbara Clapham, Professor W Jacobson .

**BENEFICIAL AREA:** National and international

**INFORMATION:** Accounts are on file at the Charity Commission but without a grants schedule. The information in this entry has been supplied by the trust.

**GENERAL:** The trust's objects are stated as: 'primarily to provide grants for the research into the prevention of human suffering, with the view to making such pioneer research work self-supporting at the earliest possible moment. The trust deed gives three principles to which the trustees should have regard in administering trust income:

• To furthering for every individual such favourable opportunities of education, service and leisure as shall enable him or her most perfectly to develop the body, mind and spirit.

• In all social life whether domestic, industrial or national, to securing a just environment, and

• In international relationships to fostering goodwill between all races, tribes, peoples and nations so as to secure the fulfilment of hope of "Peace on Earth" '.

A large proportion of the trust's funding goes to pioneer medical research but a list of the grants showed the following allocations with relevance to the scope of this guide:

Grants of £16,000 or more were given to:

Harmony Community Trust, Belfast;

Northern Ireland Council for Integrated Education;

Grants of £10,000 up to £16,000 were given to:

Charity Know How, Eastern Europe;

Churches Commission on Overseas Students, hardship fund;

UNAIS, for 2 workers in Mali;

A grant of up to £10,000 was given to:

Forum for Community Work, Belfast.

It is understood that the trust is developing a programme in South Africa.

**EXCLUSIONS:** No general appeals of any sort.

**APPLICATIONS:** A preliminary telephone call to the secretary is recommended before a written application is presented. Applications are considered three to four times a year.

## Still Waters Charitable Trust

*[handwritten: DGMT p.614 - not likely]*

**GRANT TOTAL:** £12,000 (1991/92)

**MAIN AREAS OF WORK:** General

**ADDRESS:** 10 Greenhurst Lane, Oxted, Surrey RH8 0LB

**CORRESPONDENT:** R H H Kendall

**BENEFICIAL AREA:** Unrestricted

**INFORMATION:** Accounts are on file at the Charity Commission.

**GENERAL:** This trust was established in 1990. No list of grants is available, but it is known that Survival International received a grant of £500 in 1992.

**APPLICATIONS:** In writing to the correspondent.

*[handwritten margin notes: no funding equipment in isolation; after 2 yr subject to satisfactory report; meetings Feb/June/Oct each yr. Application beginning month before; small grants up to £2,000 don't have to be seen at meeting salary 15-18,000 yr max 3 yrs.]*

# Eric Stonehouse Trust Ltd

**GRANT TOTAL:** £3,000 (1992/93)

**MAIN AREAS OF WORK:** Relief of suffering and disease

**ADDRESS:** The Old Rectory, Starston, Harleston, Norfolk IP20 9NG

**CORRESPONDENT:** Rev Dr M N France

**TRUSTEES:** Rev M N France, Mrs E France, P N Hepworth, Miss C S France, Miss M L France

**BENEFICIAL AREA:** National and to national groups working abroad

**INFORMATION:** Accounts are on file at the Charity Commission.

**GENERAL:** Grants with relevance to the scope of this guide were given:

In 1992/93 –

Medical Aid for Poland (£100);

Voluntary Service Belfast, Cooperation Ireland, Prisoners Abroad (£50 each);

In 1991/92 –

Anglo-Thai Foundation (£100).

**EXCLUSIONS:** Grants only to registered charities. None for individuals or political activities.

**APPLICATIONS:** In writing to the correspondent. Decisions are made three times a year. Acknowledgements are not made.

# Strathspey Charitable Trust

**GRANT TOTAL:** Not known

**MAIN AREAS OF WORK:** Overseas relief

**ADDRESS:** David Blank & Co, 90 Deansgate, Manchester M3 2QJ

**TELEPHONE:** 061-832 3304

**CORRESPONDENT:** John Alcock

**TRUSTEES:** P M Rose, A H Alcock, J G Baker.

**BENEFICIAL AREA:** National and international

**INFORMATION:** No accounts are filed with the Charity Commission.

**GENERAL:** This trust was established in 1989 and is believed to have an income of some £100,000. Its trust deed states that it will support Oxfam, Christian Aid, Save the Children, the British Red Cross and other charities selected by the trustees.

**APPLICATIONS:** In writing to the correspondent.

# The Sumray Charitable Trust

**GRANT TOTAL:** £8,000 (1978)

**ADDRESS:** Davis, Frankel & Mead, Solicitors, 8 Queen Anne Street, London W1M 9LD

**CORRESPONDENT:** See above

**TRUSTEES:** M Sumray, Mrs C Sumray, M Marcus Davis, P M Emanuel

**BENEFICIAL AREA:** National and international

**INFORMATION:** No accounts have been filed with the Charity Commission since 1978.

**GENERAL:** It is only possible to give information from very out of date accounts. These show that in 1978, and in the two previous years, the major grant was given to the Society of Friends of Jewish Refugees (£6,225 with £7,175 and £3,600 in the two preceding years). In 1976 £450 was given to the Victims of Persecution Fund.

# The Bernard Sunley Charitable Foundation

**GRANT TOTAL:** £2,834,000 (1992/93)

**MAIN AREAS OF WORK:** General

**ADDRESS:** 53 Grosvenor Street, London W1X 9FH

**TELEPHONE:** 071-409 1199

**CORRESPONDENT:** D C Macdiarmid, Director

**TRUSTEES:** John B Sunley, Sir William Shapland, Joan M Tice, Mrs Bella Sunley, Sir Donald Gosling

**BENEFICIAL AREA:** Unrestricted

**INFORMATION:** Accounts are on file at the Charity Commission.

**GENERAL:** This large trust has assets of some £50 million and a net income of £2.9 million. Grants with relevance to this guide were made:

In 1992/93 –

Urban Foundation of South Africa (£30,000 and in the previous year);

Centre for Research in Communist Economies (£10,000 and in the previous year);

British Executive Service Overseas, VSO (£2,000 each);

Ross McWhirter Foundation (£1,000 and in the previous year);

Raleigh International (£1,000);

Cornerstone Belfast, Northern Ireland Children's Holiday Scheme (£1,000 each);

In 1991/92

Atlantic College of the United World Colleges (£550,000);

British Institute of International and Comparative Law (£30,000);

GAP Activity Projects Ltd (£5,000);

**EXCLUSIONS:** No grants to individuals.

**APPLICATIONS:** In writing to the correspondent with latest audited accounts. The trust regrets that no replies are made to unsuccessful applicants.

## Joan Tanner Charitable Settlement

*will consider an application*

**GRANT TOTAL:** £2,550 (1978)

**MAIN AREAS OF WORK:** General

**ADDRESS:** PO Box 356, 45 Mosley Street, Manchester M60 2BE

**TELEPHONE:** 061-242 3637

*Andrea Bakewell*

**CORRESPONDENT:** Philip Carlton, Royal Bank of Scotland plc, North of England Trustee Office

**BENEFICIAL AREA:** National, international and local.

**INFORMATION:** Accounts have not been filed with the Charity Commission since 1978.

**GENERAL:** The information available on public record is very out of date. However the accounts for 1978 show the following grants with some relevance to the scope of this guide:

Save the Children Fund, Friends Service Council, Pestalozzi Children's Village Trust (£100 each).

The trustees have returned this entry and revised the contact information but have not updated the information about grants and scale of giving.

## C B & H H Taylor Trust

**GRANT TOTAL:** £90,000 (1992)

**MAIN AREAS OF WORK:** General with a particular interest in Quaker concerns

**ADDRESS:** 16 Stocks Wood, Birmingham B30 2AP.

**CORRESPONDENT:** Mrs H H Taylor.

**TRUSTEES:** Mrs H H Taylor, Mrs C H Norton, Mrs E J Birmingham, J A B.Taylor, W J B Taylor, Mrs C M Penny.

**BENEFICIAL AREA:** National, with an interest in the Birmingham area, and some organisations working overseas.

**INFORMATION:** Accounts have not been filed at the Charity Commission since 1985.

**GENERAL:** Apparently this family trust limits its grants to charities in which family members have a personal interest. It has a strong Quaker commitment and it is understood the 3/4 of its funding goes to Quaker work. Many grants are recurrent. The most recent accounts at the Charity Commission were for 1985 when the following organisations received support:

Quaker Peace and Service (£4,000);

Friends World Committee of Consultation (£2,500);

Voluntary Service Belfast, Oxfam, Quaker Council for European Affairs (£250 each);

Woodbrooke College (£100).

**APPLICATIONS:** New applications can be submitted for trust meetings in April and November. These organisations need to make their applications when they are due accompanied by a copy of the accounts of the previous year.

## Thompson Charitable Trust

*No – DGinT p-634 vol 2*

**GRANT TOTAL:** £72,000 (1992)

**ADDRESS:** 13A Pond Road, London SE3 0SL

**TELEPHONE:** 081-852 8893

**CORRESPONDENT:** A P Thompson

**TRUSTEES:** Alison Way, Jeremy Way

**INFORMATION:** Accounts are on file at the Charity Commission.

**GENERAL:** In 1992 the trust made the following grants with relevance to this guide:

Opportunity Trust (£5,000);

Charity Know How Network (£2,000).

**APPLICATIONS:** In writing to the correspondent.

*not educat*
*Enaiser*

# The Tudor Trust *don't fund individuals*

**GRANT TOTAL:** £19,335,000 (1992/93)

**MAIN AREAS OF WORK:** Social welfare, health, education

**ADDRESS:** 7 Ladbroke Grove, London W11 3BD

**TELEPHONE:** 071-727 8522

**CORRESPONDENT:** Roger Northcott, Secretary, or Jill Powell, Grants Administrator

**TRUSTEES:** Grove Charity Management Ltd. of which the Directors are: M K Graves, H M Dunwell, Dr D J T Graves, A A Grimwade, P J Buckler, C J M Graves, C M Antcliff, Sir James Swaffield, R W Anstice, L K Collins, E H Crawshaw, M S Dunwell, J W D Long.

**BENEFICIAL AREA:** Unrestricted

**INFORMATION:** Guidelines for applicants, and an annual report are available. Full reports and accounts are on file at the Charity Commission.

**GENERAL:** This is the largest general purpose trust in Britain. It makes over 1,600 grants a year, ranging from £200 to £1 million, with an average value of over £12,000.

There is an overall emphasis on social welfare in disadvantaged urban and rural parts of the United Kingdom. Grants are categorised as follows: Accommodation; Arts; Crime Prevention; Education; Employment and Training; Environment and Conservation; Health; Leisure; Overseas; Welfare Generally. Grants with some relevance to the scope of this guide are mostly made under the two latter categories.

Grants given in 1992/93 under **Welfare Generally** included a total of £110,500 to 13 refugee organisations with the largest grants given to:

Refugee Arrivals Project (£30,000);

Refugee Council (£24,000);

Community of Refugees from Vietnam, Somali Refugee Action Group, Greenwich (£10,000 each).

Under the **Education** category two grants were given to refugee work:

World University Service (UK) (£10,000);

Minority Rights Group (£1,000).

A total of £147,000 was allocated to 18 groups working in aspects of **family conciliation** with the largest grants given to:

National Association of Family Mediation & Conciliation Services (£27,500);

Hackney and East London Family Mediation Service Project (£25,000);

Family Mediation Scotland (£15,000).

A total of £452,550 was allocated in the **Overseas** category to 26 organisations with grants of particular interest to this guide given to:

Charity Know How (£25,000);

Bucharest Independent Living Centre (£30,000);

Homeless International (£36,000).

Some 4% of total grants given were made to **Northern Ireland** comprising 3.5% of total value of grants, these grants included:

Corrymeela Community, Belfast (£20,000);

Enniskillen Community Development Project (£10,000);

Northern Ireland Council for Voluntary Action (£6,000);

Ulster Quaker Peace Committee (£3,000).

**APPLICATIONS:** Applications in writing may be sent at any time to the Grants Administrator, Mrs Jill Powell. There is a continuous process of assessment. However because of the volume of requests it takes about two months for a decision to be notified. Obtain the note on how to make an application from the trust.

*Community*

# ~~Tyne & Wear~~ Foundation

**GRANT TOTAL:** £731,700 (1992/93)

**MAIN AREAS OF WORK:** General

**ADDRESS:** MEA House, Ellison Place, Newcastle-on-Tyne, NE1 8XS

**TELEPHONE:** 091-222 0945

**CORRESPONDENT:** Carol Meredith, Grants Officer

**TRUSTEES:** Board Members: Sir Tom Cowie; David Francis; Richard Harbottle (Chair); Carole Howells (Vice-Chair); Grigor McClelland; Lucy Milton; Sylvia Murray; Pauline Nelson; Frank Nicholson; Brian Roycroft; Roger Spoor; John Squires; Sir Michael Straker; Tony Tompkins; Alan Wardropper (Treasurer); Mike Worthington, Pummi Mattu, Alma Caldwell, Alastair Balls, Brian Latham.

**BENEFICIAL AREA:** Tyne and Wear, Durham and Northumberland.

**INFORMATION:** Annual review and grants policy available from the foundation.

**GENERAL:** The Tyne and Wear Foundation was established in 1988. It is based on an American model of community foundations which aims to raise an endowment fund to benefit a wide range of charitable causes in the local community.

The foundation's review for 1992 shows one grant with relevance to this guide:

North East Refugee Service (£8,000, with £5,000 given in the previous year).

**APPLICATIONS:** Contact Caroline Meredith for further information of application form and guidelines.

# Tzedakah

**GRANT TOTAL:** £172,000 (1989/90)

**ADDRESS:** Messrs Leonard Finn & Co, 8 Brentmead Place, London NW11 9LHuk

**TELEPHONE:** 081-4581141

**CORRESPONDENT:** L I Finn

**TRUSTEES:** Tzedakah Limited.

**BENEFICIAL AREA:** National

**INFORMATION:** Accounts have not been filed with the Charity Commission since 1989/90.

**GENERAL:** The trust gives mainly to Jewish charities. Grants with some relevance to this guide have been given:

In 1989/90 –

Relief of Russian Jewry (£870);

Russian Immigrants Aid Fund (£336);

Council of Christians and Jews (£180);

In 1988/89 –

Project Seed Educational Trust (£1,025);

UNICEF (£132);

Friends of Refugees of Eastern Europe (£50).

**APPLICATIONS:** It is understood that funds are committed and that unsolicited applications are unlikely to be considered.

# Van Neste Foundation

**GRANT TOTAL:** £177,000 (1992/93)

**MAIN AREAS OF WORK:** General

**ADDRESS:** 15 Alexandra Road, Clifton, Bristol BS8 2DD

**CORRESPONDENT:** F J F Lyons, Secretary

**TRUSTEES:** M T M Appleby (Chairman), F J F Lyons, Mrs B Stevens, G J Walker

**BENEFICIAL AREA:** National and international

**GENERAL:** The foundation's main areas of interest are the Third World and Eastern Europe, the handicapped and elderly, the advancement of religion, community and Christian family life, respect for the sanctity and dignity of human life. Grants relevant to this guide have been given in 1991/92 to:

CAFOD (£25,000);

Prisoners Abroad (£3,000);

Polish Trust (£1,300).

**APPLICATIONS:** In writing to the correspondent at any time: the trustees meet quarterly. Enclose a SAE to receive an acknowledgement.

# Edward Vinson Charitable Trust  *u o*

**GRANT TOTAL:** £13,500 (1992)

**MAIN AREAS OF WORK:** General, with a particular interest in overseas relief and human rights

**ADDRESS:** 34 Lavender Grove, Milton Keynes, Herts MK7 7DB

**TELEPHONE:** ~~0908 667122~~  *person moved on + died*

**CORRESPONDENT:** Ruth Matthews, Trustee

**TRUSTEES:** Ruth Matthews, John Matthews, Sarah Maitland.

**BENEFICIAL AREA:** National and international

**INFORMATION:** Accounts are on file at the Charity Commission.

**GENERAL:** In 1992 the trust made 14 grants which included the following:

CAFOD (£2,000);

United Reform Church (£1,000);

Medical Foundation for the Victims of Torture (£1,000);

Traidcraft Exchange (£1,000);

Canon Collins Educational Trust for South Africa (£1,000);

Foundation for Peace and Justice in South Africa (£1,000);

UNICEF UK (£500).

In the previous year grants of £1,000 each were given to: Christian Aid; Medical Aid for Palestine; Cusichaca Project Trust.

**APPLICATIONS:** In writing to the correspondent.

## Howard Walker Charitable Trust

**GRANT TOTAL:** £56,000 (1992/93)

**MAIN AREAS OF WORK:** General

**ADDRESS:** Messrs Bury & Walkers with Smith Ibberson, Solicitors, Britannic House, Regent Street, Barnsley, South Yorkshire S70 2EQ

**TELEPHONE:** 0226-733533

**CORRESPONDENT:** See above. *Ben Nicholson*

**TRUSTEES:** Mrs C Walker, Mrs D M Grunwell, Miss M Moxon

**BENEFICIAL AREA:** National and international

**INFORMATION:** Accounts are on file at the Charity Commission.

**GENERAL:** The following grants relevant to the scope of this guide have been given:

In 1992/93 –

Development Education Centre (location not given) (£500);

Tear Fund, CARE (£250 each);

Ockenden Venture (£200 with £100 in the previous year);

UNICEF (£150 with £200 in the previous year);

Medical Foundation for the Care of Victims of Torture (£150 with a grant also in the previous year);

In 1991/92 –

Y Care International (£1,250);

VSO (£250);

Amnesty International, Christian Aid, British Red Cross (£200 each);

UNA Trust Appeal (£150).

**APPLICATIONS:** There is no application form. Applications are considered periodically. Only successful grantees are acknowledged.

## Anne Wall Trust

**GRANT TOTAL:** £12,000 (1990/91)

**ADDRESS:** Messrs Peachey & Co, Arundel House, Arundel Street, London WC2R 3ED

**CORRESPONDENT:** See above

**TRUSTEES:** Mrs M A Wall, P A Williamson, I D Wilson, A W Hawkins

**BENEFICIAL AREA:** National

**INFORMATION:** Accounts are on file at the Charity Commission.

**GENERAL:** The trust has general charitable purposes. It has been included because in 1990/91 it gave a small grant relevant to this guide:

British Atlantic Committee (£80).

**APPLICATIONS:** In writing to the correspondent.

## Warbeck Fund Ltd

**GRANT TOTAL:** £690,600 (1992/93)

**MAIN AREAS OF WORK:** General

**ADDRESS:** 32 Featherstone Street, London EC1Y 8QX

**TELEPHONE:** 071-490 1922

**CORRESPONDENT:** The Secretary

**TRUSTEES:** The Directors: J Gestetner, M B David, N Sinclair

**BENEFICIAL AREA:** National and international

**GENERAL:** The fund gives predominantly to Jewish causes. The most recent accounts for 1992/93 showed the following grants with relevance to the scope of this guide:

British Red Cross (£13,000);

Central British Fund for World Jewish Relief (£6,680);

Group Relations Education Trust (£3,000);

Federation of Hungarian Jews in Great Britain (£1,000);

Schools Partnership Worldwide (£100);

Rainforest Foundation UK (£65).

**APPLICATIONS:** In writing to the correspondent though it is understood that funds are likely to be committed.

# The Wates Foundation

**GRANT TOTAL:** £1,173,000 (1992/93)

**ADDRESS:** 1260 London Road, Norbury, London SW16 4EG

**TELEPHONE:** 081-764 5000

**CORRESPONDENT:** Sir Martin Berthoud, Director

**TRUSTEES:** Anne Ritchie (Chairman), Andrew Wates, David Wates, Jane Wates, John Wates, Susan Wates.

**BENEFICIAL AREA:** Unrestricted, but see below.

**INFORMATION:** An information sheet and an annual report and accounts is available from the foundation. Accounts are on file at the Charity Commission.

**GENERAL:** The foundation's information leaflet states its present policy as: 'the alleviation of distress and the improvement of the quality of life, especially in the urban community. Within these broad aims, which are reflected in a wide pattern of grants, the trustees currently have a special interest in the well-being of young people in all its aspects, both spiritual and physical ... The majority of grants are made to projects in the London area, particularly in South London, and nearby. A few are made in Northern Ireland, Merseyside, and the North East. Applicants outside these areas should consider carefully whether their project is exceptional enough to justify a departure from the foundation's normal practice. A substantial proportion of the foundation's income is at present committed to three year projects, some of which are very large. The disposable income is therefore restricted'. The normal grant range is £1,000 to £25,000. Grants with some relevance to this guide were given:

In 1992/93 –

Charity Know How (£10,000 with £5,000 in the previous year);

Bearr Trust, core funding for work in Russia and the Republics (£5,000);

Charities Aid Foundation, Central Europe, visits for people active in the voluntary sector in Czechoslovakia (£1,000);

United Nations Association International Service (£4,450);

Voluntary Service Overseas (£4,000 also in the previous year);

Jointly Funded Scholarships for Students from Eastern Europe and the Soviet Union, funded with the FCO (£5,590 with £2,756 in the previous year);

Project Spark, relief and rescue of Bosnian children (£1,000);

Voluntary Service Overseas (£4,000);

South London Refugee Project (£5,000);

Medical Foundation for Victims of Torture (£1,000);

Somali Welfare Association (£200);

Older Refugees from Vietnam, Lewisham (£200);

Newham Conflict and Change Project (£8,000 with £6,500 in the previous year);

Corrymeela Community (£5,000 and in the previous year);

In 1991/92 –

Extra Care Belfast (£10,000);

Northern Ireland Council for Voluntary Action (£7,000);

Marie Stopes International (£5,000);

LEAP training costs for volunteers working with small groups to resolve conflict and violence (£3,000);

London Tamil Academy, for training of Tamil refugees (£2,000);

Association of Charitable Foundations towards the cost of Eastern European attending a conference in the UK (£609);

**EXCLUSIONS:** Grants are not normally made to general appeals from large well-established charities, to umbrella organisations or national associations or in response to national appeals. Grants are also not normally made for research, fundraising, travel and foreign conferences. A few grants for overseas projects are made to UK organisations working in Eastern Europe and the Third World; no grants are made in the Republic of Ireland.

**APPLICATIONS:** In writing to the correspondent with a description of the project and latest accounts. Grant allocation meetings normally January, April, July, October.

# Mary Webb Trust

**GRANT TOTAL:** £172,500 (1991/92)

**MAIN AREAS OF WORK:** Environment, Third World, Health

**ADDRESS:** 15 Bourne End Road, Northwood, Middlesex HA6 3BP

**CORRESPONDENT:** D C Morgan

**TRUSTEES:** D C Morgan, J M Fancett, C M Nash, G H Webb

**BENEFICIAL AREA:** National and international

**INFORMATION:** Accounts are on file at the Charity Commission.

**GENERAL:** It is worth noting that in 1991/92 total grants more than doubled from the previous year when £74,500 was disbursed. Grants with some relevance to the scope of this guide were given in 1991/92 to:

Ethiopia Aid (£20,000);

Concern Worldwide, SOS Sahel (£10,000 each);

Cyclone in Bangladesh (£5,000);

Tools for Self Reliance (£1,500).

In the previous year £10,000 was given to the Gulf Crisis Appeal.

**APPLICATIONS:** The trustees prefer to make their own enquiries and do not want unsolicited appeals.

# Weinberg Foundation

**GRANT TOTAL:** £140,000 (1991/92)

**ADDRESS:** 9-15 Sackville Street, Piccadilly, London W1X 1DE

**CORRESPONDENT:** M G M Torok

**TRUSTEES:** F Mauwer, N Ablitt

**INFORMATION:** Accounts are on file at the Charity Commission

**GENERAL:** In 1991/92 the following grants with some relevance to this guide were given:

Groups Relations Education Trust (£6,000);

SOS Yugoslavia (£1,000);

Cambodia Trust (£500).

**APPLICATIONS:** In writing to the correspondent.

# The Weinstock Fund

**GRANT TOTAL:** £238,000 (1991/92)

**MAIN AREAS OF WORK:** General

**ADDRESS:** 1 Stanhope Gate, London W1A 1EH

**CORRESPONDENT:** Miss J M Elstone

**TRUSTEES:** D Lewis, M Lester, S A Weinstock

**BENEFICIAL AREA:** National

**INFORMATION:** Accounts are on file at the Charity Commission.

**GENERAL:** Grants with some relevance to the scope of this guide have been given:

In 1991/92 –

Save the Children Fund (£11,000);

Israel Diaspora Trust (£1,000);

Pestalozzi Trust (£750);

C B F World Jewish Relief (£500 with £1,000 in the previous year);

Northern Ireland Council for Voluntary Action, Amnesty International, Oxfam (£500 each);

Cooperation Ireland, English Speaking Union, Holocaust Education Trust (£500 each, also given in the previous year);

In 1990/91 –

United Nations Commission for Refugees (£10,000);

Group Relations Education Trust (£7,000);

Friends of the Earth (£1,000);

UNICEF (£500 with £1,000 in the previous year);

In 1989/90 –

21st Century Trust (£2,000).

**APPLICATIONS:** In writing to the correspondent.

# Welton Foundation

**GRANT TOTAL:** £730,000

**MAIN AREAS OF WORK:** Medical

**ADDRESS:** c/o KPMG Peat Marwick, 1 Puddle Dock, London EC4V 3PD

**TELEPHONE:** 071-286 8000

**CORRESPONDENT:** Richard Reid, Secretary; R R Jessel, Grants Administrator

**TRUSTEES:** G C Seligman, Sir Ronald Leach, D B Vaughan, H A Stevenson.

**BENEFICIAL AREA:** National, including Jersey

**INFORMATION:** Accounts are on file at the Charity Commission.

**GENERAL:** This charity gives predominantly to medical work. In 1990/91 the Medical Foundation for the Care of Victims of Torture received a grant of £2,500.

The Welton Foundation also supports Charity Know How (see separate entry).

**APPLICATIONS:** In writing to the correspondent.


# The Westcroft Trust

**GRANT TOTAL:** £76,000 (1992/93)

**MAIN AREAS OF WORK:** General

**ADDRESS:** 32 Hampton Road, Oswestry, Shropshire SY11 1SJ

**CORRESPONDENT:** Dr Edward Cadbury.

**TRUSTEES:** Edward P Cadbury, Mary C Cadbury, Richard G Cadbury, James E Cadbury, Erica R Cadbury

**BENEFICIAL AREA:** National

**INFORMATION:** Accounts are on file at the Charity Commission.

**GENERAL:** The five areas of interest of the trust are: 'international understanding; religious causes, particularly of social outreach, usually of the Society of friends but also those originating in Shropshire; needs of those with disabilities, primarily in Shropshire; development of the voluntary sector in Shropshire; development of community groups and reconciliation between different cultures in Northern Ireland'. Grants with relevance to this guide were given:

**Under International Understanding**

In 1992/93 –

Quaker Peace Studies Trust, Bradford University Department of Peace Studies (£5,200 with £9,000 in the previous year);

Medical Educational Trust, projects of MEDACT (£3,660);

UNA Trust (£1,000);

Lansbury House Trust Fund (WRI) (£500 also in the previous year);

Amnesty International (£104 with £500 in the previous year);

Oxford Project for Peace Studies (£500);

In 1991/92 –

Northern Friends Peace Board (£940);

United World Trust/National Peace Council (£600);

University College, London Centre for the Study of Conciliation and Conflict (£500);

Canterbury University Asian Peace Research Association, Bradford University Department of Peace Studies, Oxford Research Group, International Alert, Poland Young People Exchange, Brighton Peace Centre (£500 each).

**Under Religious Society of Friends**

In 1992/93 –

Quaker Peace and Service (£3,010 with £2,895 in the previous year);

Northern Friends Peace Board (£1,500);

Friends World Committee (£250 with £875 in the previous year);

Cape Town Quaker Peace Centre (£300 with grant also in previous year);

**Under Social Service**

In 1992/93 –

Ulster Quaker Peace Education Project (£1,000);

Peace and Reconciliation Group (£500);

Voluntary Service Belfast (£356 with similar grant in previous year);

Northern Ireland Council for Voluntary Action (£300 with £140 in the previous year);

In 1991/92 –

IVS Northern Ireland (£350);

**Under Overseas**

In 1992/93 –

Guardian Fund for Africa (£1,500);

Oxfam (£1,387 with grant also in previous year);

Miriam Dean Refugee Trust Fund (£720 with grant also in previous year);

Canon Collins Educational Trust for Southern Africa (£500 with grant also in previous year);

In 1991/92 –

Anglo-Thai Foundation, UNICEF Emergency Relief for Kurdish Refugees (£500 each);

Sheffield Somalian Refugees Trust (£350);

Medical Foundation for the Care of Victims of Torture (£200);

**EXCLUSIONS:** Well funded and patronised national appeals are usually rejected as are appeals to build up capital funds.

**APPLICATIONS:** Applications are dealt with at about 2 month intervals.

# Westminster Foundation for Democracy

**GRANT TOTAL:** £2 million from the government (1993/94) and contributions sought from the private business sector

**ADDRESS:** Clutha House, 10 Storey's Gate, London SW1P 3AY

**TELEPHONE:** 071-976 7565; Fax 071-976 7464

**CORRESPONDENT:** Diana Warwick, Chief Executive

**TRUSTEES:** Board of Governors: Sir James Spicer MP (Chairman), George Robertson MP (Vice-Chairman), Sir Russell Johnston MP (Vice-Chairman), Tony Clarke, Mrs Margaret Ewing MP, Professor Peter Frank, Timothy Garton Ash, Lady Howe, Gavin Laird, Ralph Land, Sir Archie Hamilton MP, Dr Michael Pinto-Duschinsky, Ian Taylor MP, Ms Carole Tongue MEP

**INFORMATION:** Information leaflets and informative lists of projects given support.

**GENERAL:** The foundation was established by Royal Prerogative in March 1992 to provide assistance in building and strengthening pluralist democratic institutions overseas, following consultations between the British Government and the British political parties. The three main political parties in Britain are each represented on the Board of Governors, appointed by the Secretary of State for Foreign and Commonwealth Affairs after consulting the parties; there is also a representative of the smaller political parties; and non-party figures drawn from business, the trade unions, the academic world, and the non-governmental sector. A non-voting advisory member of the board from the Foreign and Commonwealth Office acts as a channel of communication with the Government and provides factual advice as required. The foundation is however fully independent in its decision-making.

The foundation may support any project aimed at building pluralist democratic institutions abroad. These may include:

- election systems, administration, or monitoring;
- parliaments or other representative institutions;
- political parties;
- free media;
- trade unions;
- human rights groups;
- other organisations in the voluntary sector.

The foundation will concentrate its efforts initially on Central and South-Eastern Europe, on the former Soviet Union, and on Anglophone Africa. Projects elsewhere in the world will be considered sympathetically. Preference will be given to projects with clear action plans, designed to achieve concrete results; to projects with lasting effects; to projects which build up self-sustaining organisations rather than ones dependent on outside assistance. Where possible projects will be supported by the foundation in co-operation with other organisations and foundations.

Examples of grants given in the second series of projects between April 1993–1994:

> Common Purpose, an assessment visit to Hungary by the trust which aims to build community involvement and leadership through the participation of potential leaders in activities centred on a particular city (£5,000);

> Future of Europe Trust, a two-week course to assist the development of young politicians from the national/regional offices of Hungary's main political parties and local government (£6,800);

> Thames Valley University and the British Association for Central and Eastern Europe, a series of three-week visits for two groups of deputies of the Polish Sejm, drawn for all parties (£42,540);

> European Institute for the Media, for a one-week study visit to recommend ways of assisting the media in Serbia/Montenegro (£2,790);

> Amnesty International, for production of education materials and training of educators in human rights education in Eastern Europe and the former Soviet Union (£41,000);

International Alert, towards a seminar on conflict prevention and resolution in Georgia (£7,025);

Penal Reform International, for a one-week training programme in Kazakhstan for emerging human rights organisations (£10,100);

Birmingham University and Voronezh University Centre for Academic and Business Co-operation, to encourage the development of independent voluntary organisations (£24,790);

Nicaraguan Solidarity Campaign, for a civic education programme (£7,909).

**EXCLUSIONS:** General budgetary assistance and organisations which advocate or support the use of force will not be supported.

**APPLICATIONS:** In writing to the correspondent. Applicants are advised to first obtain its pamphlet "Overview" which includes some guidelines for applicants. Project evaluations are part of the conditions of assistance from the foundation.

## The Garfield Weston Foundation

**GRANT TOTAL:** £7,959,000 (1992/93)

**ADDRESS:** c/o Weston Centre, Bowater House, 68 Knightsbridge, London SW1X 7LR

**TELEPHONE:** 071-589 6363

**CORRESPONDENT:** Harold W Bailey

**TRUSTEES:** Garfield Weston (Chairman), Guy Weston, Galen Weston, Grainger Weston, Miriam Burnett, Barbara Mitchell, Nancy Barron, Gretchen Bauta, Wendy Rebanks, Camilla Dalglish.

**BENEFICIAL AREA:** National

**INFORMATION:** Accounts are on file at the Charity Commission.

**GENERAL:** The foundation has general charitable objects (with a particular interest in education, medicine and religion). In 1992/93 the following grants with relevance to the scope of this guide were given:

English Speaking Union (£52,000 in 2 grants);

Justice Trust Appeal, Population Concern (£10,000 each);

Marie Stopes International (£5,000);

Runnymede Trust (£2,500);

VSO (£1,500);

Quaker College Belfast, Council of Christians and Jews (£1,000 each);

Voluntary Service Lisburn (£500);

Women Caring Trust (£150).

**EXCLUSIONS:** No grants to individuals.

**APPLICATIONS:** In writing to the correspondent.

## The Westward Trust

**GRANT TOTAL:** £31,600 (1992)

**MAIN AREAS OF WORK:** General

**ADDRESS:** 4 The Chestnuts, Winscombe, Avon BS25 1LD.

**CORRESPONDENT:** D J Ironside

**TRUSTEES:** D.J Ironside, Mrs J Ironside, J M Ironside, Mrs R M Dodd

**BENEFICIAL AREA:** National

**INFORMATION:** Accounts are on file at the Charity Commission.

**GENERAL:** The trustees do not encourage unsolicited applications because of the breadth of their charitable contacts.

The accounts for 1992 show grants to the Religious Society of friends of £12,400 for its local, national and international work. In addition a loan of £100,000 made to the Society in the previous year for building a meeting house was converted to a grant. Small grants under £100 were given to the Corrymeela Centre, Quaker Peace Studies Trust, Tools for Self Reliance and the Conflict Research Society.

**APPLICATIONS:** Unsolicited applications are not welcomed.

## The Whitaker Charitable Trust

**GRANT TOTAL:** £99,000 (1992/93)

**MAIN AREAS OF WORK:** General

**ADDRESS:** 21 Buckingham Gate, London SW1E 6LS

**TELEPHONE:** 071-828 4091

**TRUSTEES:** P E D Dunning, D W J Price.

**BENEFICIAL AREA:** National and international

**INFORMATION:** Accounts are on file at the Charity Commission.

**GENERAL:** The trust's main interest is educational, in particular in the United World College of the Atlantic, which consistently receives the lion's share of its grant allocation. Grants included:

In 1992/93 –

United World College of the Atlantic (£80,000 with £40,000 and £50,000 in the 2 previous years);

Intermediate Technology Development Group (£1,000 also given in the previous year);

Medical Aid for Poland (£500);

In 1991/92 –

Minority Rights Group (£500);

Enniskillen Integrated Primary School, Omagh Integrated Primary School (£500 each and in the previous year);

Belfast Charitable Trust for Integrated Education, Fermanagh Integrated Primary School (£250 each and in the previous year).

**APPLICATIONS:** In writing to the correspondent.

# Humphrey Whitbread's First Charitable Trust

**GRANT TOTAL:** £60,700 (1990/91)

**ADDRESS:** Flat 22, 34 Bryanston Square, London W1H 7LQ

**CORRESPONDENT:** Humphrey Whitbread

**TRUSTEES:** H Whitbread, S C Whitbread, H C Whitbread, C R Skottowe

**BENEFICIAL AREA:** National and international

**INFORMATION:** Accounts are on file at the Charity Commission.

**GENERAL:** The trust has general charitable objects. In 1990/91 some 300 grants were given, the majority of which were a few hundred pounds and less. Only 20 grants were £1,000 or more with the largest grant of £3,028.

Grants in 1990/91 with some relevance to the scope of this guide were:

Red Cross Gulf Appeal (£1,000);

Christian Aid (£1,000);

Save the Children Fund (£150);

Prisoners Abroad, Oxfam (£100 each);

Survival International (£53).

**APPLICATIONS:** In writing to the correspondent though it is understood that funds are already committed.

# The H D H Wills 1965 Charitable Trust

**GRANT TOTAL:** £384,660 (1991/92)

**ADDRESS:** 12 Tokenhouse Yard, London EC2R 7AN

**TELEPHONE:** 071-588 2828

**CORRESPONDENT:** Mrs I R Wootton

**TRUSTEES:** J Kemp-Welch, Hon V M G A Lampson, J B S Carson, Lady E H Wills

**BENEFICIAL AREA:** United Kingdom, Channel Islands and the Irish republic

**INFORMATION:** Accounts are on file at the Charity Commission.

**GENERAL:** In 1991/92 the trust made about 15 grants over £1,000 with the remainder (over 100 grants) of between £100 and £500. Grants with relevance to this guide were given:

In 1992/92 –

21st Century Trust (£150,000 with £140,625 in the previous year);

United World College of the Atlantic (£1,500);

Belfast Charitable Trust for Integrated Education (£200);

Cooperation Ireland, Enniskillen Integrated Primary School (£100 each);

Medical Aid for Palestinians, Relief Fund for Poland, Y Care International, Population Concern (£100 each);

In 1990/91 –

Ditchley Foundation (£10,000);

Cooperation North, Northern Ireland Voluntary Trust, All Children Together, Women Caring Trust (£100 each);

Relief Fund for Romania, UNICEF, English Speaking Union (£100 each).

**APPLICATIONS:** In writing to the correspondent but it is understood that few new applications are likely to be considered.

# Women Caring Trust

**GRANT TOTAL:** £122,420 (1992)

**ADDRESS:** 154 Buckingham Palace Road, London SW1W 9TR

**TELEPHONE:** 071-730 8883; Fax: 071-730 8885

**CORRESPONDENT:** Mrs Elizabeth F Kennedy, General Secretary.

**TRUSTEES:** Mrs Michael Garland and Lady Hayhoe (Co-Chairmen),Lady Bidwell, Lady Fisher, Mrs S Darling (NI), Mrs J Herdman (NI), D J R Ker, Mrs D Lindsay (NI), Mrs Betty Lushington, Mrs L McGown, Lady Quinlan, Michael MacLoughlin (Treasurer).

**BENEFICIAL AREA:** Northern Ireland

**INFORMATION:** An annual report with full list of organisations which have received support is available from the trust. Applicant guidelines are also available.

**GENERAL:** The trust is a non-political, non-sectarian fund-raising charity formed in 1972 to help women and children in Northern Ireland. It provides the opportunity for people in Britain to express their sympathy for the suffering of their fellow citizens in Northern Ireland by giving practical help and enabling the trust to continue its work among families who, through no fault of their own, are caught up in the Troubles. The trust supports community organisations all over the Province. It has helped to supply and maintain a fleet of playbuses for 3-5 year olds, enabling them to play in comparative safety off the streets for a few hours every day. Playschemes, Youth Clubs, Community Centres and holidays by the sea and in the countryside for groups of 'mixed' children have all been helped. Integrated schools receive support.

During 1992 as many as 170 different groups and organisations received grants ranging from £100 to £10,000.

**EXCLUSIONS:** Individuals, major capital costs, salaries.

**APPLICATIONS:** There is no application form; the trustees meet four times a year. All profits are carefully reviewed with advisers in Northern Ireland, including Voluntary Service Belfast.

# Zephyr Charitable Trust

**GRANT TOTAL:** £15,000 (1992/93)

**MAIN AREAS OF WORK:** General

**ADDRESS:** New Guild House, 45 Great Charles Street, Queensway, Birmingham B3 2LX

**TELEPHONE:** 021-212 2222

**CORRESPONDENT:** Roger Harriman

**TRUSTEES:** Elizabeth Breeze, Roger Harriman, David Baldock, Donald I Watson.

**BENEFICIAL AREA:** Unrestricted

**INFORMATION:** Accounts are on file at the Charity Commission.

**GENERAL:** This new trust was established in 1991 and its accounts for 1992/93 showed assets of £498,000. It gave 11 subscriptions including:

Intermediate Technology Development Group (£2,500);

Earth Resources Research Ltd, Survival International (£1,250 each);

Quaker Peace Studies (£500).

Its donations included:

Save the Children (Somalia/Sudan) (£1,000).

**APPLICATIONS:** In writing to the correspondent. However the trustees commit the bulk of the income by way of recurring subscriptions and the balance is usually made available for emergency one-off assistance so positive response to unsolicited appeals is not very frequent.

# Zochonis Charitable Trust

**GRANT TOTAL:** £679,000 (1992/93)

**MAIN AREAS OF WORK:** General

**ADDRESS:** P O Box 500, Abbey House, 74 Mosley Street, Manchester M6O 2AT

**TELEPHONE:** 061-228 3456

**CORRESPONDENT:** Touche Ross & Co

**TRUSTEES:** J B Zochonis, G A Loupos, Alan Whittaker

**BENEFICIAL AREA:** Unrestricted

**INFORMATION:** Accounts are on file at the Charity Commission.

**GENERAL:** A review of the trust's accounts over recent years showed the following grants with some relevance to the scope of this guide:

In 1992/93 –

V S O, One World Broadcasting Trust (£5,000 each);

CARE, Churches Commission on Overseas Students (£2,000);

In 1991/92 –

Police Foundation (£35,000 in 2 grants);

Royal African Society (£25,000);

African Welfare and Development (£5,000);

In 1990/91 –

British Executive Service Overseas Corporate Scheme (£40,000);

Project Orbis International (£10,000);

Minority Rights Group (£2,000).

**APPLICATIONS:** In writing to the correspondent.

# UK SOURCES

## UK Governmental

**Contents**

## Economic and Social Research Council (ESRC)

**GRANT TOTAL:** Research grants: £30,176,000; Postgraduate training: £12,156,000 (1992/93)

**ADDRESS:** Polaris House, North Star Avenue, Swindon SN2 IUJ

**TELEPHONE:** 0793- 413000; Fax: 0793 413001

**CORRESPONDENT:** Tim Whitaker, Head of Information

**TRUSTEES:** Council members: Professor Howard Newby (Chairman), Miss Jenny Abramsky, Professor Michael Anderson (Chair, Research Resources Board), Professor Vicki Bruce (Chair, Research Programmes Board), William Daniel, Mrs Elizabeth Filkin, Professor Janet Finch, Professor Roderick Floud, Jonathan Fox, Richard Freeman, Norman Glass, Professor John Goodman, Miss Christine Hancock, Dr Jeremy Harbison, Professor David Hargreaves (Chair, Research Centres Board), Professor Alan Hay (Chair, Training Board), Professor Dennis Kavanagh, Professor Stephen Nickell (Chair, Research Grants Board), Mrs Mary Tuck.

**INFORMATION:** Annual report with grants information, information leaflet.

**GENERAL:** The ESRC is the UK's leading research agency for the social sciences. It is an independent organisation, established by Royal Charter in 1965 and funded mainly by government. The ESRC's aim is to provide high quality research and data to help the government, businesses and the public to understand and improve the UK's economic performance and social well-being.

Subject areas supported by the ESRC include: Area Studies; Economic and Social History; Economics; Education; Environmental Planning; Human Geography; Linguistics; Management and Business Studies; Political and International

Relations; Psychology; Social Administration; Social Anthropology; Socio-legal Studies; Sociology; Statistics, Computing and Methodology.

All ESRC-supported research is contracted to higher education institutions and independent research centres; the ESRC does not employ researchers directly. The Council funds research in three ways: through Research Programmes, Research Centres and Research Grants.

There are over 30 Research Programmes which are programmes of independent but related research projects lasting three to five years. The projects are commissioned and managed by the Research Programmes Board.

Some 20 Research Centres undertake long-term research. They are funded for a period of ten years and are built around established research teams. The Research Centres Board manages the ESRC's portfolio of centres and the annual competition for new centres.

About 200 Research Grants are awarded to researchers each year. Each grant is assessed and graded by the Research Grants Board. The award for a single project must not exceed a total of £750,000 or exceed £300,000 in any one year. The council also sponsors through an annual competition, a range of workshops, seminars and conferences.

The council also funds studentships for outstanding postgraduates. The council supports some 750 research training students and 700 students on advanced courses. From 1993, studentships became available for part-time research degree study.

**APPLICATIONS:** Contact the Information Division for general enquiries; the Research Grants and Research Administration Division about research grants and the Postgraduate Training Division about postgraduate training awards.

## Foreign and Commonwealth Office: Diplomatic Wing

**ADDRESS:** London SW1A 2AH

**GENERAL:** The department grant-aids certain organisations. There is no formalised procedure for making applications and recipients develop appropriate working contacts within the Foreign and Commonwealth Office.

The following list of non-governmental, and statutory organisations supplied by the Resource and Finance Department shows a total of £6,474 million provision for grants in aid in 1993/94. Almost half this sum (44.4%) was provided to the Commonwealth Institute.

Commonwealth Institute £2,874,000

Westminster Foundation for Democracy £2,000,000

British Association for Central and Eastern Europe £190,000

British Russia Centre £218,000

GB/China Centre £215,000

Franco-British Council £79,000

British Youth Council £42,000

United Nations Association £24,000

Anglo/German Foundation £175,000

Encounter £31,000

West India Committee £16,000

Canning House £40,000

Commonwealth Trust £25,000

Commonwealth Games Grant £50,000

UK/Japan 2000 Group £4,000

UK/Canada Colloquia £6,000

ABEENA £1,000

International Committee of the Red Cross £300,000

International Commission of Jurists £13,000

College of Europe, Bruges £3,000

Hague Academy of International Law £7,000

Atlantic Council of the UK £150,000

Spanish Tertulias £8,000

## How Know Fund, Joint Assistance Unit (E) or (CE), Foreign & Commonwealth Office

**GRANT TOTAL:** £54.3 million (budget for 1993/94)

**ADDRESS:** Old Admiralty Building, Whitehall, London SW1A 2AF

**TELEPHONE:** See below

CORRESPONDENT: JAU (CE) Head: David Coates, Deputy Head: Dick Jenkins; JAU (E) Head: Michael McCulloch, Assistant Head: John Jenkins

INFORMATION: Annual report and see list of enquiry points below.

GENERAL: The Know How Fund (KHF) is Britain's programme of bilateral technical assistance to the countries of Central and Eastern Europe and the former Soviet Union. The aim of the fund is to provide expertise to support the transition to democracy and market economy in the countries of the region. This includes helping to establish the appropriate environment and democratic and market-related institutions. The fund also encourages investment in the region by British companies.

The KHF began in Poland in 1989. It now operates in Albania, Belarus, Bulgaria, Czech Republic, Estonia, Hungary, Kazakhstan, Latvia, Lithuania, Moldova, Poland, Romania, Russia, Slovak Republic, Slovenia and Ukraine as well as other countries of Central Asia and the Transcaucasus.

The fund focuses on a number of priority sectors: banking and financial services, privatisation, small business development and management training. In addition agriculture, and particularly the food sector, was made a priority both in the former Soviet Union and in a few Central and Eastern European countries, and the energy sector, and particularly energy efficiency, in the former Soviet Union. KHF has also expanded into the reform of health services management (Russia), public administration (Hungary, Poland, Bulgaria), help to employment services (Russia, Poland, Hungary and the Czech and Slovak Republics) and the establishment of 'job centres' (Russia).

The fund responds to requests and proposals put to it not just by governments, but by local authorities and a range of other credible organisations – and sometimes individuals – in recipient countries. The fund awards contracts to British partners on the basis of competitive tenders. Projects are monitored and evaluated.

The Joint Assistance Unit is split into two sections. **The Joint Assistance Unit (Central Europe) – JAU (CE)**: covers Albania, Bulgaria, Czech Republic, Hungary, Poland, Slovak Repub-

lic, Slovenia. **The Joint Assistance Unit (Eastern) – JAU (E)**: covers: The Baltic States, Russia, Ukraine and the rest of the former Soviet Union. These Units are staffed by officers from the Diplomatic Service, Overseas Development Administration and the Department of Trade and Industry.

The **Environmental Know How Fund** was launched with funding from the Department of the Environment in 1992 in response to the threat posed to the natural environment in the region. There are examples of voluntary organisations receiving support, such as the Field Studies Council to develop environmental education in Hungary.

**Charity Know How** (see separate entry) was established by the KHF and a group of British charitable trusts to provide support and assistance to the emerging voluntary sector in the countries covered by the main Know How Fund.

Details of individual country programmes and some of the projects are given in the annual report. The following are enquiry points for specific countries within the Units:

Albania (071-210 0012);

Bulgaria (071-210 0007);

Czech Republic (071-210 0006);

Hungary (071-210 0007);

Poland (071- 210 0005);

Romania (071-210 0008);

Slovak Republic (071-210 0006);

Slovenia (071-210 0003);

Central and Eastern Europe/General (071-210 0004);

Russia (071-210 0028);

Baltic States, Ukraine, Kazakhstan and other FSU (071-210 0029);

Fax JAU (CE) (071-210 0010);

Fax JAU (E) (071-210 0030).

# Ministry of Defence

ADDRESS: Directorate of Defence Policy, Main Building, Whitehall, London SWlA 2HB

GENERAL: **Ministry of Defence Lectureship Scheme**: The Ministry of Defence (MOD) currently funds four Defence Lectureships at British universities. The scheme began in 1968 with the aim 'to improve the scope and level of discussion of defence subjects among informed public opinion'. The MOD finances each lectureship for an initial five years, renewable for a further five years if the performance of the lecturer is considered by the MOD and university to be satisfactory. At the end of the ten-year period it is hoped that the university can absorb the post on its own payroll. The lecturers teach courses such as Strategic Studies and undertake defence-related research, and enable a department to devote more attention to the defence aspects of its discipline.

As at 1 January 1994, Defence Lectureships were held at:

- The Centre for Defence Studies, University of Aberdeen;
- The Department of International Politics, University College of Wales, Aberystwyth;
- The Centre for Russian and Eastern European Studies, University of Birmingham;
- The Department of War Studies, King's College, University of London.

**Research and Development Contracts in Higher Education Institutes:** The MOD continues to place agreements and contracts with Higher Education Institutes (HEIs) for scientific research and development. The research and development work carried out by HEIs on behalf of the MOD forms a vital part of the MOD research programme. In the financial year 1992/93 agreements in place with HEIs formed some 12% of the MOD research programme budget available to be put outside the MOD. The cost of this research and development in the academic sector was £36 million in 1992/93.

**Joint Grant Scheme:** This scheme is aimed at supporting research in Higher Education Institutes, which is not only of high academic quality but also likely to be of relevance to defence, thereby contributing to the strengthening of both the UK science and engineering base and the defence research programme. The scheme operates alongside the Research Councils' research grant award procedures, with the MOD participating. The MOD will fund up to 50% of a joint research grant, the decision being based mainly on the level of defence relevance. There are currently 130 joint grants in operation with £5.3 million MOD funding in 1992/93.

# Youth Exchange Centre

**GRANT TOTAL:** £1,405,000 (1992/93);

**ADDRESS:** c/o The British Council, 10 Spring Gardens, London SW1 2BN

**TELEPHONE:** 071-389 4030

**CORRESPONDENT:** Ian Pawlby, Head; Gordon Blakely, Head of Programmes

**INFORMATION:** Information leaflet (also listing the kind of exchanges that are not considered).

**GENERAL:** The centre gives grants to support continuing and constructive links between British youth groups and young people in another country. (In 1992/93 1,300 grants were given.) The aim is to foster better understanding and establish firm contact with a partner community. Young people without the opportunity for international experience are the main target group.

Grants are considered for two way, reciprocally arranged projects with Western and Eastern Europe, the USA, Israel and Japan. (Programmes for other Commonwealth countries are arranged by the Commonwealth Youth Exchange Council which has a separate entry. The CYEC is, however, supported financially by the Youth Exchange Centre.) The YEC is interested to learn of exchanges taking place elsewhere. In very exceptional circumstances it may help and support an innovative exchange as a pilot project. The centre cannot underwrite the full cost of an exchange. Support is given to the round-trip travel costs and the hosting costs in Britain. Typical travel grants cover about one third of the costs. There is increasing competition for the limited funds available and priority is given to the development of new exchanges or to innovative projects.

**APPLICATIONS:** Application forms are available and must be submitted at least 12 weeks before a visit is scheduled. They are considered by Regional Grants Committees which meet between October and June.

# NORTH AMERICAN SOURCES

## FUNDING FROM THE USA

by Michael Norton, Directory of Social Change

Spending two days examining grants information on foundations at the Foundation Center library in New York is an eye opener. Every grant made by a foundation has to be listed on an IRS return which is available for public scrutiny. And agencies such as the Foundation Center, itself a non-profit, make a living by cataloguing and analysing all major grants (of $10,000 of more) made by all US foundations. The Center publishes directories of grants categorised by type of beneficiary and indexed by the geographical location of the grant and by the name of the beneficiary receiving the grant. This makes it particularly easy to identify overseas organisations benefiting from US foundation support.

From a scrutiny of the information at the Foundation Center, most of which relates to the calendar year 1991, the following conclusions can be drawn which are relevant to UK non-profit organisations active in the field of peace or international affairs:

**1)** The scale of US foundation giving is enormous and far outstrips on a per capita basis the contribution made by grant-making trusts in the UK.

**2)** There is considerable interest in international affairs amongst US foundations (again unlike the UK), with a wide range of causes supported, from policy research to citizen advocacy, from all political perspectives from those promoting the leading role of the USA in the world to those encouraging community action by the oppressed, from those fervently supporting the status quo to those equally fervently trying to oppose it.

**3)** Some individual foundations give enormously in this area – Rockefeller, Ford, MacArthur to name just three.

**4)** The vast majority of US giving is to US non-profits. Mostly this is for their own projects and their own expenditure. Some will involve partnerships with foreign organisations, and for a small number the US agency will be acting as a 'half-way house' receiving the grant on behalf of a foreign agency and then remitting the money overseas to be spent locally.

**5)** Only a tiny number of grants are made each year to non-US agencies. However because of the scale of US giving to international affairs, this still represents a significant sum for overseas fundraisers.

Peace and international affairs are international concerns. Work being done in Britain can be and often is of international significance. The fact that most US foundation money goes to US agencies does not imply that the work being done by those agencies is any better or any worse than that being done over here and elsewhere. It is just far easier for US foundations to give to a US agency. There are three main reasons why US money goes to the US:

**a)** US agencies will be addressing issues from a US perspective, and often these issues will be of particular concern to the US (for example hemispheric issues for the Americas, such as the foreign policy, trade and migratory relationships between the USA and its poorer neighbours).

**b)** The Internal Revenue Service requires additional documentation for all grants made directly to foreign beneficiaries. This makes it administratively far simpler for US foundations to give to US agencies.

**c)** The recipients are on the doorstep. They have easier access to the donors and are more likely to be known to them and to be able to develop good personal working relationships.

Given the paucity of UK trust funding for international issues and the difficulty of gaining access to US foundation support, UK agencies could adopt a number of possible strategies:

**1)** They can accept the situation as it is and try harder to raise the money they need. This might mean taking whatever opportunities exist to meet grant officers. It will mean keeping in touch by sending copies of annual reports and other relevant literature. It could mean an occasional trip to the US to renew contact. It must mean getting hold of foundation annual reports and guidelines for applicants. It will require focusing on those projects which will be of particular interest to US foundations and stressing the quality, relevance and cost-effectiveness of the work (this last should not be too difficult given the lower salary levels in the UK). Better grantsmanship may lead to better chances of success, but still this is likely to be marginal, given the structural difficulties facing overseas applicants.

**2)** Strategy number two is to form working partnerships with US equivalents. The Harvard/Southampton University joint programme on nuclear non-proliferation is a good example of this approach. A partnership can bring the best of both (or more) organisations' efforts and talents to bear on a problem, thereby improving the quality of the work over and beyond what either organisation could do individually. And most importantly, it can put the overseas organisation on an equal footing with its US partner when applying for a grant. This strategy could be applied to:

- Major research programmes of global significance;
- Bilateral issues and programmes;
- European issues and concerns (and in Eastern Europe and the former Soviet Union there are plenty of these today) where a UK agency will be 'on the doorstep of the problem' and have a common language with the US agency and donor. This could give UK agencies a special role;
- Conferences and international events, not just for the

staging of such event, but also towards publications or bringing delegates from poorer nations to the events. Trying to raise money in the UK for such items is more difficult and there is much less money available. A partnership approach might make access to funding very much easier. There is another reason too for developing partnerships. Global issues and the search for solutions to global problems are being seen as of increasing importance and urgency. A greater degree of internationalism in tackling international issues can only be to the good.

**3)** The final strategy is 'if you can't beat them, join them'. Why not set up a US non-profit of your own? As in the UK, there is a fundamental freedom in the US to join together with others to address issues or problems of common concern. There is no reason why the impetus for setting up a US non-profit should not come from the UK, provided all the necessary legal and fiscal requirements are met. There are two possible approaches:

- Set a US non-profit simply to receive funds and channel them to the UK to pay for your work in the UK. The US entity would make it administratively simpler to receive the funding. It could also have a fundraising capacity to promote the organisation and the work it is doing, and to build good relationships with potential donors, or
- Set up a US non-profit to undertake its own work programme and to work in partnership with you in the UK. This will be a sister organisation to your own, with shared aims and mission. Work could be shared where appropriate. And there could be cross representation at board level. This would require some investment up front. But in the long run it could create access to substantial funding.

If we are living in a global age with issues of international concern, with researchers and key staff members geographically mobile, and with a skew in funding opportunities, why should not UK agencies of 'world class' which are dealing with international issues begin to deal with these on an international basis and develop a transnational structure to do this? An organisation such as the LSE, which has international recognition and potential, might set up affiliate bodies in Tokyo, Berlin, Washington and Moscow to develop programmes which relate to its special interests in these and other countries and it would raise the money it needs to undertake these programmes from local and international sources and create an appropriate structure for this effectively.

The clear conclusion from studying the availability of grants from US sources for international affairs is that there are more opportunities for action by fundraisers in the UK than might seem immediately apparent.

# US FOUNDATIONS

## Contents

# American Express Philanthropic Program

**GRANT TOTAL:** $22 million (1992); Grant range $300 – $2m

**MAIN AREAS OF WORK:** Community Service; Education and Employment; Cultural Programmes

**ADDRESS:** American Express Tower, World Financial Center, New York 10285-4710, USA

**TELEPHONE:** (212) 640-5661

**CORRESPONDENT:** Cornelia W Higginson, Vice-President, International Philanthropic Programme

**INFORMATION:** Grants list and application guidelines.

**GENERAL:** The Philanthropic Program includes the American Express Foundation, The American Express Minnesota Foundation, the American Express Cultural Affairs and certain corporate gifts. The programme is committed to supporting projects which create public-private partnership. In 1992 the Community Service programme disbursed $2.7 million. It addresses other critical needs in American Express communities worldwide. Over 200 grants were given in the USA and 22 internationally. These included the following which are relevant to this guide (no grant sizes were given):

Centre for European Policy Studies (CEPS);

Centre for Economic Policy Research; Royal Institute for International Affairs;

Co-operation North Limited, Ireland;

Institute for International Economics.

**EXCLUSIONS:** No support for Individuals, fundraising activities, travel, religious or political organisations, publications, endowments or capital campaigns.

**APPLICATIONS:** There are no deadlines or application forms. The board meets in March and September. A final notification is given within three to four months. All applications should contain proof of non-profit status, geographical areas served by the organisation, history of previous support from the programme, description of project with detailed budget, latest annual report, funding sources. For full details obtain the guidelines with the grants schedule (see above).

# Arca Foundation

**GRANT TOTAL:** $1,524,600 (1991); Grant range: $1,000 – $100,000

**ADDRESS:** 1425 21st Street, NW, Washington, DC 20036, USA

**TELEPHONE:** (202) 822-9193

**CORRESPONDENT:** Janet Shenk, Executive Director.

**INFORMATION:** Annual report.

**GENERAL:** The Arca Foundation was established in 1952 'to help promote the well being of mankind throughout the world'. It is concerned to help citizens shape public policy, particularly on economic and political issues affecting the Western Hemisphere, north and south. It is especially interested in human rights and in Latin America, the Caribbean and southern Africa. There are no geographical limitations but grants are not made to individuals. Recent grants have included:

In 1990 –

US Forum, to fundraise for Mandela Freedom Fund in the US ($30,000);

Amnesty International, for human rights worldwide ($25,000).

In 1989 –

International Human Rights Law Group, election monitoring in Central America ($20,000);

Lawyers Committee for Civil Rights Under Law, election in Nambia ($20,000);

**APPLICATIONS:** Written proposals should be sent in writing to meet deadlines on 1 October and 1 April. Board meetings are in December and June and notification can be expected 2 weeks after the board's decision.

# AT&T Foundation

**GRANT TOTAL:** £27,692,000 (1991): Grant range: $1,000- $1m

**ADDRESS:** 1301 Avenue of the Americas, Rm 3100, New York, NY 10019, USA (see also below)

**TELEPHONE:** (212) 841-4747

**CORRESPONDENT:** Sam A Gronner, Secretary

**INFORMATION:** Biennial report and information brochure, including application guidelines.

**GENERAL:** This large foundation has been included because of its scale and a couple of relevant grants rather than a clear policy interest in the scope of work covered by this guide. International affairs and public policy are mentioned as interests but emphasis is on support for private higher education and institutions and projects in the areas of health care, social action and the arts. Giving is on a national basis.

Grants relevant to this guide were given in 1990 to:

Council on International and Educational Exchange ($12,000);

Institute for East-West Security Studies ($10,000).

**APPLICATIONS:** Write for reports and guidelines to P O Box 45284, Department FC, Jacksonville, Florida 32232-5284. There are no application forms. Deadlines are January, April, June and September. The board meets in March, June, September and December.

# Banyan Tree Foundation

**GRANT TOTAL:** $1,668,000 (1990)

**ADDRESS:** c/o O'Melveny & Myers, 1999 Avenue of Stars, Los Angeles, California 90067, USA

**CORRESPONDENT:** Stuart Tobisman, Assistant Treasurer

**GENERAL:** The foundation's policy is to support international development and relief programmes, literacy journals and centres.

A grant was made in 1990 to the Prince's Youth Business Trust, London ($15,000).

**APPLICATIONS:** The foundation makes its own choices and unsolicited applications are not accepted.

# The Lynde and Harry Bradley Foundation, Inc

**GRANT TOTAL:** $27.2 million (1992); Grant range: $150 – $750,000

**ADDRESS:** 777 East Wisconsin Avenue, Suite 2285, Milwaukee, Wisconsin 53202, USA

**TELEPHONE:** (414) 291-9915

**CORRESPONDENT:** Michael Joyce, President

**INFORMATION:** A full report with details of policy and grants is available accompanied by notes to guide applicants.

**GENERAL:** The foundation supports research and education in domestic, international and strategic public policy. It aims: 'to encourage projects that focus on cultivating a renewed, healthier, and more vigorous sense of citizenship among American people, and among peoples of other nations, as well'.

The following grants relevant to this guide were given between 1990 and 1992:

Cambridge University, for History fellowships ($21,500);

Centre for Research into Communist Economies, London, to support its general programme ($101,040);

Institute for European Defence and Strategic Studies, for publications programme ($85,000 in 3 grants);

LSE, London, for 2 studies, one on American economic policy, the other on the impact of price reforms on the Chinese economy ($103,500 and $308,200);

Society for Central Asian Studies, London, for conference on Central Asian Republics of the Soviet Union and for general programme; ($50,000 in 2 grants);

**EXCLUSIONS:** No grants to individuals or support for endowment funds or strictly denominational projects.

**APPLICATIONS:** The application process is in two steps. First a brief letter of enquiry describing the organisation and the intended project should be sent. If the foundation decides the proposal falls within its policy guidelines, applicants are sent a brochure describing the foundation's programme, guidelines and a checklist of information required. Final authority for making grants rests with the board which meets four times a year, February, May/June, September and November. To be considered at one of these meetings proposals need to be submitted by the 15th of December, March, July, and September.

# The Samuel Bronfman Foundation, Inc

**GRANT TOTAL:** $6,253,000 (1990) Highest grant $1.5m

**ADDRESS:** 375 Park Avenue, New York, NY 10152-0192, USA

**CORRESPONDENT:** William K Friedman, Vice-President

**GENERAL:** The foundation aims to perpetuate the ideals of American democracy. It finances research programmes for the study of democratic business enterprise by means of fellowships and professorships in colleges and universities.

Grants in 1990 included:

East West Forum, DC ($420,000 with a similar grant in the previous year);

Edgar M Bronfman East-West Fellowships, NYC ($88,000 with $38,000 in the previous year).

**APPLICATIONS:** There are no application forms or deadlines. The board meets in January, April, July and October.

# Bydale Foundation

**GRANT TOTAL:** $555,000 (1990); Grant range: $500 – $50,000

**ADDRESS:** 11 Martine Avenue, White Plains 10606, New York, USA

**TELEPHONE:** (914) 428 3232

**CORRESPONDENT:** Milton D Solomon, Vice President.

**GENERAL:** The foundation supports international understanding, public policy research, environmental quality, cultural programmes, the law and civil rights, social services, higher education and economics. Grants have included:

In 1989 –

Center for Strategic and International Studies ($15,000);

US-South Africa Leader Exchange Program, DC ($10,000);

Council on Foreign Relations, NYC ($10,000);

Foreign Policy Association, NYC ($10,000).

**APPLICATIONS:** There are no application forms.

The board meets in December. Proposals are preferably submitted in July and August. The deadline is 1 November.

# C S Fund

**GRANT TOTAL:** $412,000 (1991) Grant range; $1,500 – $45,000

**ADDRESS:** 469 Bohemian Highway, Freestone, C A 95472, USA

**TELEPHONE:** (707) 874 2942; Fax (707) 874 1734

**CORRESPONDENT:** Martin Teitel, Executive Director

**INFORMATION:** Annual report and information brochure both containing applicant guidelines.

**GENERAL:** The fund makes grants to programmes that demonstrate national or international impact and that lead directly to changes in policy or practice. It makes grants within the areas of dissent, the environment and peace.

Its 1993 statement about its peace work is as follows: 'There is a growing recognition that military strength alone does not provide national security. The tools of war and the habits of mind that engender their use threaten all people and the earth itself. The C S Fund's peace grants:

- acknowledge both the pluralistic world and our global interdependence;
- address root causes of conflict;
- promote non-violence, alternative behaviours, and new models for resolving differences.'

Its dissent category includes:

- protecting the right to dissent and hold divergent opinions;
- preserving society's right to hold accountable all of its institutions and officials, both public and private;
- preventing human rights violations and civil rights limitations.

Grants in 1993 included:

Institute for Defence and Disarmament Studies ($25,000);

Pacific Campaign for Disarmament and Security ($7,500);

Fund for Peace ($20,000).

**EXCLUSIONS:** No grants for film and video production.

**APPLICATIONS:** There is no application form. The fund prefers a written proposal to a telephone call, meeting or letter of intent. The fund has three granting cycles each year. In 1994 the deadlines were: 15th April for a decision in July 1994; August 15th for a decision in November 1994; December 15th for a decision in April 1995.

# Carnegie Corporation of New York

**GRANT TOTAL:** $48.4 million (1992)

**MAIN AREAS OF WORK:** Cooperative Security, Strengthening Human Resources in Developing Countries, Education and Healthy Development of Children and Youth

**ADDRESS:** 437 Madison Avenue, New York 10022, USA

**TELEPHONE:** (212) 371-3200

**CORRESPONDENT:** Dorothy Wills Knapp, Secretary

**INFORMATION:** A general information brochure and newsletter of grants are available.

**GENERAL:** The corporation makes this statement about its Cooperative Security programme: ' While the superpower conflict has ended, the world remains a dangerous place. Threats to larger nations may be less direct and less apparent, but threats to smaller nations have grown, and great powers cannot remain aloof from these conflicts. In particular, the widespread availability of advanced weapons technology provides a powerful incentive for great powers to cooperate in addressing the new danger posed by the Cold War's legacy. This technology is available to adversaries in regional "hotspots" around the world, and poses a new dimension of threat.'

'Governments are likely to turn to independent experts, scholars, and academic institutions for help in spelling out a vision and designing a strategy to cope with these dangers. The corporation has chosen as its contribution to the post-Cold War restructuring an investment in scholarly research and leadership debate on the scope and detail of cooperative security. '

'The program's first priority is to explore the operational detail and practical appeal of overlapping cooperative security regimes. The program supports selected research and educational efforts designed to help:

• define the military strategy and arms control approach best suited to cooperative security regimes;

• encourage continued economic and political reform in the former Soviet Union and East Central Europe with activities designed to build civil societies and strengthen democratic institutions in the former Soviet sphere;

• build and strengthen international institutions and procedures to support a stable peace, with special attention given to methods and means for conflict prevention, conflict resolution, peacemaking, and peacekeeping;

• anticipate emerging threats to and requirements for security so that preventive measures can be taken by the world community;

• build an American consensus for new policies, educating policy makers and the public on options before them.'

The programme does not support fellowships programmes or curriculum development.

In 1993 the corporation has budgeted £52 million for grants primarily in the USA, although 7.4% of that amount may be used for research and education benefiting some countries that are or have been members of the British overseas Commonwealth.

During 1990 the following international grants were given to organisations based in the UK:

Action in International Medicine, London ($25,000);

Association of Commonwealth Universities, London ($150,000).

Whilst there are limitations to its international giving this entry is included because of the corporation's specific interest in cooperative security and the prospect that joint proposals between American and European institutions might be successfully developed.

**EXCLUSIONS:** No scholarship and travel grant programmes.

**APPLICATIONS:** An initial approach should be made by letter or telephone. This may lead to a request for a more detailed application. There are no deadlines. The board meets October, January, April and June. Notification is six months.

# The Carthage Foundation

**GRANT TOTAL:** $3,241,000 (1991); Grant range: $5,000 – $556,000

**ADDRESS:** Three Mellon Bank Center, 525 William Penn Place, Suite 3900 Pittsburgh, PA 15219-1708, USA

**TELEPHONE:** (412) 392-2900

**CORRESPONDENT:** Richard M Larry, Treasurer.

**INFORMATION:** Annual report.

**GENERAL:** The Carthage Foundation confines most of its grant awards to programmes that will address public policy questions concerned particularly with government and international affairs. It provides support for general purposes, conferences and seminars. Grants made in 1990 included:

Heritage Foundation, for European/US scholarly exchanges ($100,000);

National Defense University Foundation, general support ($100,000);

Hudson Institute, Soviet affairs research ($50,000).

**EXCLUSIONS:** No grants are given to individuals.

**APPLICATIONS:** There are no application forms or deadlines. The initial approach should be by letter. The board meets in Spring and Autumn and notification should be within two to three weeks.

# Columbia Foundation

**GRANT TOTAL:** $2.2 million (1991/92); Grant range: $1,000 – £200,000

**ADDRESS:** One Lombard Street, Suite 305, San Francisco, California 94111, USA

**TELEPHONE:** (415) 986-5179

**CORRESPONDENT:** Susan Clark Silk, Executive Director

**INFORMATION:** Application guidelines, annual report.

**GENERAL:** The foundation's current focus is on projects that address critical issues and offer promise of significant positive impact in the following areas:

• preservation for the natural environment;

- enhancement of urban community life and culture;
- the interdependence of nations and understanding among people from different cultures;
- reversal of the arms race worldwide;
- the protection of basic human rights.

The foundation focuses its programme primarily on projects that seek common ground between the San Francisco community and the shared global concerns facing an interdependent world.

Grants relevant to the scope of this guide include;

In 1991 –

Government Accountability Project, to expose illegal and hazardous practices of nuclear weapons industry ($30,000);

In 1990 –

20/20 Vision Education Fund, to teach local communities citizen advocacy on environmental and arms control issues ($15,000);

Physicians for Social Responsibility, for programme on public health, safety and environmental impact of US nuclear weapons and production facilities ($25,000);

Arias Foundation for Peace and Human Progress, Costa Rica (2 grants totalling $50,000).

**APPLICATIONS:** In writing. Deadlines are 1 August and 1 February.

# Compton Foundation, Inc

**GRANT TOTAL:** $3,458,000 (1991) Grant range $500 – $200,000

**ADDRESS:** 545 Middlefield Road, Suite 178, Menlo Park 94025, California, USA

**TELEPHONE:** (415) 328-0101

**CORRESPONDENT:** James R. Compton, President; Edith T Eddy, Executive Director

**INFORMATION:** A biennial report and leaflet on policies and guidelines are available.

**GENERAL:** The foundation addresses community, national and international concerns in the fields of peace and world order, population and environment, equal educational opportunity, community welfare and social justice, and culture and the arts. In 1991 the following major distributions were made:

Peace and world order $708 500;

Population $805,500;

Environment $2,028,000.

The foundation makes the following statement about its policy for peace and world order: 'The foundation is concerned with the elimination of war as a means of settling international disputes, and the construction of a mutual global security system as an alternative to war.". The foundation's priorities include:

- preventing the proliferation of nuclear and other weapons of destruction;
- influencing public policy to promote peaceful means of settling international disputes;
- supporting multilateral approaches to international issues;
- strengthening existing international institutions so that they may evolve into organisations that can improve law and order among peoples of the world;
- addressing the interrelationship between peace and world order, population growth, and environmental degradation.'

Grants are made for the following kinds of activities:

- Fellowships support, through the Institute for the Study of World Politics;
- Education of the public;
- Education of reporters, editorial writers, and policy makers;
- Advocacy and public activism through selected organisations;
- Collaboration across national boundaries among groups with similar interests;
- Scholarly research in selected academic centers of excellence with special priority given to projects which define the problem, are interdisciplinary, are policy related, lead to action.

Content areas of special interest include:

- conflict resolution;
- definition of national security and human rights;

- equitable distribution and management of technology, resources, energy, and food;
- the relation between economic interdependence and peace in developing countries;
- economic conversion.'

Grants in 1991 included:

University of Southampton, Nuclear Non-Proliferation Programme ($25,000);

World Resources Institute ($30,000);

Fund for Peace ($65,000);

Center for National Security Studies ($35,000);

Institute for the Study of World Politics ($239,000 mainly for fellowship programme);

National Security Archive ($43,600)

Soviet Peace Fund, distinguished fellows exchange ($25,000);

Carnegie Endowment for International Peace ($25,000).

**APPLICATIONS:** All applicants are first advised to obtain up to date information about priorities and concerns to determine the relevance of their proposal. A brief 3-4 page proposal should be sent.

# Patrick and Anna M Cudahy Fund

**GRANT TOTAL:** $1.58 million (1991); Grant range: $400 – $88,000

**ADDRESS:** PO Box 11978, Milwaukee, Wisconsin 53211, USA

**TELEPHONE:** (708) 866-0760

**CORRESPONDENT:** Sr Judith Borchers, Executive Director

**INFORMATION:** Annual report and application guidelines.

**GENERAL:** The fund supports social services, international development, human rights, environment, youth and homelessness. The international programme is mainly concerned with organisations working in South Africa or Latin America.

Grants in 1990 included:

Cambridge University, England for research on causes of contemporary crime ($15,000);

Lawyers Committee for Human Rights Under Law, South Africa programme ($15,000).

**EXCLUSIONS:** No grants for individuals or for endowments, No loans.

**APPLICATIONS:** Initial contact should be made with the proposal and a covering letter. After that an application form may be forwarded. The deadlines are eight weeks before the board meetings which are usually in April, June, September and December. Final notification is two weeks after the meeting.

# Damien Foundation

**GRANT TOTAL:** $150,000 – $250,000 annually

**ADDRESS:** 235 Montgomery Street, Suite 1010, San Francisco, California 94104, USA

**TELEPHONE:** (415) 421-7555: Fax (415) 421 0712

**CORRESPONDENT:** Mark Rabine, Secretary

**INFORMATION:** A brochure of basic information and a selective grants list is available.

**GENERAL:** The foundation supports grass-roots organisations and projects whose work reflects compassion, consciousness and commitment. It takes an international approach to grantmaking. 'We believe that only a holistic approach will bring solutions that can heal our fractured world'. The foundation is particularly interested in the environment, women and aspects of the spiritual.

Its giving is primarily in the USA, Brazil and the UK. Grants with particular relevance to this book have been given to:

The Network Foundation, UK which supports projects on the environment, human rights and social justice ($4,000);

Gaia Foundation, UK for Amazon Basin projects ($10,000);

Findhorn Community Youth Centre (£5,000).

**EXCLUSIONS:** No grants to individuals.

**APPLICATIONS:** The foundation does not accept unsolicited applications 'but, we engage in dialogue with like-minded individuals and collaborate with activists and other philanthropists'.

# Earhart Foundation

**GRANT TOTAL:** $2.36 million (1992)

**ADDRESS:** 220 Green Road, Suite H, Ann Arbor, Michigan 48105, USA

**TELEPHONE:** (313) 761-8592

**CORRESPONDENT:** David B Kennedy, President; Antony T Sullivan, Secretary and Director of Program

**INFORMATION:** Summary annual report is available on request

**GENERAL:** H B Earhart Fellowships are awarded through a special nominating process for graduate study. Research Fellowships are awarded on direct application to individuals who have established themselves professionally. The areas of interest are international affairs, political science, economics and history.

No details or current grants are available but it is known that the Institute of Economic Affairs, London, received support in 1988 for the Centre for Research into Communist Economics.

**EXCLUSIONS:** Direct applications from candidates or uninvited sponsors for H B Earhart Fellowships are not accepted.

**APPLICATIONS:** Application should be by letter. There are no deadlines. The board meets monthly except in August.

# The Educational Foundation of America

**GRANT TOTAL:** $4.3 million (1990); Grant range: $7,000 – $375,000

**ADDRESS:** 35 Church Lane, Westport 06880, Connecticut, USA; Grant application office: 23161 Ventura Boulevard, Suite 201, Woodlands Hills CA 91364, USA

**TELEPHONE:** Grant application office: (818) 999-0921

**CORRESPONDENT:** Diane M Allison, Executive Director

**INFORMATION:** Annual report, application guidelines

**GENERAL:** Grants are primarily given for the arts, education including higher education, the environment and population control and the medical sciences.

Recent grants have included:

In 1991 –

International Peace Academy ($180,000);

In 1990 –

World Policy Institute, NY, for expanded Public Education Programme focusing on three key areas in post-Cold War Period: East-West Europe, Asia, and future global financial, environmental and military policies ($30,000);

Human Rights Watch, NYC ($42,000);

Union of Concerned Scientists, for Advanced Reactor Assessment Project ($25,000).

Support includes general purposes and operating budgets, special projects, research and publications.

**APPLICATIONS:** There is no application form and the initial approach should be made by letter. The board meets in March, July and November.

# Eurasia Foundation

**GRANT TOTAL:** See below

**ADDRESS:** 2021 K Street, Suite 215, Washington, DC 20006, USA

**TELEPHONE:** (202) 872-0933; Fax: the same number

**INFORMATION:** Information sheet

**GENERAL:** The Eurasia Foundation was set up in 1993 as a private non-profit organisation with start-up funds from the Agency for International Development. It total annual expenditure is expected to be in the order of $16 million.

Its purpose is to make grants in support of economic reform and democratic institution building in the New Independent States (NIS) of the former Soviet Union. Its general criteria for grantmaking are that the grant:

- support private sector development and /or democratic institution building;
- produce a significant and sustained effect on the ground in the NIS;
- represent a genuine transfer, adaptation, or creation of skills in the NIS.

Initial programme priorities will be management training and economics education. The foundation may also fund policy research, technical assistance, training, and educational and implementation activities in economic and political reform, law, business development and public management reform. The foundation also expects to play a major role in working with non-governmental organisations in fields such as environment, health and human rights. It may also fund in the fields of media and communications, and science and technology.

Several field offices in Russia, Ukraine and Central Asia are being set up.

# Ford Foundation

**GRANT TOTAL:** $264.4 million (1992); Grant $500 – $5 million

**ADDRESS:** 320 East 43rd Street, New York, NY 10017, USA

**TELEPHONE:** (212) 573-5000

**CORRESPONDENT:** Barron M Tenny, Secretary

**INFORMATION:** Annual report, booklet – 'Current Interests'.

**GENERAL:** The Ford Foundation seeks 'to identify and contribute to the solution of problems of national or international importance. It works primarily through granting funds to institutions for experimental / demonstration and developmental efforts that promise to produce significant advances in various fields. It sometimes makes grants to individuals and also makes loans to or otherwise invests in enterprises that will advance its objectives.'

The foundation operates six programme areas: urban poverty; rural poverty and resources; rights and social justice; governance and public policy; education and culture; international affairs; reproductive health and population; media projects.

Within the area of international affairs, the foundation approved $35.6 million of expenditure in 1992 of which $9.2 million was for developing country programmes. Working closely with the foundation's field offices in Africa, Asia, and Latin America, the international affairs programme supports worldwide initiatives directed toward:

- the prevention of war and the strengthening of peace and security through arms control and disarmament and the promotion of international means for averting and resolving conflicts;
- the promotion of democratic values and respect for human rights as set out in the International Bill of Human Rights;
- the creation of an equitable international economic system that fosters growth and development for all nations and groups;
- the strengthening of international and regional institutions and of international law as means to resolve international problems;
- the analysis of United States foreign policy in light of the above goals. This programme is also responsible for work in Eastern Europe and the former Soviet Union. The programme seeks to help integrate into the international community the countries of the region – especially Hungary, Poland, Russia, and the Czech and Slovak republics.

The foundation's interests in each programme area are amplified in the booklet: 'Current Interests of the Ford Foundation 1992 and 1993'. It is too long to reproduce here but it seems worth quoting: 'Although the foundation will continue its long-standing interest in international security and arms control, it will pay increasing attention to the political, economic, environmental, and social dimensions of regional security arrangements'.

Grants given to organisations in the UK in 1992 from within the international affairs programme included (with the headings under which they are categorised):

Under its international law programme –

Cambridge University ($200,000);

Oxford University ($30,000);

Under its international development and economics / refugee and migrants programme –

Overseas Development Institute Ltd ($216,000);

Foundation for International Environmental Law and Development ($150,000);

Edinburgh University ($45,000);

Under its international human rights programme –

International Centre for the Legal Protection of Human Rights ($425,000);

Article 19 Research and Information Centre on Censorship ($45,000);

Under its former Soviet Union and Eastern Europe programme –

Writers and Scholars Educational Trust ($500,000);

Under its developing countries programme –

Hugh Pilkington Charitable Trust, refugee development programme in Eastern and Southern Africa ($72,610);

International Centre for Legal Protection of Human Rights, for human rights programme in West Africa ($29,000);

International Institute for Strategic Studies, for Middle East and North Africa programme ($45,000);

Penal Reform International, for Middle East and North Africa programme ($21,825);

London School of Economics, for refugee and migrant programme in Sri Lanka, Nepal and India ($75,000);

London University, international relations programme in Sri Lanka, Nepal and India ($75,000);

Queen Elizabeth House, for refugee and migrant programme in Southeast Asia ($50,000)

**APPLICATIONS:** Applications are considered throughout the year. There are no forms. Applicants are advised to send a brief proposal first. Notice is usually sent within one month as to whether it falls within the foundation's programme interests and budgetary limitations.

## Ford Motor Company Fund

**GRANT TOTAL:** $22 million (1991); Grant range: $100 – $1m

**ADDRESS:** The American Road, Dearborn 48121, Michigan, USA

**TELEPHONE:** (313) 845-8711

**CORRESPONDENT:** Leo J Brennan Jr, Executive Director

**INFORMATION:** Annual report and application guidelines.

**GENERAL:** The fund gives support for education and higher education, community funds and urban affairs, civic and cultural programmes. Giving is primarily in areas of company operations nationwide, however the following grants for international programmes have been given:

In 1991 –

Co-operation Ireland, NY ($10,000, also given in the previous year);

Council for Foreign Relations ($10,000 also given in the previous year);

In 1990 –

American Near East Refugee Aid, DC, ($15,000);

Institute for East-West Security Studies, NYC ($10,000);

Foreign Policy Association, DC, ($35,000 in 2 grants).

**APPLICATIONS:** There is no application form or deadlines. The board meets in April and October. Notification takes about six months.

## General Electric Foundation, Inc

**GRANT TOTAL:** $799,353 (1990); Grant range: $250 – $80,000

**ADDRESS:** 3135 Easton Turnpike, Fairfield, Connecticut 06431, USA

**TELEPHONE:** (203) 373-3216

**CORRESPONDENT:** Clifford V Smith, Jr President

**INFORMATION:** Annual report including application guidelines.

**GENERAL:** The foundation is one of two company foundations; this one focuses exclusively on international programmes. Whilst the majority of the grants appear to be awarded to organisations in the USA the funds have to be spent outside the country. The foundation's objective is: 'to give primarily to innovative organisations that will play a significant role internationally in advancing charitable, scientific, literary or educational programmes'. Its fields of interest centre on intercultural relations, international relief and international development.

Recent grants with relevance to this guide have been:

US-South Africa Leadership Exchange Program ($15,000);

Co-operation Ireland ($25,000);

Eisenhower Exchange Fellowships ($50,000).

**APPLICATIONS:** An application form is not required. Applications are largely by invitation only.

# General Motors Foundation, Inc

**GRANT TOTAL:** $23 million (1990); Grant range: £200 – $2 million

**ADDRESS:** 13/145 General Motors Building, 3044 West Grand Boulevard , Detroit, Michigan 48202-3091, USA

**TELEPHONE:** (313) 556-4260

**CORRESPONDENT:** D R Czarnecki

**INFORMATION:** Information brochure.

**GENERAL:** Grants are largely for higher education, hospitals and health, social services, cultural programmes and urban and civic affairs. A wide range of types of support may be considered, from equipment and technical assistance to research and publications as well as operating budgets and campaigns. Giving is primarily in cities where the company has significant plant operations.

Grants for international programmes have included:

In 1990 –

Center for Strategic and International Studies, DC, for general support ($60,000 also given in the previous year);

Co-operation Ireland, NY, for general support ($20,000 also given in the previous year);

**APPLICATIONS:** There are no application forms or deadlines. The contributions committee meets annually.

# General Service Foundation

**GRANT TOTAL:** $1.4 million (1991); Grant range: $700 – $150,000

**ADDRESS:** 411 East Main Street, Suite 205, Colorado 81611, USA

**TELEPHONE:** (303) 447-9541

**CORRESPONDENT:** Robert W Musser, President.

**INFORMATION:** Annual report including application guidelines.

**GENERAL:** The foundation's major areas of interest are population, resources, and international peace.

The foundation's more detailed guidelines about its international peace programme are as follows: 'to address the root causes of conflict and to promote peaceful and stable communities, primarily in Mexico, Central America and the Caribbean.'

Programmes and projects which 'address the following issues, as well as their inter-relationships:

• political rights and civil freedoms

• international law and relations

• economic, environment and development concerns.'

Funding will be given primarily for education and policy analysis and formation, rather than for research.

'The foundation will also make contributions to organisations working to accomplish the following objectives:

• develop leadership and participation in the non-governmental organisation community

• further communication and collaborative efforts among non-governmental organisations

• strengthen inter-regional organisations, both governmental and non-governmental.'

Grants in 1990 included:

International Peace Research Association, for Latin American delegate to attend conference in the Netherlands ($15,000);

International Institute of Education, NY, leadership development for human rights organisations in developing countries ($15,000).

**APPLICATIONS:** An application form is sent if a project is appropriate. It is strongly recommended that a letter of enquiry describing the project be sent before a formal proposal is sent. Application deadlines are 1 February and 1 September for board meetings in Spring and Autumn. Final notification takes about six months.

# German Marshall Fund of the United States

**GRANT TOTAL:** $4,029,000 (1991); Grant range: $1,500 – $525,000

**ADDRESS:** 11 Dupont Circle, NW, Suite 750, Washington, DC 20036, USA

**TELEPHONE:** (202) 745 3950

**CORRESPONDENT:** Frank E Loy, President.

**INFORMATION:** Berlin Office: The German Marshall Fund of the United States, Clara-Zetkin-Strasse 112, 10117 Berlin (30) 391 62 01/(30) 229 92 02; Fax: (30) 391 64 33; Special Representative for France: Mary Fleming, 20 rue Tournefort, 75005 Paris, France (010 331 45 87 18 24; Fax: 010 331 43 31 65 70) A newsletter, information brochure with guidelines and grants list can be obtained.

**GENERAL:** The fund was founded in 1972 by a gift from the Federal Republic of Germany in appreciation of American post-war recovery assistance, to assist in the understanding and resolution of certain contemporary and emerging problems common to industrial societies. Its publication 'Transatlantic Perspectives' offers the following summary of purpose: 'To promote a more informal understanding of differences that arise between Western Europe and the US, and to stimulate exchanges of practical experience on common problems confronting modern industrial societies'.

Programme areas include common domestic problems, international relations, European/American comparative studies of industrial societies, and encouraging media interest in coverage of events in Europe. The fund sponsors a number of fellowship programmes for Europeans. These include employment fellowships, minority fellowships, environmental fellowships and journalism fellowships.

Grants with relevance to this guide have included:

In 1992 –

Twenty-First Century Trust, England, 2 grants for Central and Eastern European workshop participants ($20,000);

Transatlantic Policy Network, Brussels, to launch and develop the organisation in US and Europe ($20,000);

LADO (League for the Defence of Human Rights), Bucharest, Romania ($10,000);

In 1991 –

European Strategy Group, task force on US military presence in Europe ($70,000);

Charter 77 Foundation, travel programme for Czech leaders to broaden experience and to link projects with US donors ($40,000);

International Human Rights Law Group, to train Romanian lawyers ($24,500);

Confederazzione Nazionale dell Artigianato, Bologna, for study tour in US ($11,000).

In 1990 –

Centre for International Environmental Law, London ($60,000);

Centre for Economic Policy Research, London ($40,000).

**EXCLUSIONS:** No support for arms control and diplomatic studies.

**APPLICATIONS:** An application form is required for the fellowship programmes. An initial approach can be made by telephone, letter or proposal. Deadlines vary. The board meets three times a year.

# The Global Fund for Women

**GRANT TOTAL:** $857,000 (1992)

**ADDRESS:** 2480 Sandhill Road Suite 100, Meadow Park, California 94025-6941, USA

**TELEPHONE:** (415) 854-0420

**CORRESPONDENT:** Gretchen Stuphen, Grants Manager

**GENERAL:** The fund, established in 1987, has a policy is to support international women's rights and issues, focusing especially on grassroots women's initiatives in developing countries.

As an international grantmaking organisation its aims are to:

• provide funds to seed, strengthen and link groups that are committed to women's well-being and that work for their full participation in society;

• encourage increased support for women's programmes globally;

• provide leadership in promoting a greater understanding of the importance of supporting women's full participation internationally.

Examples of recent grants:

In 1993 –

SOS Hotline for Women and Children Victims of Violence, Belgrade ($10,000);

Maypole Fund, London (see separate entry) ($10,000);

In 1992 –

Federation for Women and Planned Parenthood, Warsaw ($8,000);

Women's Centre, Belfast ($6,000);

Global Forum for Women, Dublin ($4,000);

Feminista Halozat, Budapest ($10,000);

**APPLICATIONS:** Priority is given to grassroots initiatives in developing countries. In dealing with requests from wealthier countries priority is usually given to minority female populations. There is no application form or deadlines. A proposal of no more than five pages should be sent.

# The William and Mary Greve Foundation, Inc

**GRANT TOTAL:** $687,300 (1990); Grant average: $1,000 – $5,000

**ADDRESS:** 630 Fifth Avenue, Suite 1750, New York 10111, New York, USA

**TELEPHONE:** (212) 758-8032

**CORRESPONDENT:** Anthony C M Kiser, President

**INFORMATION:** Programme policy statement and applicant guidelines.

**GENERAL:** The foundation gives grants mainly for education and related fields, US-Eastern bloc relations and the performing arts.

**APPLICATIONS:** There are no application forms or deadlines.

# Harry Frank Guggenheim Foundation

**GRANT TOTAL:** $1.6 million (1991); Grant range for organisations: $300 – $100,000; for individuals: $8,000 – $30,000.

**ADDRESS:** 527 Madison Avenue, New York, NY 10022-4304, USA.

**TELEPHONE:** (212) 644-4907

**CORRESPONDENT:** Karen Colvard, Programme Officer.

**INFORMATION:** Annual report and application guidelines.

**GENERAL:** The foundation administers an international, interdisciplinary programme of scientific research and study concerning human social problems related to dominance, aggression, violence. It makes grants for research at post-doctoral level (not necessarily requiring a PhD D). Work may be undertaken by individuals or small teams with an average of $25,000 per year for projects with a duration of one to two years. Grants, known as Dissertation Fellowships, are also made to PhD candidates who are in the writing stage of a dissertation.

A substantial review of the foundation's grant-making was undertaken late in 1989. It was agreed 'not to restrict the disciplinary range of the programme, but to emphasise an interest in research with the promise of addressing contemporary human social problems, and specified six broad problems of pressing concern:

• violence, aggression, and dominance in relation to social change;

• the socialisation of children;

• intergroup conflict;

• drug trafficking and use;

• family relationships;

• investigations of the control of aggression and violence.

Examples of past grants include:

University College, London on 'Nationalism, Ethnicity and the Cultural Structure of Violence' ($24,572 1990);

Oxford University, for individual research project ($24,790 1990)

135

**EXCLUSIONS:** No grants for endowments of capital funds. No conference or work expenses.

**APPLICATIONS:** Initial approaches should be made including the proposal and the CV of the researcher. All applicants must obtain the guidelines to be sure they get the formalities correct, for instance six copies of the complete application are required. Deadlines; for research grants, August 1st and February 1st; for Dissertation Fellowships, February 1st. Board meetings June and December. Notification within a week of the meetings.

# The W Averell and Pamela C Harriman Foundation

**GRANT TOTAL:** $2,178,000 (1991)

**ADDRESS:** 63 Wall Street, 23rd Floor, New York 10005, USA

**CORRESPONDENT:** William F Hibberd, Secretary

**GENERAL:** The foundation, set up in 1969 by the distinguished former US government official and his wife, gives support in higher education, cultural programmes and foreign policy. In 1991 the foundation gave a greatly increased sum of over $2 million in 36 grants. The increase was caused by one massive grant of $1.5 million. (In 1990 two grants totalling $393,500 had been made.)

**APPLICATIONS:** There are no application forms or deadlines.

# William and Flora Hewlett Foundation

**GRANT TOTAL:** $39,569,000 (1992); Grant range: $1,000 – £1 million.

**ADDRESS:** 525 Middlefield Road, Suite 200, Menlo Park, CA 94025-3495, USA

**TELEPHONE:** (415) 329-1070

**CORRESPONDENT:** David P Gardner, President

**INFORMATION:** Annual report including guidelines for applicants.

**GENERAL:** The Hewlett Foundation programmes cover: Conflict Resolution; Environment; Population; Children, Youth and Families; Education; Performing Arts; Regional Grants; Special Projects.

The programme description for Conflict Resolution states that the foundation favours general support grants that build the institutional capacity of promising conflict resolution organisations. It does not generally provide funding for specific projects or research, nor is support typically given for start-up efforts. Grants are made in five categories:

- theory development, with 'a particular interest in university-based centres that demonstrate both a strong academic commitment to systematic, interdisciplinary research on conflict resolution and also an ability to contribute to the improvement of conflict resolution practice';

- mediation and other practitioner organisations, with a particular interest in 'opportunities to help effective and stable groups increase their capacity for growth and outreach. Grants support the development of new approaches or new applications of conflict resolution methods, the achievement of greater organisational maturity, the evaluation of programme effectiveness, and numerous other efforts to enhance the overall impact of practitioner organisations';

- training and promotional organisations;

- public policy decision-making organisations. This category recognises that the origins of conflict can often be traced to defects in methods of communication and participation in policy-making. Assistance is given to organisations that demonstrate means of improving the processes of decision-making on issues of major public importance. The foundation is particularly interested in new ways of developing 'collaborative action that protects the legitimate interests of all involved parties'. This area was formerly part of the environment programme and it is expected that this category will remain largely committed to organisations working on environmental issues.

- international organisations, support is given to a limited number of organisations 'working on the international application of conflict resolution techniques and the development of practice-relevant theory related to ethnic, ideological, religious, racial, and other intergroup conflicts around the world'.

Recent grants have included:

The Network: Interaction for Conflict Resolution, Ontario, Canada, for general support ($120,000 1991);

The foundation's Education programme includes support for international and area studies at major research institutions. Participation is by invitation. The following grant was made under this programme:

Royal Institute of International Affairs, London ($300,000 1990).

The foundation's Population programme has included support to:

International Planned Parenthood Federation, London, ($540,000 1991).

The foundation's Special Projects programme has includes grants for International Security, for example:

Institute for East-West Security Studies ($300,000 1992);

Center for International Security and Arms Control, Stanford University, ($600,000 1992).

**EXCLUSIONS:** Basic research, capital construction, fund-raising drives, grants or loans to individuals.

**APPLICATIONS:** There are no application forms. Because programme policies are continually under review, applicants are advised first to write a letter of enquiry to the president with enough information to enable staff to determine whether or not the application falls within the areas of preferred interest or warrants consideration as a special project. There is no fixed minimum or maximum with respect to size of grants.

There are deadlines for the five categories in the Conflict Resolution programme: Practitioner Organisations – October 1 for review in January; International Organisations and Theory Organisations – 1 January for review in April; Training and Promotional Organisations and Public Policy Decision-making Organisations – July 1 for review in October.

# HKH Foundation

**GRANT TOTAL:** $1,461,5000 (1991)

**ADDRESS:** 33 Irving Place, 10th Floor, New York, NY 10003, USA.

**CORRESPONDENT:** Harriet Barlow, Advisor.

**GENERAL:** The foundation has written that it is pleased to receive information which pertains to its general programme areas of Reversing the Arms Race, Environmental Protection and Civil Liberties. Its approach is 'to gain as complete a sense of the current state of work in each of our focus areas as is possible given the enormous scope of each issue and its limited staff'. It consults with activists and researchers in each area and formulates strategic plans for promoting work in these areas. Sometimes this results in support for an existing project, sometimes for a new project and occasionally to foster co-operative planning and action between organisations.

**APPLICATIONS:** The HKH Foundation does not review proposals on a competitive basis instead it consults with activists and researchers to formulate strategic plans for promoting work in these areas. It states, however, that it is interested in discussing 'its thinking and choices with anyone who cares to help us improve the effectiveness of HKH's part in our collective effort to achieve peace, environmental health and freedom of expression'.

# Ira-Hiti, Foundation for Deep Ecology

(formerly the Foundation for New Paradigm Thinking)

**GRANT TOTAL:** $1,478,000 (1991)

**ADDRESS:** 950 Lombard Street, San Francisco, California 94133, USA

**TELEPHONE:** (415) 771-1102

**CORRESPONDENT:** Quincey Tompkins, Executive Director

**INFORMATION:** Information brochure.

**GENERAL:** The foundation focuses on the following key ecological issues:

- Population, including campaigns for international family planning and women's rights to control their own decisions;
- Forests and habitats;
- Grassroots activism in agriculture, bioregionalism and economics;
- Support to traditional native societies;
- Public educational campaigns to resist the growth of macro economic trends.

Giving is on an international basis.

A grant in 1992 was given to:

Mission Rainforest, Hertfordshire, England for land purchases ($81,525).

**EXCLUSIONS:** No support for research, TV, video or film productions.

**APPLICATIONS:** An application form is needed. The board meets once a year and notification can be expected within three months of this meeting.

# W Alton Jones Foundation, Inc

**GRANT TOTAL:** Over $13 million; Grant range: $5,000 – $250,000

**ADDRESS:** 232 East High Street, Charlottesville, Virginia 22902-5178, USA.

**TELEPHONE:** (804) 295-2134

**CORRESPONDENT:** John Peterson Myers, Director.

**INFORMATION:** Biennial report and application guidelines.

**GENERAL:** The foundation has two areas of funding: environmental protection and prevention of nuclear war. Most of the foundation's grantmaking occurs through foundation-initiated programmes. Unsolicited enquiries are considered as long as they fall within the foundation's priorities.

Its Secure Society Program – Preventing Nuclear Warfare covers:

- Nuclear disarmament;
- Non-proliferation;
- Common security strategies;
- The nuclear weapons production complex.

Initiative grants in 1991 and 1992 particularly relevant to this guide were:

Cambridge University, Global Security Programme ($135,000);

International Institute for Strategic Studies, London ($100,000 for 2 years);

Verification Technology Information Centre, London ($85,000);

King's College, London, Centre for Defence Studies ($50,000);

Saferworld Foundation ($25,000);

Oxford Research Group ($10,000).

**APPLICATIONS:** There are no application forms or deadlines. The initial approach should be by letter. The board meets quarterly and notification periods vary.

# The J M Kaplan Fund, Inc

**GRANT TOTAL:** $6,307,600 (1992); Grant range: $1,000 – $200,000

**ADDRESS:** 30 Rockefeller Plaza, Suite 4250, New York 10112, USA

**TELEPHONE:** (212) 767-0630; Fax: (212) 767-0639

**CORRESPONDENT:** Joan K Davidson, President

**INFORMATION:** Annual report including application guidelines.

**GENERAL:** The fund's programme was under review so some modifications may have been made. The grants are given mostly in New York City and State within the following groupings:

- the natural and built environment;
- social programmes and public policy, including civil liberties, social justice, human rights and human services;
- arts and culture.

In addition the fund has a programme of trustee-initiated grants which consider grant requests that are invited by trustees.

Grants in 1992 included:

Fund for Free Expression, for their 6 Human Rights Watch Committees that work throughout the world ($100,000 and a trustee-initiated grant of $28,200);

Lawyers Committee for Human Rights, for their international human rights programme concentrating on refugee rights ($30,000);

Soros Foundation for an Open Society, legal assistance for gypsy communities in Bulgaria, Romania and Czechoslovakia ($60,000 as a trustee-initiated grant).

In 1990 the Plough shares Fund (see separate entry) was given $35,000.

**APPLICATIONS:** The initial approach should be by telephone or letter. An application form is required. Proposals should be submitted between 1 March and 15 October.

# W K Kellogg Foundation

**GRANT TOTAL:** $144,252,000 (1991); Grant range: $300 – $2.8m

**ADDRESS:** One Michigan Avenue East, Battle Creek, Michigan 49017-4058, USA

**TELEPHONE:** (616) 968-1611

**CORRESPONDENT:** Nancy Sims, Executive Assistant, Programming

**INFORMATION:** Annual report and information brochure, each with application guidelines.

**GENERAL:** The support of the foundation is limited to programmes concerned with application of existing knowledge rather than research. It supports pilot projects which, if successful, can be continued by the initiating organisation and emulated by other communities or organisations with similar problems. Interest in Southern Africa, Latin America, the Caribbean is also noted.

Recent grants with relevance to this guide have been given:

In 1991 –

National Association of the Partners of the Americas, US hemispheric decision-making ($250,000);

Institute for Global Ethics, to promote ethics to decision-makers and leaders (£150,000);

Global Tomorrow Coalition, to promote sustainable decision-making ($75,000).

**APPLICATIONS:** Applications must conform to the given programme priorities, so all prospective applicants need to obtain full, up-to-date information. There are no application forms or deadlines. The board meets monthly.

# Henry P Kendall Foundation

**GRANT TOTAL:** $2.688 million (1990); Grant range: $2,000 – $2m

**ADDRESS:** 176 Federal Street, Boston 02110, USA

**TELEPHONE:** (617) 915-2525

**CORRESPONDENT:** Salvatore F Battinelli

**GENERAL:** The Kendall Foundation's primary concern is the overall welfare and vigour of the movements it serves: arms control and peace; defence of the natural environment and conservation of energy and resources. The foundation prefers grants to organisations that can create legislative, and/or regulative action. Towards this goal, the foundation encourages research and publicity to influence public policy; grassroots efforts to improve local and national voter registration and voter education; and the education of elected and appointed officials.

**APPLICATIONS:** There are no application forms. A brief proposal should be sent initially. Deadlines are the 15th of February, May August and November for board meetings during the following month.

# The LeBrun Foundation

**GRANT TOTAL:** $193,000 (1991)

**ADDRESS:** 2100 Main Place Tower, Buffalo, New York 14202, USA

**TELEPHONE:** (716) 853-1521

**CORRESPONDENT:** Thomas R Beecher, Trustee

**INFORMATION:** Guidelines are available.

**GENERAL:** The foundation has forwarded its revised guidelines for November 1992. These state its grantmaking policy as focusing in the following two areas:

• Famine relief and economic development – US and abroad;

• Refugee relief and resettlement – US and abroad.

To qualify for a grant applicants must be a certified US tax exempt organisation.

An annual report has not been made available and other directories do not list exemplary grants either.

**APPLICATIONS:** In writing and no longer than 4 pages. The trustees meet quarterly in March, June, September and December. Proposals must be received by the 15th of the month preceding the next quarterly meeting.

# Max and Anna Levinson Foundation

**GRANT TOTAL:** $788,000 (1991) Grant range: $150 - $60,000

**ADDRESS:** 1411 Paseo de Peralta Santa Fe 87501, New Mexico, USA

**TELEPHONE:** (05 982-3662)

**CORRESPONDENT:** Charlotte Talberth, Executive Director.

**GENERAL:** The Levinson Foundation aims to develop 'a more humane and rewarding society in which people have greater ability and opportunity to determine directions for the future'. Funding is allocated in three categories:

• The environment;

• Jewish/Israel including the Israeli Peace Movement;

• Social including conflict resolution and aid to survivors of violence, human rights and multiculturalism.

Proposals are accepted 'from any and all locations but projects with broad implications for society are preferred'. Proposals for seed funding, start-up and small organisations are especially preferred.

Grants awarded in October 1993 included:

International Azerbaijan Research and Development Institute, Washington ($7,500);

Pacific Institute for Studies in Development, Environment and Security, policy recommendations on water and conflict in the Middle East ($7,500);

Center for Human Rights Advocacy, protecting human rights for Jews and others in the former Soviet Union ($7,500).

**EXCLUSIONS:** Organisations with budgets in excess of £500,00 a year are rarely considered.

**APPLICATIONS:** An application form is supplied.

Grants are awarded every eight months. Proposals may be submitted at any time. Deadlines vary each year.

# Richard Lounsbery Foundation, Inc

**GRANT TOTAL:** $1,755,000 (1990); Grant Range: $250 – $100,000

**ADDRESS:** 159A East 61st Street, New York, NY 10021, USA

**TELEPHONE:** (212) 319-7033

**CORRESPONDENT:** Alan F McHenry, President

**GENERAL:** The foundation gives support primarily to biomedical research, the improvement of the teaching and learning of science and mathematics at secondary and elementary levels, and human rights. Grants are given for seed money, matching funds, fellowships and research.

Grants relevant to this guide have been given: In 1990 –

Lawyers Committee for Human Rights, for refugee project ($20,000);

American Committee on US-Soviet Relations, DC ($20,000).

**EXCLUSIONS:** No grants for individuals, for capital or building funds, endowment funds, conferences or seminars.

**APPLICATIONS:** Applications are not encouraged as funds are mainly committed to projects developed by the directors. Proposals may be mailed to reach the deadlines six weeks prior to board meetings which are held the last Wednesday of January, April, July and October.

# Henry Luce Foundation Inc

**GRANT TOTAL:** $16,588,000 (1991); Grant range: $2,000 – $2,500,000

**ADDRESS:** 111 West 50th Street, Room 3710, New York, NY 10020, USA

**TELEPHONE:** (212) 489 -7700

**CORRESPONDENT:** John Wesley Cook, President

**INFORMATION:** Biennial report; application guidelines.

**GENERAL:** The foundation's programmes and activities are focused on:

- understanding between the peoples of Asia and the United States;
- intellectual exploration in American higher education;
- the fine and decorative arts;
- theological education;
- opportunities for women in science and technology;
- major issues of public and international policy.

Grants in 1990 with relevance to the scope of this guide include:

The Brookings Institution, towards a seminar on foreign and domestic policy for newly elected members of Congress ($35,000);

United States Global Strategy Council, for Global Water Policy and Technology Summit ($10,000);

United Nations Association of the United States of America, to support the Quadrilateral Dialogue on Asian Security, Vladivostock, Russia ($25,000);

United States Committee for UNICEF, towards project on children in especially difficult circumstances/armed conflicts in the Philippines ($75,000).

**APPLICATIONS:** For the general funding programme no application form is required. The application may be made by letter. The board meets in June, October and December. Notification length varies greatly. Most are notified in late Autumn and the end of the year.

# John D and Catherine T MacArthur Foundation

**GRANT TOTAL:** $154,387,000 (1992)

**ADDRESS:** 140 South Dearborn, Suite 700, Chicago, IL 60603, USA

**TELEPHONE:** (312) 726-8000

**CORRESPONDENT:** Grants Management, Research and Information

**INFORMATION:** Annual report, brochure on programmes and policies, more detailed information on applying to specific programme areas is available in separate brochures.

**GENERAL:** The MacArthur Foundation's grants are made through a series of eight programmes: Community Initiatives; Education; General; Health; MacArthur Fellows; Peace and International Cooperation; Population; World Environment and Resources.

In addition the foundation seeks to be an active rather than a reactive force. For instance in 1992 the foundation started a three-year initiative funded with $9 million to help in the transition to a democratic government and improved quality of life in the former Soviet Union. In 1992 grants included:

King's College, London, Department of War Studies, in support of security studies in the former Soviet Union ($50,000);

United Nations, Non-Governmental Liaison Service, Conches, Switzerland, to enable young and lesser-known scientists from the former Soviet Union to attend the United Nations Conference on Environment and Development.

In 1992 the programme on Peace and International Cooperation developed a greater focus addressing issues in four interrelated areas: US foreign policy and national priorities; arms control, disarmament and demobilisation; international governance and civil society; sustainable democracy. A total of $13,440,000 was donated in grant-aid to this programme in 1992. Kennette Benedict is Programme Director.

Grants in 1992 included:

British American Security Information Council, Washington ($97,500);

Hellenic Foundation for Defence and Strategic Studies, Athens, for an international seminar ($25,000);

International School on Disarmament and Research on Conflicts, Rome, in support of interdisciplinary courses on arms control and conflict and related research activities ($390,000 over 3 years);

King's College London, Department of War Studies, for research and interaction among young security scholars in the former Soviet Union and their counterparts in King's College ($10,000);

Pugwash Conferences on Science and World Affairs, Rome, general support over 2 years ($500,000);

American Refugee Committee, for a national congress on new strategies for refugees in the 1990s ($50,000);

FAFO, Oslo, in support of the Common Security Forum, an international research network, in collaboration with Harvard University and King's College Cambridge ($225,000 in 2 grants).

**APPLICATIONS:** Preliminary application is made through a brief letter of inquiry (not to exceed four pages) that describes the proposed project and the applicant organisation and presents a timetable and budget for completing the work.

# J Roderick MacArthur Foundation

**GRANT TOTAL:** $2.2 million (1992); Grant Range: $1,200 – $450,000

**ADDRESS:** 9333 North Milwaukee Avenue, Niles, Illinois 60714, USA

**TELEPHONE:** (708) 966-0143

**CORRESPONDENT:** See below

**GENERAL:** The foundation's objectives have been for projects throughout the world which:

"1) Eliminate censorship and protect freedom of expression, including the freedom to hold and express opinions in all media of communication, both within and between all nations;

2) Foster human rights, including political, social, economic and cultural rights;

3) Protect and foster civil liberties in the United States (including all constitutional rights) and to encourage their eventual observance in the rest of the world;

4) Foster social justice and the elimination of political, economic, social, religious and cultural oppression.'

The foundation has been in a state of transition with the end of tenure of the President, Lance Lindblom in January 1994. It has been taking stock of its policies and looking at 'potential new approaches and directions'.

The foundation wrote in February 1994: 'Unsolicited requests for funding are no longer accepted ... All grants will be made by the initiative of the board.' Its staff has been cut to one, so enquiries will not generally be answered.

The foundation has recently made a major commitment to fund three specific projects: The MacArthur Justice Center in Chicago; the Death Penalty Information Center in Washington, D C; and Article 19 in London. The first two projects have been merged with the foundation. Collectively, they will consume a significant portion of the foundation's funding.

**APPLICATIONS:** See above.

# McDonnell Douglas Foundation

**GRANT TOTAL:** $7.76 million (1991); Grant range: $25 – $1m

**ADDRESS:** c/o McDonnell Douglas Corporation, P O Box 516, Mail Code 1001510, St Louis, Missouri 63166, USA

**TELEPHONE:** (314) 232-8464

**CORRESPONDENT:** Walter E Diggs, Jr President

**INFORMATION:** Information brochure and annual report, both containing application guidelines.

**GENERAL:** The foundation gives emphasis in its grantmaking policy to education, both higher and other, and community funds. It also supports aerospace and aviation organisations, engineering, the environment, and public, civil and cultural affairs.

The foundation is included in this guide because grants made in 1989 were relevant to this guide:

Georgetown University, Center for Strategic and International Studies, DC, for general support ($40,000);

Institute for Foreign Policy Analysis, DC, for general support ($20,000);

United Nations Association of the United States, for general support ($59,500).

Southwest Missouri State University, for McDonnell Douglas Fellowship in Defence ($10,000).

**APPLICATIONS:** The initial approach should be by letter. There are no application deadlines.

# The McKnight Foundation

**GRANT TOTAL:** $46,577,000 (1991); Grant range: $400 – $1m

**ADDRESS:** 600 TCF Tower, 121 South Eighth Street, Minneapolis, Minnesota 55402, USA

**TELEPHONE:** (612) 333-422

**CORRESPONDENT:** Michael O'Keefe, Executive Vice-President

**INFORMATION:** Annual report, application guidelines, grants list.

**GENERAL:** The emphasis of the foundation's grantmaking is on the areas of human and social services. Its giving is limited to organisations in Minnesota except for special programmes initiated by the board of directors. Grants with relevance to the scope of this guide were given:

In 1991 –

Asia Foundation, small business training for Khmer refugees in Thailand ($100,000);

Council for Foreign Relations, to promote understanding of US foreign policy;

Institute for East-West Security Studies ($50,000 for research and $100,000 in 1990 for start-up costs for European Center in Czechoslovakia);

In 1990 –

C and J B Morrell Trust, York, England, for follow-up activities relating to international disaster relief, including a conference on NATO's emerging role in disaster relief ($25,000);

International Peace Academy, NYV, general support ($100,000);

University of Cape Town Fund, NYC, for scholarship assistance for black students ($50,000).

**APPLICATIONS:** There are no application forms. The initial approach should be by letter. Three copies of any proposal are required, Deadlines are the 1st of March, June, September, and December. The board meets during these months.

# Andrew W Mellon Foundation

**GRANT TOTAL:** $93,277,000 (1992)

**ADDRESS:** 140 East 62nd Street, New York, NY 10021, USA

**TELEPHONE:** (212) 838-8400

**CORRESPONDENT:** Richard Ekman, Secretary

**INFORMATION:** Annual report with guidelines for applicants.

**GENERAL:** The 1992 annual report states that the foundation continues to give its largest share of funding to its traditional areas of emphasis: higher education and scholarship, the arts and culture, conservation and the environment, and population.

However the foundation has become an increasingly active grant maker in public affairs, with some 20% of all grants in 1992 under this broad title. A major area of concentration has been Eastern Europe and Professor Richard E Quandt, economist at Princeton University, serves as senior advisor to the foundation. In 1992 $20 million was appropriated for projects and programmes in the region and this is expected to rise by an additional $12 to $15 million by the end of 1994.

The foundation concentrates on programmes in the Czech Republic and Slovakia, Hungary and Poland and limits its activities within two major areas:

- assisting the restructuring of the East European economies by funding training in economics, management, and business and by promoting the development of market-oriented institutions;

- strengthening the infrastructure of universities and other institutions of higher learning, primarily by assisting research libraries and by providing higher educational institutions with computing and computer networking capabilities.

Grants have also been made for a number of special projects:

A programme of short-term fellowships for East European humanities scholars at centres in Western Europe;

Lawyers Committee for Human Rights, New York , for its refugee and European human rights projects ($100,000).

Other grants were made to:

Atlantic Council of the United States, Washington, towards the cost of its Eastern Europe Program ($375,000);

Center for Strategic and International Studies, Washington, for use by its Government Relations Program ($400,000);

Charter Seventy-Seven Foundation ($30,000).

Apart from its support in Eastern Europe very few grants seem to be made to organisations based outside the USA though in the mid 1980s the International Institute for Strategic Studies, London, received support.

**APPLICATIONS:** Applications are reviewed throughout the year and no special forms are required. Applicants are encouraged to request further information about the nature and extent of the foundation's activities in a certain field, and to explore their proposal informally with staff, preferably in writing, before submitting a formal application.

# The John Merck Fund

**GRANT TOTAL:** $5.34 million (1992); Grant range: $1,000 – $225,000

**ADDRESS:** 11 Beacon Street, Suite 600, Boston, Massachusetts 02108, USA

**TELEPHONE:** (617) 723-2932

**CORRESPONDENT:** Francis W Hatch, Chairman

**INFORMATION:** An annual grants list and guidelines for support are available.

**GENERAL:** In 1992 the fund gave 17% of its grant-aid to each of the following areas: disarmament, international human rights, population policy. The two latter programmes are directed at US-based organisations.

Its disarmament policy aims to support projects that seek to restrain the spread of nuclear, chemical/biological and conventional weapons. Special emphasis is given to projects that relate to: 'renewal and strengthening of the Nuclear Non-Proliferation Treaty in 1995; improving export controls governing weapons technology suppliers; fostering the international community of professionals and activists devoted to this field'.

Grants relevant to this guide were:

British American Security Information Council ($35,000);

University of Southampton, for the Programme for Promoting Nuclear Non-proliferation ($90,000 over 3 years);

Peace Research Institute, Frankfurt, to promote European involvement in nuclear non-proliferation ($150,000 over 3 Years).

**EXCLUSIONS:** No support for individuals, endowment or capital fund projects, large organisations, or general support grants except for small organisations.

**APPLICATIONS:** The fund does not encourage submission of unsolicited applications. Instead the trustees request individuals to submit proposals for grants to support projects within their institutions.

# Joyce Mertz-Gilmore Foundation

**GRANT TOTAL:** $9.5 million (1992)

**ADDRESS:** 218 East 18th Street, New York, New York 10003, USA

**TELEPHONE:** (212) 475-1137

**CORRESPONDENT:** Robert Crane, Vice-President, Programme

**INFORMATION:** An biennial report including application guidelines and schedule of grants is available.

**GENERAL:** The foundation's human rights programme provides support in the following areas:

- protection and support of human rights worldwide;
- protection and support of refugee rights worldwide;
- protection and extension of rights in the United States;
- democratic development, in particular the voluntary sectors in Central Europe and the former Soviet Republics.

The foundation's world security programme is interested in initiatives which explore viable approaches to restructuring the industrial base in the United States. In addition it supports ' a limited number of projects that explore new thinking about regional or global institutions and structures that can promote and increase world security. Of particular interest are: projects exploring an expanded, more effective role for the United Nations; new configurations of political or economic institutions in post-Cold War Europe; new structures and institutions to establish, regulate or monitor agreements affecting the "global commons" or to establish regional consortia, networks or policy groups to work on common defense, environment or human rights concerns'.

Grants made in 1991 and 1992 with relevance to this guide were:

Refugee Studies Programme, Oxford ($50,000 in both 1991 and 1992);

Helsinki Citizen's Assembly, Prague ($15,000 in 1992 and 1993);

British American Security Information Council ($20,000 in 1991 and $30,000 in 1992).

**APPLICATIONS:** Applicants should first submit a letter of enquiry of no more than two pages. A full proposal may then be invited, although this does not imply that funding is necessarily forthcoming. Decisions on grants are made at twice yearly board meetings. Proposals received between the beginning of June and the end of November will be considered at the Spring meeting and proposals received from the beginning of December to the end of May will be considered at the Autumn meeting.

# Morgan Guaranty Trust Company of New York Charitable Trust

**GRANT TOTAL:** $9.3 million (1992)

**ADDRESS:** 60 Wall Street, New York NY 10260-0060, USA

**TELEPHONE:** (212) 648-9673

**CORRESPONDENT:** Roberta Ruocco, Vice-President

**INFORMATION:** An annual report is available which includes guidelines for grant applications.

**GENERAL:** The trust gives support to: the arts; education; environment; health; international affairs; urban affairs; United Way. In 1992 a total of $646,428 was donated under international affairs. The following statement on its international relations policy accompanies the report:

'Morgan supports organisations that promote an improved quality of life in the developing regions of the world where we do business. We target our support to organisations working in the fields of economic development, environment, population, primary health care, and disaster relief. While most of our grants are to US non profits, we are chiefly interested in organisations that rely on the involvement of local groups in designing and operating their programs. Most of our contributions assist organisations with programs in Asia, Latin America, and Africa, including several working to create better educational, social, and economic opportunities for black South Africans.'

'Morgan additionally supports organisations whose research and other programs in the field of international affairs promote increased understanding among countries and people of different cultural and ethnic backgrounds.'

Grants in 1992 included:

Co-operation Ireland ($10,000);

Institute for East-West Security Studies, for the Assistance Center for Banking Institutions and Financial Markets in Eastern Europe ($12,500, 1st of 2 grants);

Southern Africa Legal Services and Legal Education Project ($10,000);

World Resources Institute, for Center for International Development and Environment ($10,000, 2nd of 2 grants);

Oxfam America ($15,000);

International Voluntary Services ($10,000);

Refugees International ($7,500);

**APPLICATIONS:** An application form is required. The initial approach should be by letter. The deadline is September 15th.

# Charles Stewart Mott Foundation

**GRANT TOTAL:** $44.05 million

**MAIN AREAS OF WORK:** Civil society, environment, Flint, poverty

**ADDRESS:** 1200 Mott Foundation Building, Flint, Michigan 48502-1851, USA

**TELEPHONE:** (313) 238-5651

**CORRESPONDENT:** Judy Samelson, Director of Communications

**INFORMATION:** Annual report including application guidelines, programme policy statement, newsletter

**GENERAL:** This entry largely quotes from the foundation's brochure 'Philosophy, Programs and Procedures 1993'. A new programme structure was adopted at the end of 1992. A new, five-year plan for the Environment programme was adopted in March 1993. Extensive refinement of the other programme areas is anticipated during the next two years.

The foundation's programme is now organised in four programmes:

* Civil society;
* Environment;
* Flint;
* Poverty.

Its Civil Society programme aims 'to encourage the emergence of new civil societies and to strengthen mature civil societies in selected areas of the world'. Grantmaking is focused in four areas:

* Central Europe and the Independent (Soviet) States with a focus on four areas: Environment, the Non-profit Sector, Political/Economic Infrastructures, Other Activities.
* Philanthropy and Voluntarism with a focus on: Community Foundations, Philanthropic Membership Organisations, Strengthening the Non-profit Sector.
* South Africa
* Special Initiatives 'that offer unusual opportunities for resolution of significant international and/or national civil society problems or that have potential as future program areas'.

The Environment programme is directed towards threats of international, national and regional significance. Internationally the programme focuses on select geographic areas, largely in the Western Hemisphere with a limited number of grants also made through the Civil Society programme. Grantmaking is focused in four areas:

* Prevention of Toxic Pollution

* Reform of International Lending and Trade Policies
* Protection of the Great Lakes Ecosystem
* Special Initiatives

Recent grants have included the following:

> Foundation for International Security, Oxon ($35,000 1990);

> European Cooperation Fund, Brussels, for European Foundation Centre membership ($67,000 and $27,000 1990);

> Ulster University, Community Education Centre ($10,000 1990);

> Charities Aid Foundation, England for United Kingdom Community Foundation Endowment Challenge Grant Programme ($1,000,000 1990)

**APPLICATIONS:** Applications in writing. there are no deadlines. The board meets in March, June, September and December. Notification takes between 60 to 90 days.

# Ruth Mott Fund

**GRANT TOTAL:** $1,770,000 (1991); Grant range: $1,000 – $40,000

**ADDRESS:** 1726 Genesee Towers, Flint, Michigan 48502, USA

**TELEPHONE:** (313) 232 3180

**CORRESPONDENT:** Deborah E. Tuck, Executive Director.

**INFORMATION:** General guidelines for applicants and specific programme guidelines.

**GENERAL:** The fund makes grants in four programme areas: arts; environment; health promotion; national/international security.

The fund 'seeks to foster public review and discussion of those domestic and foreign policy issues and initiatives that can contribute to the security of nations.' It is especially interested in receiving applications that address the following:

* Deepening of examination by the public of national and international security issues in terms of their implications for global security;
* Strengthening the processes of accountability to the public of national security agencies;
* Monitoring the Department of Energy's and

Department of Defense's impacts on the environment and human health;

- Examining the level and quality of expenditures for national security.

The fund states that projects outside the United States are given low priority and are rarely funded.

**APPLICATIONS:** Grants are limited to qualifying charitable organisations with IRS tax exemption status of through a sponsoring organisation with such status. There is no application form but applicants are advised to obtain the details of grant application format. Two copies of a summary page, grant request and financial/organisational material are required. The board meets three times a year, generally the first week of February, June and October. Deadline dates are the first of November, March and July.

# Stewart R Mott Charitable Trust

**GRANT TOTAL:** Under $250,000 a year; Grant Range: $100 to $2,000

**ADDRESS:** 14 East 96th Street, Suite 2, New York, New York 10128, USA

**TELEPHONE:** (212) 289-0006

**CORRESPONDENT:** Steve Cheifetz, Administrative Director

**INFORMATION:** Spectemur Agenda has dissolved and its function assimilated into the trust.

**GENERAL:** The trust provides very little information itself in marked contrast to most US foundations. It replies to information requests on a single A4 sheet which states: 'We do not publish official annual reports, forms for guidelines nor applications. We do not review proposals on a fixed schedule'. The trust's focus is in support of 'nationally-based organisations active in these areas of advocacy:

- peace and foreign policy/prevention of nuclear war;
- population issues/family planning/ reproductive rights;
- civil rights/civil liberties'.

**EXCLUSIONS:** No funding for individuals, travel or cultural exchange programmes, conferences.

**APPLICATIONS:** Send a request for funding in a brief letter (2-3 pages) describing the project, including a description of the organisation and a budget showing other sources of funding obtained or intended. Applicants will be contacted is the request is being considered or if further information is needed.

# National Foundation for Democracy

**GRANT TOTAL:** See below

**ADDRESS:** 1101 Fifteenth Street, NW, Suite 700, Washington DC 20005, USA

**TELEPHONE:** (202) 293-9072; Fax: (202) 223-6042

**CORRESPONDENT:** Carl Gershman, President

**INFORMATION:** Annual report, information leaflets

**GENERAL:** The endowment's purpose is to strengthen democratic institutions around the world through private, non-governmental efforts. Its worldwide grant programme assists those outside the USA who are working for democratic goals.

The endowment was set up in 1983. Its funds are from a grant awarded by the United States Information Agency (USAID) with an annual appropriation from the US Congress. Its annual expenditure is over $26 million. Its Board of Directors is comprised of leading citizens from the mainstream of American political and civic life. The endowment ordinarily funds programmes on an annual basis. The activities supported are guided by six purposes:

- to encourage free and democratic institutions throughout the world through private-sector initiatives;
- to facilitate exchanges between United States private-sector groups and democratic groups abroad;
- to promote United States non-governmental participation in democratic training programmes and democratic institution building abroad;
- to strengthen democratic electoral processes abroad;
- to support the participation of the two major

American political parties, labour, business, and other US private-sector groups in fostering co-operation with those abroad dedicated to the cultural values, institutions and organisations of democratic pluralism;

- to encourage the establishment and growth of democratic development in a manner consistent with both the broad concerns of United States national interests and with the specific requirements of the democratic groups in other countries.

Programmes are funded in five main areas:

- Pluralism
- Democratic Governance and Political Processes
- Education, Culture and Communications International Co-operation.

Its fields of operation cover: Africa, Asia, Central and Eastern Europe, Commonwealth of Independent States, Latin America, the Caribbean and the Middle East.

For instance, in the northern tier countries of central and eastern Europe – Poland, Hungary and the Czech and Slovak Republics – the endowment has aimed to strengthen democratic institutions by providing support for the formation of trade unions and business associations, for the creation of effective parliamentary structures and policy institutes, and for the establishment of a truly independent press. Civic education programmes promoted mutual tolerance and respect among ethnic and other minorities.

Regional wide grants throughout Central and Eastern Europe promoted independent publishing, teacher training, trade union rights and issues, political party development, youth exchanges, independent student movements, and political participation by women and youth.

Grants have included:

Free Trade Union Institute, essential support for the emerging independent trade unions in the republics of the former Soviet Union (£1 million);

Freedom House, for equipment purchase and operating expenses of the Moscow-based Express Chronicle, an independent Russian-language newspaper ($55,000).

**EXCLUSIONS:** Programmes supported encourage democratic political development, not projects aimed at promoting economic and social development. No grants to individuals.

**APPLICATIONS:** Contact the endowment for full details of information required.

# The New World Foundation

**GRANT TOTAL:** £1,458,000 (1991); Grant range: $250 – $125,000

**ADDRESS:** 100 East 85th Street, New York, N Y 10028, USA

**TELEPHONE:** (212) 249-1023

**CORRESPONDENT:** Colin Greer, President

**INFORMATION:** Biennial report including application guidelines.

**GENERAL:** The foundation's programme places emphasis on:

- equal rights and opportunity, especially minorities rights;
- public education, especially the roles of parents and the community working together;
- public health, particularly helping the disadvantaged, raising occupational health and safety standards, and reducing environmental hazards to health;
- community initiative for rural and urban communities;
- the avoidance of war, especially nuclear war, and seeking peace.

Research programmes must be action or policy oriented with regard to current issues.

**APPLICATIONS:** There are no application forms or deadlines. The board meets three times a year.

# The New-Land Foundation, Inc

**GRANT TOTAL:** $1,400,000 (1991); Grant range: $1,000 – $50,000

**ADDRESS:** 1345 Avenue of the Americas, 45th Floor, New York 10105, USA

**TELEPHONE:** 212-841-6000

**CORRESPONDENT:** Robert Wolf, President

**INFORMATION:** Application guidelines

**GENERAL:** The foundation makes grants for civil rights, mental health, environmental preservation, public interest, arms control and disarmament, cultural programmes, minority and medical education, and social service and youth agencies. Its support includes assistance towards campaigns, research, general purposes and special projects

Grants in 1990 included:

Centre for Innovative Diplomacy ($30,000);

Institute for Defense and Disarmament Studies ($16,000);

Ploughshares Fund ($10,000).

**APPLICATIONS:** Applicants should obtain the guidelines with an application form. Deadlines are 1 of February and August. The board meets in Spring and Autumn and only positive replies are made.

# John M Olin Foundation

**GRANT TOTAL:** $15 million (1992); Grant range: £100 – $3m

**ADDRESS:** 100 Park Avenue, Suite 2701, New York, NY 10017, USA

**TELEPHONE:** (212) 661-2670

**CORRESPONDENT:** James Piereson, Executive Director

**INFORMATION:** Annual report including guidelines for applicants.

**GENERAL:** The foundation provides support for projects that reflect or are intended to strengthen the economic, political and cultural institutions upon which the American system of democratic capitalism is based. It also seeks to promote a general understanding of these institutions by encouraging research on the connections between economic and political freedoms, and on the cultural heritage that sustains them. The board of trustees authorises grants in four areas:

- public policy and research;
- American institutions;
- law and the legal system;
- strategic and international studies, where grants are awarded for the purpose of

examining the relationship between American institutions and the international context in which they operate. Such projects include studies of national security affairs, strategic issues, American foreign policy and the international economy.

The foundation attempts to advance its objectives through support of the following kinds of activities including: research; institutional support; fellowships; professorships; lectures and lecture series; books; scholarly journals; journals of opinion; conferences and seminars; and, on occasion, television and radio programmes.

Grants in 1992 included the following:

London School of Economics, to support a programme bringing American economists to Britain ($25,000 1992);

Oxford University, Templeton College, to support the Olin fellowship and lectures in political economy ($420,000 1992);

Harvard University, Center for International Affairs, to establish and support for 2 years the John M. Olin Institute for Strategic Studies (over $2 million 1992);

John Hopkins University, School of Advanced International Studies, 2 grants to support the Securities Studies Programme ($558,000 1992);

Center for Strategic and International Studies, Washington ($100,000 in 2 grants 1992);

Freedom House, New York, to support the East European Freedom fund, and to support the broadcast of TV documentaries in Russia (2 grants of $50,000 each 1992);

Congressional Human Rights Foundation, Washington, to support the Interparliamentary Human Rights Network ($10,000 1992);

Christian Rescue Effort for Emerging Democracies (CREED) Princetown, NJ, to support education programmes for Christians in countries formerly dominated by the USSR ($5,000 1992);

**APPLICATIONS:** In writing to the correspondent. There are no application forms or deadlines. The board meets four times a year and notification is usually given within 90 days.

# Open Society Fund

(see also the Soros Foundations)

**GRANT TOTAL:** $3,702,00 to 40 organisations; $64,000 to individuals (1990)

**ADDRESS:** 888 Seventh Avenue, 33rd Floor, New York 10106, USA

**TELEPHONE:** (212) 262-6300

**CORRESPONDENT:** Susan Weber Soros, Vice-President

**GENERAL:** This is the first foundation established by George Soros, the international financier, in 1979. Since then this address has also become the centre for an extensive network of autonomous foundations based in Central and Eastern Europe (see Soros Foundations entry). The fund gives grants for higher education, including scholarships for disadvantaged or minority students and fellowships for scholarly research or analysis; international studies and affairs; human rights; and the medical sciences. Applicants must be affiliated with an institution. Recent grants have included:

In 1990 –

    Charter 77 Foundation, Prague ($177,000);

    Charter 77 Foundation, Stockholm ($650,000);

    International Fund for the Development of Tibet ($25,000);

In 1989 –

    Central and Eastern European Publishing Project, England ($50,000);

    Great Britain East Europe Centre, London ($19,800);

    Inter University Foundation, Oxford ($24,000);

**APPLICATIONS:** Applicants will be solicited through contacts with educational institutions.

# Albert Parvin Foundation

**GRANT TOTAL:** $399,000 (1991); Grant range: $100 – $100,000

**ADDRESS:** c/o Lewis Joffa & Co, 10880 Wiltshire Blvd, No 2006, Los Angeles 90024, USA

**TELEPHONE:** (310) 475-5657

**CORRESPONDENT:** Albert B Parvin, Vice-President

**GENERAL:** The foundation was established in 1960 'to promote peace, understanding and goodwill among the nations of the world through education, enlightenment and recognition of achievements toward this objective'. It operates both nationally and internationally in the fields of social welfare and education through grants for construction projects, for higher education and child welfare, and through fellowships tenable at Princeton University and the University of California by students from new and underdeveloped nations.

**APPLICATIONS:** There are no deadlines.

# PepsiCo Foundation, Inc

**GRANT TOTAL:** $7,441,000 (1990); Grant range: $100 – $750,000

**ADDRESS:** 700 Anderson Hill Road, Purchase, NY 10577, USA

**TELEPHONE:** (914) 253-3153

**CORRESPONDENT:** Jacqueline R Millan, Vice-President, Contributions

**INFORMATION:** Information brochure, application and policy guidelines.

**GENERAL:** The foundation is particularly interested in education, higher education, education for minorities, health services, economics, youth, community funds, international affairs, civic affairs, the arts, and business education. Grants relevant to this guide were given:

In 1989 –

    Institute for East-West Security Studies, NY ($35,000);

    Center for Strategic and International Studies, DC ($30,000);

    American Committee on US-Soviet Relations, DC ($20,000);

    Council on Foreign Relations, NY ($10,000).

It should be noted that giving is primarily in areas of company operations in New York.

**APPLICATIONS:** There are no application forms or deadlines. The initial approach should be with a proposal.

# Pew Charitable Trusts

**GRANT TOTAL:** $143,538,000 (1992); Grant range: $1,500 – $2.2 million

**ADDRESS:** One Commerce Square, 2005 Market Street, Suite 1700, Philadelphia 19103-7017, USA

**TELEPHONE:** (215) 975-9050

**CORRESPONDENT:** Rebecca W Rimel, Executive Director

**INFORMATION:** Annual report, grants list, application guidelines.

**GENERAL:** The Pew Charitable Trusts, represent seven individual charitable trusts funded between 1948 and 1982 by the sons and daughters of Joseph N Pew, founder of the Sun Oil Company. The trusts support non-profit organisations dedicated to improving the quality of life for individuals and communities and encouraging personal growth and self-sufficiency. Grants are awarded in the areas of conservation and the environment, arts and culture, education, health and human services, public and foreign policy, and religion. There is also an inter-disciplinary fund. The Public Policy programme has two main goals:

• Promoting economic and political freedom by supporting collaborative efforts among US and international partners to consolidate democratic, market-oriented transitions, especially in Eastern and Central Europe, and in Southeast Asia and Latin America.

• Global security, to promote effective interdisciplinary approaches to understanding and responding to emerging threats to global peace and security. The programme concentrates primarily on issues of ethnic and sectarian conflict. The programmes are reviewed every two years. New guidelines will appear in 1995.

Grants have included:

In 1992 –

University of Cambridge, England for global security fellowship programme ($1,900,000);

In 1991 –

American Council of Learned Societies, to strengthen constitutionalism in Eastern Europe ($300,000);

Center for Strategic and International Studies, for Asia/Pacific security co-operation ($220,000);

In 1990-

International Institute for Strategic Studies, London ($130,000);

Center for Democracy in the USSR, NYC, to improve Western understanding of ongoing changes in the Soviet Union through better access to independent news sources ($150,000).

**APPLICATIONS:** The trusts' guidelines and information about limitations in each programme area should be obtained. An application form is required. An initial approach by letter (of no more than 2 to 3 pages) may be made. There are deadlines only for the cultural programme. The board meets four times a year. Final notification is about three weeks after the board meeting.

# Ploughshares Fund

**GRANT TOTAL:** $4.1 million (1992/93); Grant range: $1,000 – $40,000

**ADDRESS:** Fort Mason, San Francisco, CA 94123, USA

**TELEPHONE:** (415) 775 -2244

**CORRESPONDENT:** Sally Lilienthal, President; Karen R Harris, Executive Director

**INFORMATION:** An annual report with guidelines for applicants is available.

**GENERAL:** The Ploughshares Fund was founded in 1981 with one purpose – to prevent nuclear war. Its 1993 report states that in the coming years it will concentrate on the following areas of concern:

• halting the spread of nuclear weapons;

• controlling the international trade in conventional weapons;

• promoting new approaches to international security;

• confronting the legacy of the arms race.

The fund can give grants to individuals and for direct lobbying programmes, There is no geographical limitation on grants.

Grants in 1993 included:

Centre for Defence Studies, King's College, London, for a newsletter for analysts in the international development community to encourage them to consider militarisation and security issues when developing economic and aid policies ($25,000);

Centre for Defence Studies, King's College, London, for summer training programme in Pakistan on South Asian defence and security issues ($10,000);

Dfax Associates, Bradford, UK, for an electronic news summary service on conventional arms transfers, directed to some 100 organisations around the world addressing arms issues. ($18,000);

International Security Information Service, London, to brief MPs on nuclear proliferation ($15,000);

Saferworld, Bristol, to organise a broad coalition of NGOs to build political support in Europe for tighter controls on arms exports ($15,000);

University of Bradford, Department of Peace Studies, to monitor the development of the UN Arms Register, make recommendations on its strengthening for the 1994 review, and to support an international conference in Beijing on the international arms trade. ($15,000);

Vipin Supta, Middlesex, to acquire and analyse satellite imagery of the Chinese nuclear weapons test site ($10,000);

Interdisciplinary Research Group in Science, Technology, and Security Policy (IANUS), Darmstadt, Germany for a conference to launch the International Network of Engineers and Scientists Against Proliferation ($20,000);

Jaffee Center for Strategic Studies, Tel Aviv, Israel, to assess the status of nuclear weapons in the Middle East and promote policies for controlling their spread in the region ($20,000);

Peace Research Institute, Frankfurt, Germany, to support briefings for government officials in west and east European countries on what can be done to stop nuclear weapons proliferation and to control exports of sensitive nuclear materials ($21,000);

BUKO – Campaign to Stop Arms Exports, Bremen, Germany, for a public education and lobbying campaign in Germany and other European countries to ban the production and sale of land mines ($10,000);

European Nuclear Test Ban Coalition, Brussels, to set up a coalition of groups from six European countries ($10,000);

**EXCLUSIONS:** The production of films, videos or books is not funded, neither is research of writing of academic dissertations.

**APPLICATIONS:** There are no application forms or application deadlines. The board meets four times a year (in February, May, September and December) with additional meetings for small grants up to $10,000. A detailed note of the information required from applicants is set out by the fund and should be obtained before making an approach.

# The Prospect Hill Foundation, Inc

**GRANT TOTAL:** $1,767,000 (1992); Grant range: $2,000 – £300,000

**ADDRESS:** 420 Lexington Avenue, Suite 3020, New York, NY 10170, USA

**TELEPHONE:** (212) 370-1144

**CORRESPONDENT:** Constance Eiseman, Executive Director

**INFORMATION:** A grants list and guidelines for applicants are available.

**GENERAL:** The foundation has the following fields of interest: arms control, conservation, environment, family planning. It gives grants for a range of activities including seed money, operating budgets, matching funds and special projects.

Examples of grants in 1990 include:

University of Southampton, Nuclear Non-Proliferation Programme ($15,000);

Natural Resources Defence Council ($20,000);

Nuclear Control Institute, DC ($20,000);

New York University Center for War, Peace and the News Media ($23,000);

Ploughshares Fund ($15,000)

**EXCLUSIONS:** No grants for research.

**APPLICATIONS:** Applicants are advised to obtain guidelines from the foundation before submitting an enquiry. There is no application form. The initial approach should be by letter enclosing two copies of the proposal. There are no deadlines.

# Public Welfare Foundation

**GRANT TOTAL:** $16,750,570 (1991); Grant range: $1,000 – $250,000

**ADDRESS:** 2600 Virginia Avenue NW, Suite 505, Washington DC 20037-1977, USA

**TELEPHONE:** (202) 965-1800

**CORRESPONDENT:** Larry Kressley, Executive Director

**INFORMATION:** Annual report including application guidelines

**GENERAL:** The foundation supports grassroots organisations with an emphasis on environment, population, the elderly, youth underclass, and criminal justice. The programmes must serve low-income populations with a preference for short-term needs.

Examples of international grants relevant to this guide:

In 1992 –

International Planned Parenthood Federation, London for increased awareness of family planning in the following countries: Bangladesh programme ($27,000); Thailand programme ($35,000); Vietnam programme ($25,000);

Marie Stopes International, London, family planning programme in Pakistan ($50,000); programme in Cairo ($75,000);

In 1991 –

Arms Control Association, for information and education ($70,000);

International Human Rights Law Group, rule of law project in Central and South America ($47,000);

In 1990 –

Council for a Liveable World Education Fund, Boston, education and projects for a meaningful solution to the arms race ($50,000);

In 1987 –

Community of the Peace People, Belfast, for general support (£10,500).

**EXCLUSIONS:** These include building funds, endowments, publications, grants for scholarship, research and conferences.

**APPLICATIONS:** The initial approach should be in writing including a summary sheet with the proposal. The board meets four times a year. Notification can be expected within three to four months.

# Rockefeller Brothers Fund

**GRANT TOTAL:** $10,509,000 (1992); Grant range: $1,000 – $285,000

**ADDRESS:** 1290 Avenue of the Americas, New York, NY 10104-0233, USA

**TELEPHONE:** 212-373 4200

**CORRESPONDENT:** Benjamin R Shute, Jr, Secretary-Treasurer

**INFORMATION:** Annual report, including application guidelines.

**GENERAL:** The fund makes grants under the following headings:

- One World: Sustainable Resource Use;
- One World: World Security;
- Non-profit Sector;
- Education;
- New York City;
- Special Concerns: South Africa.

The major portion of the grant funds are given under the One World programmes (over $6 million). Projects are located for the most part in East Asia, East Central Europe, the former Soviet Union or the United States.

The goal of its World Security programme is 'To improve political, security, and economic relations among nations and strengthen arms control – recognising that world peace is threatened not by conflicts among competing political philosophies, differing religions, and varying cultural traditions but also by frustration and aggression arising from inequities in the sharing of the food, energy, goods, and services the world economy produces.' It states its strategy at the global level 'restraining horizontal nuclear proliferation – the spread of nuclear weapons capability to additional countries. Emphasis is given to issues related to the extension of the Nuclear Non-Proliferation Treaty, tightening nuclear export controls, controlling surplus plutonium, and exploring promising means of containing the nuclear weapons capability that has already been developed around the globe'.

Under its One World programme the fund assists efforts to analyse the connections between global resource management and global security.

Grants in 1992 included:

Southampton University, Nuclear Non-proliferation Programme ($330,000 total over several years);

Sussex University, Surplus Plutonium in Europe and Japan project ($64,000 over two years);

Verification Technology Information Centre, London, publication on arms control verification issues ($95,000 total over several years);

Central and East European Publishing Project, Oxford, general support ($120,000 total over several years);

APPLICATIONS: There is no application form. The first approach should be by a letter of no more than 2 to 3 pages. There are no deadlines. The board meets in February, June and November and notification should take about three months.

# The Rockefeller Foundation

GRANT TOTAL: $68,410,000 (1991)

ADDRESS: 1133 Avenue of the Americas, New York, NY 10036, USA

TELEPHONE: (212) 869 8500

CORRESPONDENT: Lynda Mullen, Secretary.

INFORMATION: Annual report, programme policy statement, application guidelines.

GENERAL: The foundation aims 'to promote the well-being of mankind throughout the world'. Its strong international programme to support science-based development provides a focus for four of the foundation's divisions, Global Environment, Agricultural Sciences, Health Sciences, Populations Sciences, and for its special African Initiatives programme.

The major part of its funding is given to organisations but a considerable number of scholarships are also awarded.

The foundation also runs a small grant programme on International Security which supports 'projects which focus on limiting or reversing proliferation of nuclear, chemical, and biological weapons of mass destruction. Funding primarily follows four major themes: confidence-building measures; developing South-North non-government organisational partnerships; encouraging the intellectual linkage between development and non-proliferation; and strengthening barriers to proliferation. In all of these areas, the officers seek projects coming from the developing world, with priority given to Asia and the Middle East.'

The programme gave about £550,000 in 1992 with grants ranging between $15,000 and $150,000. Grants with some relevance to this guide:

In 1992 –

International Peace Academy, New York ($100,000);

Center for Study of Soviet Change ($75,000);

Peace Research Institute, Frankfurt ($25,000).

APPLICATIONS: There are no special forms or application deadlines The board meets four times a year. A proposal should be sent containing: a description of the proposed project with clearly stated plans and objectives, a comprehensive plan for total funding during and, where applicable, after the proposed grant period, a listing of the applicant's qualifications and accomplishments, and if applicable, a description of the institutional setting. Organisations may be asked to supply information on their own affirmative action, including data on the gender and minority composition of the leadership of the organisation.

# Samuel Rubin Foundation

GRANT TOTAL: $795,000 (1991); Grant range: $500 – $200,000

ADDRESS: 777 United Nations Plaza, New York, NY 10017, USA

TELEPHONE: (212) 697 8945

**CORRESPONDENT:** Cora Weiss, President.

**INFORMATION:** Programme policy statement.

**GENERAL:** The foundation makes grants to national and international organisations for programmes concerned with the pursuit of peace and justice, the search for an equitable reallocation of the world's resources, and the fullest implementation of social, economic, political, civil and cultural rights.

Its fields of interest are in particular: law and justice, peace, arms control, international affairs, international relief, foreign policy, Africa, civil rights, women, education, higher education, human rights, economics.

Grants in 1992 included:

British American Security Information Council ($10,000);

Citizen Alert ($5,000);

Center for Ecological Socialism ($2,500);

Five Colleges Programme in Peace and World Security Studies ($2,000).

**APPLICATIONS:** A written proposal should be sent. There are no deadlines. The board meets three times a year and notification is within two weeks following these meetings.

# Sarah Scaife Foundation

**GRANT TOTAL:** $11.2 million (1991); Grant range: $1,000 – $1m

**ADDRESS:** 3 Mellon Bank Center, 525 William Penn Place, Suite 3900, Pittsburgh 15219-1708, Pennsylvania, USA

**TELEPHONE:** (412) 392-2900

**CORRESPONDENT:** Richard M Larry, President.

**INFORMATION:** Annual report including application guidelines.

**GENERAL:** The foundation directs most of its resources to support organisations addressing major domestic and international public policy issues through research, publications and education.

Grants in 1990 have included:

American Bar Association Fund for Justice and Education, for standing committee on law and national security ($130,000);

Foreign Policy Research Institute, Philadelphia, general support ($75,000).

**APPLICATIONS:** There are no application forms or deadlines. The initial approach should be by letter. The board meets in February, May, September and November.

# Schering-Plough Foundation, Inc

**GRANT TOTAL:** $2.776 million (1991): Grant range: $1,000- $250,000

**ADDRESS:** One Giralda Farms, P O Box 1000, Madison, New Jersey 07940-1000, USA

**TELEPHONE:** (201) 822-7412

**CORRESPONDENT:** Rita Sacco, Assistant Secretary

**INFORMATION:** Corporate giving report including application guidelines.

**GENERAL:** The foundation's primary objective is support of institutional activities devoted to improving the quality and delivery of health care through medical and allied education. It gives especially in areas where the company has major facilities. Grants given in 1990 included:

Co-operation Ireland ($30,000);

US South Africa Leader Exchange Programme ($10,000).

**EXCLUSIONS:** Publications and conferences are not supported.

**APPLICATIONS:** There are no application forms. Deadlines are 1 February and 1 July for board meetings in Spring and Autumn.

# Scherman Foundation

**GRANT TOTAL:** $4.1 million (1992); Grant range $5,000 – $200,000.

**ADDRESS:** 315 West 57th Street, Suite 2D, New York, NY 10019, USA

**TELEPHONE:** (212) 489 -7143

**CORRESPONDENT:** David F Freeman, Executive Director.

**INFORMATION:** An annual report is available.

**GENERAL:** The main areas of interest are disarmament and peace, conservation, family planning, human rights and liberties, the arts and social welfare. The 1992 annual report states that in the last two years particular priority has been given to organisations in New York City.

Grants in 1992 included:

Physicians for Social Responsibility, Washington ($30,000);

Parliamentarians for Global Action, New York ($25,000);

Search for Common Ground, Washington ($20,000);

National Academy of Sciences, Committee on Human Rights, Washington ($30,000);

Population Institute, Washington ($30,000).

**EXCLUSIONS:** Grants are not given for scholarships and fellowships, or to colleges, universities, higher education institutions or to individuals.

**APPLICATIONS:** In writing to the correspondent. There are no deadlines. The board meets quarterly. Notification within 3 months.

# Florence and John Schumann Foundation

**GRANT TOTAL:** $7.2 million (1991); Grant range: $5,000 – $500,000

**ADDRESS:** 33 Park Street, Montclair, New Jersey 07042, USA

**TELEPHONE:** (201) 783-6660

**CORRESPONDENT:** John W Passacantando, Executive Director

**INFORMATION:** Annual report and guidelines for applicants.

**GENERAL:** Grants are given for effective governance, environment, international relations, media.

Grants in 1991 have included:

Aspen Institute for Humanistic Studies, Queenstown MD , for conference on financing environmental reforms in Eastern Europe ($52,000);

Atlantic Council of the United States, Washington, to strengthen the non-proliferation role of the International Atomic Energy Agency ($15,000);

Rutgers University Foundation, New Brunswick MJ, to the Journalism Resources Institute advising new democracies in Europe to develop independent print and broadcast journalism ($100,000);

**EXCLUSIONS:** No grants to individuals, for endowment funds, appeals, equipment, loans.

**APPLICATIONS:** In writing to the correspondent. There is no application form and only one copy of the proposal is required. The deadlines are January 15th, April 15th, August 15th for board meetings in February, June and October.

# Sequoia Foundation

**GRANT TOTAL:** $3.82 million: Grant range: $750 – $163,000

**ADDRESS:** 820 A St, Suite 345, Tacoma, Washington 98402, USA

**TELEPHONE:** (206) 627-1634

**CORRESPONDENT:** Frank D Underwood, Executive Director.

**INFORMATION:** Policy statement and application guidelines.

**GENERAL:** The foundation aims to serve the environmental and social needs of the world community. Grants are focused on the stimulation, encouragement, and support of established, voluntary, non-profit organisations set up to meet national and international need in areas of the environment and social services with an economic development component. Current geographic and interest area priorities are Mexico, Central America and the Himalayan mountain region, but priorities may change annually.

Grants in 1990 included:

International Peace Academy ($60,000);

Amnesty International, USA ($10,000).

**APPLICATIONS:** An application form is required. The initial approach should be by letter with two copies of a proposal. There are no deadlines. The board meets at least six times a year.

# Alfred P Sloan Foundation

**GRANT TOTAL:** $36.6 million (1992): Grant average: $10,000 – $3m

**ADDRESS:** 630 Fifth Avenue, Suite 225, New York, NY 10ll-0242, USA

**TELEPHONE:** (212) 649-1649

**CORRESPONDENT:** Stewart F Campbell, Financial Vice-President and Secretary

**GENERAL:** The 1992 annual report states that the main interests and programmes of the foundation are concentrated primarily in four areas:

- Science and technology;
- Economic growth, industrial competitiveness, and standard of living;
- Education in science, technology and management;
- Selected national issues.

The foundation aims, under its Selected National Issues programme to 'contribute to the major issues of our time'. 'While no major projects were funded in 1992 studies which were funded earlier in 1990 and 1991 are ongoing and included research on the public perception of nuclear power, the long-term clean-up of radioactive waste at federal reactor sites, deep ocean waste disposal options, and a comparative analysis of American and European experiences with different programs and policies regarding illicit drugs'.

Recent international grants include:

International Council of Scientific Unions ($25,000, 1993);

Institute Francais des Relations Internationales, Paris ($30,000 1990);

Foundation for International Studies on Peace/Security ($30,000 1989);

London School of Economics ($150,000 1989).

**EXCLUSIONS:** No grants for buildings or endowment funds.

**APPLICATIONS:** An initial letter of inquiry is advisable. There are no deadlines for the programmes as the board meets throughout the year. Applications should include a detailed description of the project, amount requested, qualification of key personnel, timetable, proof of tax exempt status and the results expected from the proposed grant.

# The Soros Foundations

**ADDRESS:** 888 Seventh Avenue, Suite 1901, New York, NY 10106, USA

**TELEPHONE:** (212) 757-2323; Fax (212) 974-0367

**CORRESPONDENT:** Frances Abouzeid, Shawn Pattison

**BENEFICIAL AREA:** Central and Eastern Europe, the former Soviet Union, and South Africa

**INFORMATION:** Guide to the Soros Foundations; 'Open Society News'; information brochure; speeches and reports.

**GENERAL:** The Soros Foundation network was created by the international financier, George Soros. A list of Soros Foundations is given at the end of this entry. The New York office is able to help with additional information. The following information is taken directly from the foundations' brochure.

'The Open Society Fund, Soros' first foundation, was established in 1979. Its initial grants supported human rights organisations as well as scholarships for black students at Capetown University. Soon, it began to offer scholarships to East European dissident intellectuals. This led to the establishment of a foundation for Hungary in 1984, and since then, a network of foundations spanning Central and Eastern Europe and the former Soviet Union. In accordance with Soros' belief that "it is not enough to destroy a closed society in order to bring about an open society", the Soros Foundations seek to build the infrastructure of democracy in the region ... The Soros network also facilitates the development of programmes and institutions with regional presence, the most important of which is the Central European University'.

**Scope:** The purpose of the Soros Foundations is to support independent institutions in the countries of Central and Eastern Europe, the former Soviet Union, and South Africa during the period of transition from repression to openness. The majority of the foundations' support goes to projects and people in Central and Eastern Europe and the few other regions where the foundation operates. In exceptional cases where non-indigenous organisations receive grants, projects and people in those regions must be direct beneficiaries.

Although strategies sometimes vary, each of the foundations within the network seeks to provide educational opportunities for individuals and encourage reform of the educational system, foster political and cultural pluralism, support revision of the economic structure in order to encourage private enterprise and a market economy, and to provide direct technical assistance to address major health and environmental problems. The foundations place a high premium on voluntary activity.

The ultimate determinant of a programme's application is local need. The foundations are mainly interested in education, culture, civil society, health and the environment. In principle, no area of need is excluded from consideration. If a general trend may be discerned among all the foundations' activities, it is that they are becoming more proactive (and less reactive) grantmakers.

**Major activities:**

**Education**

The Soros Foundations place great emphasis on education as a catalyst for change. The centre-piece of their efforts is the Central European University (CEU) which opened in 1991 with a grant of £25 million for the first five years. The CEU is educating the region's future leaders through postgraduate study and research in the social sciences at its Prague and Budapest colleges.

Soros Foundations may provide support to other educational institutions and organisations for educational reform projects, student exchange programmes, equipment grants, dollar conversion for the purchase of technical equipment in the West.

Many of the foundations make grants to individuals for: Soros scholarships and fellowships, travel and incidental expenses related to scholarships at Western universities, travel grants for short-term study, research or conference attendance, and publication grants. 27 Soros Student Advising Centres give students information on educational opportunities in the West. The English language is promoted through a variety of local projects.

**Civil Society**

Democratic Infrastructure Grants may be made to individuals and organisations for: legal reform, both at the national (constitutional) and local levels; assisting a democratic and independent media; internships for government and civic groups leaders from the region in government, media, social service and non-profit offices in the West; encouraging pluralism, human rights and voter participation; and promoting the development of the not-for-profit sector.

**Management Training and Economic Reform**

Grants may be made to: encourage systemic reform in various sectors of the economy; develop indigenous business management talent; and promote the development of small businesses and the privatisation of state enterprises.

**Health and Environment**

Most foundations contribute project support to indigenous, independent organisations which address major health or environmental problems in direct and practical ways. Many foundations offer distribution networks, payment of shipping charges for donated medical supplies, internships at Western hospitals, fellowships sending American volunteers abroad to teach environmental topics, travel grants, and dollar conversion for the purchase of desired medical equipment.

**Culture**

Many of the foundations make grants for: internships and travel grants, training and management of cultural institutes and libraries, preservation of libraries and public collections, promotion of national culture abroad, and art and other cultural exhibitions.

A list of Soros foundations as at January 17th, 1994 follows:

**Albania**

Open Society Foundation for Albania
Mr Avni Mustafaj, Executive Director
Rr Labinotl No 125, Tirana
Tel: (355 42) 34 621; Fax: (355 42) 34 223

**Belarus**

Soros Foundation – Belarus
Ms Elizabeth Smedley, Executive Director
Prospekt F Skorina 65, Korpus 11 A 5th Floor, 220027 Minsk
Tel: (70172) 39 93 46; Tel/Fax: (70172) 32 80 92

**Bosnia and Herzegovina**

Open Society Fund – Bosnia Herzegovina
Dr Zdravko Grebo, Executive Director
Ise Jovanovica 2, 71000 Sarajevo
Tel: (412) 339 4736; Fax: (412) 339 4724

**Bulgaria**

Open Society Fund – Sofia
Mr George Prohsky, Executive Director
1 Bulgaria Square, NDK Office Building 11th
Floor,
PO Box 114, 1463 Sofia
Tel: (35 92) 658 177; Fax: (35 92) 658 276

**Croatia**

Open Society Fund - Croatia
Ms Karmin Basic, Executive Director
Krvavi Most 2, 41000 Zagreb
Tel: (385 41) 276 819.272017; Tel/Fax: (385 41)
275 741

**Czech Republic**

Open Society Fund – Prague
Ms Maria Kopecka, Administrative Director
c/o The Central European University,
Room 419
Taboritska 23
1390 87 Praha, POB 114
Tel: (42 2) 27 41 37; Fax: (42 2) 27 37 40

**Estonia**

Open Estonia Foundation
Ms Mall Hellam, Executive Dir
Tel: (372 2) 601 895; Fax: (372 2) 601 998

**Hungary**

Soros Foundation – Hungary Mr Lazlo Kardos,
Executive Director
PO Box 34,1525 Budapest
Tel: (36 1) 202 6211; Fax: (36 1) 175 7767

**Kazakkstan**

Soros Foundation – Kazakhstan
Mr Brian Kemple, Programme Coordinator
Ul, Panfilova 75, Kv 13, Almaty
Tel: (7 3272) 33 90 36

**Kyrgyzstan**

Soros Foundation – Kyrgyzstan
Ms Nancy Humm, Mr Sergei Kogin,
Programme Coordinators
Ul, Toktogul 92, kv 21, 720000 Bishkek
Tel/Fax: (7 3312) 223 233

**Latvia**

Soros Foundation – Latvia
Ms Vita Matiss, Executive Director
Krisjana Barona 31, LV -1722 Riga I
nt Tel/Fax: (371) 88 28 160

**Lithuania**

Open Society Fund – Lithuania
Mr Vytautas Gruodis, Executive Director
Jaksto 9, 2600 Vilnius
Tel: (370 2) 221 687/221 355; Fax: (370 2) 221 419

**Macedonia**

Open Society Fund of Macedonia
Mr Vladimir Milcin, Executive Director
Ilindenska bb, Room 310, 91000 Skopje
Tel: (389 91) 220 812 Fax: (389 91) 116 534

**Moldova**

Soros Foundation – Moldova
Ms Lorina Balteanu, Executive Director
Bulgara Str 32,
277001 Chisinsu
Tel/Fax: (373 2) 264 071 / 264 408 / 260 031

**Poland**

Stefan Batory Foundation
Mr Jacek Wojnarowski, Executive Director
ul, Flory 9, 00-586 Warsaw
Tel:(48 22) 488 055; Fax: (48 22) 493 561

**Romania**

Soros Foundation for an Open Society
Mrs Anca Maria Harasim, Executive Director
PO Box 22-196, Bucharest 71102
Tel: (40 1) 659 0696; Fax: (40 1) 312 2745

**Russia**

Cultural Initiative Foundation
Ms Yelena Karpukhina, Executive Director
Bolshoi Kozlovski pereulok 13/17
Mailing address: B78 107078 Moscow
Tel: (7 095) 921 2085/928 4632 Fax: (7 095) 288
9512/921 9025

**Slovakia**

Open Society – Bratislava
Ms Rachel Tritt, Executive Director
Staromestska 6,
811 03 Bratislava
Tel: (42 7) 316 913; Tel/Fax: (42 7) 314 730

**Slovenia**

Open Society Fund – Slovenia
Mr Rastko Mocnic, Executive Director
Mikloslceva 13,
61000 Ljubljana
Tel: (386 31) 302 912; Tel/Fax: (386 61) 312 139

**South Africa**

Open Society Foundation for South Africa
Mr Michael Savage, Executive Director
Albion Springs, 183 Main Road,
Rondebosch, 7700 Cape
Tel: (27 21) 689 8396; Fax: (27 21) 689 3266

**Switzerland**

The Soros Rroma Foundation
Cristina Kruck, Executive Director
Hoschgasse 54, 8008 Zurich
Tel: (41 1) 383 6326; Fax: (41 1) 383 6302

**Ukraine**

International Renaissance Foundation
Mr Bohdan Budzan, Executive Director
46 Artema St, 254053 Kyiv
Tel: (7 044) 216 2596/216 1324/216 1253/244
7497; Fax: (7 044) 216 7629

**Yugoslavia**

Open Society Fund – Yugoslavia
Ms Sonja Licht, Executive Director
Kralja Petra 71, 11000 Belgrade
Tel: (381 11) 626 563/624 888; Fax (381 11) 634 652

**Other Office**

**France**

Soros Foundation – Paris 38 Boulevard
Beaumarchais, 75011 Paris
Tel: (33 1) 4805; Fax: (33 1) 4021 6541

**EXCLUSIONS:** General operating expenses on an
ongoing basis, construction or endowment
funds. Except in rare circumstances, the foundations do not contribute to charities, underwrite
the costs of conferences or fund institutional
research. Also excluded are political campaigns,
organisations which discriminate by race,
colour, creed, gender etc, projects which seek to
influence legislation, fundraising events,
inventions or profit-making ventures, film
projects.

**APPLICATIONS:** Some foundations offer programmes which others do not. Before applying
to any foundation or programme, it is advised to
contact the appropriate foundation office regarding specific programmes and conditions of
eligibility.

# The Starr Foundation

**GRANT TOTAL:** $31,534,000 (1991); Grant range:
$1,000 -6m+

**ADDRESS:** 70 Pine Street, New York, NY 10270,
USA

**TELEPHONE:** (212) 770-6882

**CORRESPONDENT:** Ta Chun Hsu, President.

**GENERAL:** The foundation makes grants largely
for education with emphasis on higher education, including scholarships under specific
programmes; also limited contributions to
hospitals and medical research, cultural programmes, international affairs organisations, and
social services.

Grants in 1991 included:

Center for Strategic and International Studies,
for conference in Moscow ($50,000);

English Speaking Union of the US, for
scholarship fund ($30,000);

French American Foundation for the
Development of Relations ($10,000).

**APPLICATIONS:** There are no deadlines. The initial
approach should be made by letter. Board
meetings are held in February and September.
The foundation does not issue guidelines or a
statement of policy.

# Stewardship Foundation

**GRANT TOTAL:** $3.657 million (1991); Grant range:
$1,000 – $340,000

**ADDRESS:** Tacoma Financial Center, Suite 1500,
1145 Broadway Plaza, Tacoma, Washington
98402, USA

**TELEPHONE:** (206) 272-8336

**CORRESPONDENT:** George S Kovats, Executive
Director

**INFORMATION:** Biennial report and application
guidelines.

**GENERAL:** At least 85 per cent of funds are paid

for evangelical religious organisations whose ministries reach beyond the local community. Its fields of interest include Southern Africa, international development, education and Europe. It gives both nationally and internationally as well as within Washington.

Recent grants for international programmes in 1990 have included:

Refugees International, for general support ($24,000 with $15,000 given in the previous year);

International Peace Academy ($10,000 also given in the previous year when the grant was for a US/USSR workshop on Third World conflict resolution).

**EXCLUSIONS:** Research is excluded.

**APPLICATIONS:** There are no application forms or deadlines. The board meets in March, June, September and December.

## Texaco Foundation

**GRANT TOTAL:** $8.3 million (1990); Grant range: $500 – $200,000

**ADDRESS:** 2000 Westchester Avenue, White Plains 10650, New York, USA

**TELEPHONE:** (914) 253-4150

**CORRESPONDENT:** Maria Mike-Mayer, Secretary

**INFORMATION:** Annual report with application guidelines.

**GENERAL:** The foundation aims to enhance the quality of life by providing support for cultural programmes, higher education, social welfare, public and civic organisations, hospitals and health agencies and environmental protection. Recent grants for international programmes have included:

In 1990-

Center for Strategic and International Studies ($100,000 with $50,000 in the previous year);

Middle East Institute ($25,000 also given in the previous year);

Caribbean/Central American Action ($10,000 also given in the previous year);

In 1989 –

Foreign Policy Association ($11,000);

Council on Foreign Relations ($10,000);

**APPLICATIONS:** The are no application forms or deadlines. The board meets at quarterly intervals.

## The Tinker Foundation, Inc

**GRANT TOTAL:** $2.07 million (1992)

**MAIN AREAS OF WORK:** Understanding between the peoples of the US, Latin America, Iberia and Antarctica

**ADDRESS:** 55 East 59th Street, New York, New York 10022, USA

**TELEPHONE:** (212) 421-6858

**CORRESPONDENT:** Martha T Muse, Chair and President

**INFORMATION:** A detailed annual report with grant information is available.

**GENERAL:** Grants are awarded to organisations and institutions which promote the interchange and exchange of information within the community of those concerned with the affairs of Latin America, Iberia and Antarctica. Emphasis is placed on activities with strong public policy implications, innovative solutions to problems, and which incorporate new mechanisms for addressing environmental, economic, political and social issues. A grant in 1992 relevant to this guide was given to:

Royal Institute for International Affairs, London, for Argentine participation in the third annual Argentine-British Conference, initiated after the 1982 war ($20,000).

**EXCLUSIONS:** No grants to individuals, campaigns or operating budgets.

**APPLICATIONS:** The initial approach should be by letter. Full proposals when requested on an application form. Deadlines are the 1st March and 1st October for board meetings in June and December.

## Topsfield Foundation

**GRANT TOTAL:** About $92,000

**ADDRESS:** Route 169, Box 203, Pomfret, Connecticut 06258, USA

**TELEPHONE:** 203-928 2616

**CORRESPONDENT:** Phyllis Emigh

**GENERAL:** The foundation was established in 1983 'to support efforts concerned with world hunger, population, and peace. Because it feels a particular urgency about the nuclear arms race, grantmaking is concentrated among grassroots groups working toward nuclear disarmament. While the foundation understands that short-term political change is one step, it believes human security results from real change in the hearts and minds of people everywhere. Therefore, the foundation seeks to enlarge the circle of people involved in disarmament efforts and to translate national concern into debate over public policy. Particular emphasis is given to projects and organisations which build new constituencies and provide avenues of involvement to newcomers.

To this end, the foundation has initiated and funded projects, such as Options, a University Outreach Programme on Nuclear Policy, and Access, a Security Information Service.' These have now become well established and in 1987 largely independent of the foundation.

It is understood that in the 1990s the foundation's resources are directed mainly towards promoting Study Circle discussions on social and political issues – especially on environment, arms control, foreign policy, international relief, citizenship, adult education and health services.

**APPLICATIONS:** Applications are only made on direct recommendation of board members.

# United States Institute of Peace

**GRANT TOTAL:** About $2,310,000 (1991); Grant range $10,000- $74,000

**ADDRESS:** 1550 M Street NW, Suite 700, Washington DC 20005-1708, USA

**TELEPHONE:** (202) 457 1700

**CORRESPONDENT:** Dr Kenneth M. Jenson, Director, Grants Program.

**INFORMATION:** Biennial report and brochure on unsolicited grants containing detailed guidelines for applicants.

**GENERAL:** The Institute was established by an act of Congress as an independent, non-profit corporation to 'serve the people and the Government through the widest possible range of education and training, basic and applied research opportunities, and peace information services on the means to promote international peace and the resolution of conflicts among the nations and peoples of the world without recourse to violence'.

Through its two principal grantmaking components – unsolicited grants and solicited grants, the institute offers financial support for research education and training, and the dissemination of information on international peace and conflict resolution. Unsolicited grants are provided for any topics that fall within the institute's broad mandate while solicited grants are awarded for special priority topics identified in advance by the institute.

Topic areas for unsolicited grants include but are not restricted to: international conflict resolution; diplomacy; negotiation theory; functionalism and 'track two' diplomacy; methods of third party dispute settlement; international law; international organisations and collective security; deterrence and balance of power; arms control; psychological theories about international conflict; the role of non-violence and non-violent sanctions; moral and ethical thought about conflict and conflict resolution; and theories about relationships among political institutions, human rights, and conflict. There are no disciplinary restrictions.

Grants listed in the 1991 annual report included:

London University, Third-party Mediation in Third World Conflicts ($35,000);

Paul H Laurent, Lancs, UK, Arms Sales Policies of Czechoslovakia, France, Germany, Sweden, and Britain ($20,000);

Strathclyde University, Rules for Avoiding Conflicts ($20,000);

International Institute for Strategic Studies, London, Threats to Democracy in Eastern Europe ($30,000);

Sheffield University, Caribbean Security ($20,000);

St Catherine's College, Oxford, New International Order Conference ($30,000).

**APPLICATIONS:** Every proposal must be on an

official application form, ten copies of which must be submitted. The deadlines are the beginning of April and the beginning of October for notification in late July and early February respectively. All foreign institutions are required to provide evidence of non-profit status when submitting an application.

# United Way International

**ADDRESS:** 901 North Pitt Street, Alexandria, Virginia 22314-1594, USA

**TELEPHONE:** (703) 519-0092; Fax: (703) 519-0097

**CORRESPONDENT:** Russy Sumariwalla, President

**INFORMATION:** Annual report

**GENERAL:** United Way International (UWI) is a charitable organisation founded by United Way of America. It was established in response to increasing requests for assistance from countries interested in the United Way system of organised voluntary action.

UWI is not a funding body as such. Each affiliate in other countries raises its own funds and distributes them locally. It has been included in this guide because it is able to provide valuable support services to help develop civil societies worldwide by promoting voluntary initiatives and voluntary development. United Way organisations engage community leaders, often in co-operation with government and business leaders, to address major social problems and human needs, and to provide opportunities for people to participate in improving the well-being of their communities.

United Way start-up costs may be provided, if necessary. However its major activities are the provision of 'capacity-enhancing technical assistance' to its affiliates including on and off-site training.

United Way is active in over 30 countries. It has launched a new initiatives programme in Eastern and Central Europe and the newly independent states of the former Soviet Union. Initiatives have developed particularly in the Russian Federation, Hungary, the Czech Republic, Slovakia and Poland. Initiatives to stimulate voluntarism and volunteerism have been taken in Russia, Ukraine and Belarus.

# Weyerhaeuser Family Foundation, Inc

**GRANT TOTAL:** $392,000 (1991); Grant range: $5,000 – $30,000

**ADDRESS:** 2100 First National Bank Building, Saint Paul, Minnesota 55101, USA

**TELEPHONE:** (612) 228-0935

**CORRESPONDENT:** Nancy Weyerhaeuser, President.

**INFORMATION:** Annual report and application guidelines.

**GENERAL:** Since the 1960s the foundation has placed emphasis on the support of programmes of national and international significance that attempt to identify and correct the causes of maladjustment in our society.

Its fields of interest are education for members of minority races, conservation and environment, family planning and international affairs.

**APPLICATIONS:** An application form is required. The initial approach should be by letter. Applications can be submitted between January and April with a deadline of 1st May. Decisions are made once a year.

# The Whitehead Foundation

**GRANT TOTAL:** $2,446,000 (1991); Grant range $50 – $400,000

**ADDRESS:** 65 East 55th Street, New York, NY 10022, USA

**TELEPHONE:** (212) 755-3131

**CORRESPONDENT:** Denise Emmett

**GENERAL:** The foundation is particularly interested in: international affairs, economic and public policy, the arts and higher education. A specific interest in Europe is noted. Giving is primarily in New York.

Grants with relevance to this guide have been given:

In 1991 –

Emergency Committee for Aid to Poland ($25,000 with $50,000 given in the previous year);

Central Europe Institute, DC ($25,000);

In 1990 –

Institute for East-West Security Studies, general support ($75,000 in 2 grants);

American Friends of Bilderberg, NY (£20,000);

**APPLICATIONS:** Unsolicited applications are rarely approved.

# Winston Foundation for World Peace

**GRANT TOTAL:** $302,000 (1990); Grant range: $2,500 – $20,000

**ADDRESS:** 1875 Connecticut Avenue, NW, Suite 710, Washington DC 20009, USA

**TELEPHONE:** (202) 483-4215; Fax: (202) 483-4219

**CORRESPONDENT:** John Tirman, Executive Director

**INFORMATION:** Quinquennial report, 1986-1991, list of grants up to 1993, guidelines for applicants.

**GENERAL:** The foundation was established in 1985. For seven years the major portion of the grantmaking has been devoted to work towards the permanent prevention of nuclear war. It has also sought to curtail militarism, excessive US military spending, and regional conflicts. The foundation will continue these emphases as part of a broader set of objectives called cooperative security. This is a broader, integrated approach to the foundation's goals, and will result in supporting a wider variety of projects, falling into the following categories:

- preventive diplomacy, which may include a broad range of activities aimed to alert and spur officials to prevent or deter conflict;
- peacemaking and peacekeeping, which are best pursued by the UN or regional security organisations;
- codes of conduct, encompassing a revision of international norms that will chart a peaceful course for the post-Cold War world;
- demilitarisation, the gradual contraction of the size and scope of national military establishments;
- fostering the conditions of peace, including economic vitality and equality, human rights and democracy, and protection of natural resources.

Grants made between October 1991 and October 1993 included:

British American Security Information Council, for general support ($30,000);

Saferworld, Bristol, for efforts to bring conventional arms export constraints to the European community ($25,000);

Institute for War and Peace Reporting, London, for a special edition on Kosovo and Macedonia of its news magazine, War Report ($7,500) to publish work by indigenous journalists and broadcast new perspectives on the Balkans crisis ($20,000);

Centro Studi di Politica Internazionale, Rome, to investigate why collective security systems failed in the Balkans ($43,000);

Humanitas International Human Rights Committee, work on Soviet and East European human rights and disarmament issues ($5,000 in both 1989 and 1990).

Winston Foundation Fellowships are now offered for junior, senior or graduate students for a project in cooperation with a non-governmental organisation. A stipend is provided for the duration of the project expected to be a full-time commitment of some 2-4 months during either the academic year or the summer.

The foundation now manages and advises other funders as well. The CarEth Foundation has been managed by Winston staff since early 1991. The Executive Director is consultant to the Henry P Kendall Foundation. (See separate entry)

**APPLICATIONS:** There are no application forms. The board meets three times a year. Deadlines for submission of requests are likely to the beginning of January, May and September. Check with the office for the exact dates. The Fellowship Programme has different deadlines, for example: for Autumn 1994 by July 15th 1994; for Winter/Spring 1995 by November 1st 1994. Information requests about these should be addressed to Tara Magner.

# **CANADIAN** FOUNDATIONS

## Contents

## Blair Family Foundation

**ADDRESS:** c/o National Trust Co, 21 King Street East, Toronto, Ontario M5C IB3, Canada

**CORRESPONDENT:** Senior Foundation Officer

**GENERAL:** The foundation supports the arts, the environment, science, education and international activities.

A recent grant was given to the Canadian Centre for Disarmament ($15,000).

**EXCLUSIONS:** No support for conferences.

## Donner Canadian Foundation

**GRANT TOTAL:** Can$2,860,000 (1988)

**ADDRESS:** 402-212 King Street West, Toronto, Ontario M5H IK5, Canada

**CORRESPONDENT:** Robert Cuchman

**GENERAL:** The foundation has agreed on four focus areas. These include International Affairs and Oceans and Inland Waters. Projects must be innovative preferably with side geographical impact. Preference is given to projects which fall outside the terms of reference of other agencies.

Grants have included:

Queen's University, Ontario, Canada and the USA in a changing global economy ($60,000);

University of New Brunswick, meeting the challenge of international terrorism ($15,000).

## Walter and Duncan Gordon Foundation

**ADDRESS:** Sun Life Tower, P O Box 66, 150 King Street West, Suite 1211, Toronto, Ontario M5H IJ9, Canada

**CORRESPONDENT:** Ms Christine Lee, Executive Director

**GENERAL:** The foundation aims to strengthen Canada and the well-being of all Canadians. It supports innovative projects, with discernible impact, which influence the development of policy and encourage social action. It focuses its support within three areas:

• Canada's North;

• Peace and Disarmament;

• Secondary Education.

A recent grant was given to the Canadian Centre for Arms Control and Disarmament ($30,000).

## The Lawson Foundation

**GRANT TOTAL:** Can$1,250,000 (1987)

**ADDRESS:** 1384 Wonderland Road North, London, Ontario N6G 2C1, Canada

**CORRESPONDENT:** Colonel Tom Lawson, President

**GENERAL:** The foundation supports charitable purposes within Ontario and religious or educational purposes within Canada. Its six focus areas are:

• Peace and disarmament;

• Poverty;

• Museums;

• Hospitals;

• Salvation Army;

• Community colleges.

## George Cedric Metcalfe Foundation

**GRANT TOTAL:** Can$932,000 (1992)

**ADDRESS:** 105 Pears Avenue, Toronto, Ontario M5R 1S9, Canada

**TELEPHONE:** (416) 926-0366

**CORRESPONDENT:** Josie Romita, Co-ordinator

**GENERAL:** The foundation has six specific information areas: Social Services, Arts/Culture, Education, Environment, Wildlife, International Development It operates in Canada and the Third World (through Canadian organisations).

Recent grants include:

Canadian Centre for Arms Control and Disarmament ($65,000);

Canadian Friends Service Committee ($7,500).

**EXCLUSIONS:** These include conferences and seminars, publication of books, emergency or deficit funding.

**APPLICATIONS:** There are no application forms but the foundation will not accept incomplete applications and its criteria are set out in an information sheet. Applications should reach the co-ordinator before April 1st or September 21st to be eligible for consideration by the advisory board at its twice yearly meetings.

## George and Helen Vari Foundation

**ADDRESS:** 8 Prince Arthur Avenue, Toronto, Ontario, M5R 1A9, Canada

**CORRESPONDENT:** Donald S Rickerdt, Vice-President

**GENERAL:** Its policies cover: Humanising man's environment; Technology and education; Canada's immigrants; Canada/France relations.

# EUROPEAN SOURCES

## European Foundations

### Contents

## King Baudouin Foundation

(Fondation Roi Baudouin)

**ADDRESS:** Rue Brederode 21, Brederodestraat 21,
B-1000 Brussels, Belgium

**TELEPHONE:** 32 2 511 1840

**CORRESPONDENT:** Luc Tayart de Borms, Programme Co-ordinator (National and International)

**INFORMATION:** Annual report and information
brochure.

**GENERAL:** The foundation aims to support all
initiatives likely to improve the living conditions
of the Belgian people, taking account of the
economic, social, scientific and cultural factors,
both at national and international level, which
will have an impact on the country's evolution in
the years to come.

The foundation conducts its own projects and
seldom makes grants to institutions or individuals. It awards the King Baudouin International
Development Prize.

It has undertaken activities in Central and
Eastern Europe in two areas: Youth and Minorities in Parliaments.

## Canon Foundation in Europe

**ADDRESS:** Strawinskylaan 1443, 1077 XX Amsterdam, The Netherlands

**TELEPHONE:** (03) 20 575 3207; Fax: (03) 20 575 3167

**CORRESPONDENT:** Richard Burke, President and
Chief Executive Officer; Corrie Siahaya-Van
Nierop, Executive Assistant

**INFORMATION:** Fact sheet, corporate brochure,
newsletter, annual list of fellows.

**GENERAL:** The foundation was established in 1987
to promote, develop and spread science, knowl-

edge and understanding, particularly between Europe and Japan. It is endowed with annual contributions and managed by a board of directors assisted by an advisory board of persons eminent in the fields of economics, humanities, law, politics and science.

The foundation offers Visiting Research Fellowships to men and women who have already demonstrated unusual capacity for productive scholarship or professional achievement. Fellowships may vary from six months to two years according to the nature of the project. A significant component of the research should be carried out in the EC/EFTA countries or Japan respectively. The fellows must be nationals and permanent residents of Europe or Japan. Grants are currently in the range of DFL 50,000 per year or pro rata for other periods. Applicants should be between 30 and 45 years old.

In 1993 five Japanese and eight European Canon Fellowships were awarded.

**APPLICATIONS:** Foundation application forms must be received from candidates before 15th October each year. Final selection of fellows is generally made before 15th March each year.

# Deutscher Akademischer Austauschdienst (DAAD)

(German Academic Exchange Service)

**GRANT TOTAL:** DM 345 million (1992)

**ADDRESS:** Head Office, Kennedyallee 50, D53175, Bonn , Germany

**TELEPHONE:** (0228) 8820

**CORRESPONDENT:** Professor Dr Theodor Berchem (President), Dr Christian Bode (Secretary General). London Office: 17 Bloomsbury Square, London WC1A 2LP (071-404 4065). DAAD also maintains branch offices in Cairo, Nairobi, New Delhi, New York, Paris, Rio de Janeiro, San José and Tokyo.

**GENERAL:** Founded in 1925, DAAD promotes international university relations between the Federal Republic and foreign countries. Academic staff, researchers and students from all disciplines participate in the scheme. DAAD is funded mainly by the Foreign Office, the Minis-

try of Education and Science, the Ministry for Economic Co-operation and the states of the Federal Republic of Germany.

# European Cultural Foundation

**GRANT TOTAL:** £112,000 (1992) Grant range: £1,700 -£10,500

**ADDRESS:** Jan Van Goyenkade 5, 1075 H N, Amsterdam, Netherlands

**TELEPHONE:** (010-31200 76 02 22)

**CORRESPONDENT:** Dr R Georis, Secretary-General.

**INFORMATION:** European Cultural Foundation (UK Committee): Professor John Pinder (Chairman), James Took (Director), Pilgrims, Appledore, Ashford, Kent TN26 2AE (023 383 215).

The foundation publishes an annual report and a twice-yearly newsletter.

**GENERAL:** The foundation, set up in 1954, is a non-profitmaking organisation devoted to the promotion of activities of a multi-national character and European inspiration, in the fields of education, environment, social affairs, the arts and humanities, international relations and the media. The foundation operates a twofold programme involving grants, and since 1975, a network of institutes and centres established independently or in co-operation with other organisations throughout Europe. National committees also operate on its behalf in European countries. The address of the UK Committee is given above.

The foundation's grantmaking programme gives support to projects involving at least three European countries and of European inspiration. Requests by individuals are not usually considered.

The foundation makes grants under the following headings:

- Architecture and Archaeology;
- Fine Arts, History, Literature, Music and Cultural Co-operation; Employment and Social Problems;
- Education, Language and Youth;
- International Relations, Human Rights and European Co-operation;
- Environment;
- Media.

**APPLICATIONS:** Guidelines for grants are available. Applications should be in writing, Deadlines are mid January and mid September each year.

# The European Human Rights Foundation

**GRANT TOTAL:** 243,250 ECU

**MAIN AREAS OF WORK:** Human Rights

**ADDRESS:** Rue Van Campenhout 13, 1040 Brussels, Belgium, Europe

**TELEPHONE:** 02/734 94 24; Fax: 02/734 68 31

**CORRESPONDENT:** Peter Ashman, Director

**TRUSTEES:** Board Members: Ewa Letowksa, Kempton Makamure, Alice Marangopoulos, Peter Nobel, Martin Kriele, Nicole Questiaux, Theo Van Boven, Suriya Wickremasinghe.

**BENEFICIAL AREA:** Worldwide

**INFORMATION:** An annual report is available from the foundation.

**GENERAL:** The foundation is registered in the Netherlands with the following objects:

- the promotion and protection throughout the world of civil, political, economic, social and cultural rights as they are at present laid down in international instruments;
- the furtherance of endeavours to realise aims of a humanitarian nature in general.

It has limited funds available to distribute to individuals and non-governmental organisations for work in these human rights fields. As most of its funds are provided by the European Community, the foundation does not fund projects or organisations which have been funded by the EC in the same year for similar activities.

The policy of the foundation is to favour action projects. It does not fund educational studies, and usually only funds research projects when these are likely to have practical impact. There is no geographic limitation on work; grants seldom exceed 6,400 ECU. Recipients have to report on the expenditure of the grant within 12 months of receiving it, and acknowledge the support of the foundation in their annual report or other published material relating to the grant.

The London office of the foundation is: 95a Chancery Lane, London WC2A 1DT 071-405 6018/9

**APPLICATIONS:** All applications must be made on the foundation's form to the main office in Belgium. The board meets in May and November each year for which the closing dates are 15 April and 15 October.

# Fondazione Rui

**GRANT TOTAL:** Not known; Lit 600 Million (1987)

**ADDRESS:** Viale Ventuno Aprile, 36, 00162 Roma, Italy

**TELEPHONE:** 06-8632128; Fax: 06-86322845

**CORRESPONDENT:** Dott Ing Alfredo Razzano, Secretary General.

**GENERAL:** The foundation was established to promote the further training of university students and intellectuals; to promote cultural activities for youth; to award scholarships to Italian and foreign students and acclimatise the latter to the Italian way of life; to collaborate with national and international organisations to these ends.

It operates nationally in the field of the arts and humanities, and both nationally and internationally in the fields of education, social welfare and studies. It operates also in the fields of international relations and aid to less-developed countries. Programmes are carried out internationally through self-conducted projects and both nationally and internationally through research, fellowships and scholarships, conferences, courses, publications and lectures.

# Fonds National Suisse de la Recherche Scientifique

**ADDRESS:** Wildhainweg 20, 3001 Bern, Switzerland

**TELEPHONE:** (031) 245 424

**CORRESPONDENT:** P E Fricker, Secretary General; Dr R Bolzern, Social Sciences and Humanities Division.

**INFORMATION:** Annual Report, a brief summary in English. Also contact Dr Bolzern.

**GENERAL:** Founded in 1952 to grant financial support to basic research when sufficient financial subsidies cannot be made available from other sources, and when research is not undertaken for commercial purposes.

It operates both nationally and internationally in the fields of education, science and medicine, the arts and humanities, law and other professions, and international relations, through grants to individuals and institutions, fellowships, scholarships, conferences, courses, publications and lectures. To be eligible for a research grant, candidates must be resident in Switzerland (regardless of citizenship); candidates for fellowships must be resident in Switzerland or graduates of a Swiss university or Federal Technical Institute. In a determined field of research, the foundation may empower an external specialised institute to allocate funds. The foundation also operates an exchange programme with the Royal Society in England.

**APPLICATIONS:** Contact the office for detailed guidelines and application deadlines.

# Foundation for International Understanding

**ADDRESS:** Kultorvet 2, PO Box 85,1003 Copenhagen K, Denmark

**TELEPHONE:** 45 139 418

**CORRESPONDENT:** Folmer Wisti, Chairman

**GENERAL:** The foundation was set up, in 1973, by Folmer Wisti to contribute to international cooperation on issues of importance in daily life at local and regional level, by the encouragement of local communities, the support of decentralisation and regionalism and the exchange of experience and ideas primarily in the fields of education, social welfare and local government. It operates internationally in the field of community endeavour.

Support is given for seminars and study tours on local community issues, for intensive triennial language courses in English, French, German and Spanish for non-academic young people and for study of developments, problems and achievements in one or more countries. The

foundation supports Det Danske Selskab (the Danish Institute) in its programme of international understanding, particularly the Institute's representatives abroad in their work to organise an exchange of information and contacts. 'Europe of Regions', a conference on decentralisation and regional autonomy, is held annually in Copenhagen. Institutions eligible for support must be independent of party politics, non-profit making and non-governmental. No support is given to individuals.

The foundation has not replied to correspondence.

# Foundation Paul-Henri Spaak

**ADDRESS:** 11 Rue d'Egmont, 1050 Brussels, Belgium

**TELEPHONE:** (010) 322 511 8100

**CORRESPONDENT:** Francois Danis, Secretaire Général.

**GENERAL:** The foundation was set up as a centre of thought and action to prolong the European work of Paul-Henri Spaak, particularly in the field of the external relations of the European Communities; to promote any activity contributing to a better understanding of the European ideal and associating new generations with the construction of Europe.

The foundation was set up to operate nationally, internationally and on a European level in the field of international relations. It proposes to encourage education and scientific research related to its aims through creating specialised professorships in EEC external affairs to be occupied by distinguished foreigners, international fellowships and scholarships, the sponsoring of publications and diffusion of documentation and information on a high level.

The foundation has not replied to correspondence.

# Heinz-Schwarzkkopf-Stiftung Junges Europa

**ADDRESS:** 2000 Hamburg 56, Rissener Landstrasse 195, Germany

**TELEPHONE:** 0411-816 381

**CORRESPONDENT:** The Manager.

**GENERAL:** The foundation aims to teach young people between the ages of 16 and 35 the fundamentals of free social and economic systems and to promote contact and understanding between young people in Europe. It operates in the European countries, including those of Eastern Europe, in the fields of international relations, culture, political and economic affairs, science and education through seminars, international youth conferences and travel scholarships.

The foundation has not replied to correspondence.

# The Ireland Funds

**GRANT TOTAL:** US $ 3 million (1993)

**ADDRESS:** 20-22 College Green, Dublin 2, Ireland

**telephone:** (010) 3531 679 2743/ 6771208

**CORRESPONDENT:** Michelle Lynch-Byron, Executive Director

**TRUSTEES:** Advisory Council in Ireland: Margaret Andrews, Adrian Bourke, Colm Cavanagh, Anastasia Crickley, Niall Crowley, Gerald Dempsey, Vincent Ferguson, Mairead Furlong, Hugh Frazer, Lady Valerie Goulding, Maurice Hayes (Chairman), Kate Kelly, Tom Kenny, Tom Kenny, James King, Matt Kingston, Vincent Koziell, Ursual Leslie, Maryon Davies Lewis, T. J. Maher, T. Kevin Mallen, James McCarthy, Mairtin McCullough, Roisin McDonough, Larry McGovern, Tom McGrath, Karl Mullen, Kieran O'Donohue, Sean O'Siochain, James Sherwin, Norma Smurfit, Paul Sweeney, Bernie Wadsworth, Dennis Whelan, Derick Wilson. (This committee makes recommendations on grant-aid to the Boards of Directors of the various funds)

**INFORMATION:** An annual report and funding guidelines in the three programme areas.

**GENERAL:** The Ireland Funds is a non-political organisation established in 1976, to raise money in the United States for the promotion of peace, culture and charity in Ireland, North and South. Since that time funds have been set up in other countries; Canada, Australia, France, Germany, Great Britain and New Zealand.

The funds focus on three separate programme areas: Reconciliation; Arts Development; Community Enterprise/Leadership. Priority is given to programmes which are specifically designed to help people combat unemployment, conflict in Northern Ireland, inner city disadvantage, and rural depopulation. In particular the funds are interested in stimulating local women's contribution in society, encouraging young people's creativity and generally supporting renewal, rejuvenation and regeneration.

Since its inception, US$55 million has been raised for worthy projects. There are three grant allocations a year. Grants vary between IR£500 and IR£30,000 and are usually of a once-off nature. However, the funds may, in certain circumstances, consider supporting a project over three years where it can clearly demonstrate the need for sustained assistance. Over that period the project would be subject to monitoring by the Ireland Funds.

**APPLICATIONS:** Closing dates for applications are mid-April, mid-July, and mid-October. The advisory council makes recommendations to the boards of directors of each fund. These meet three times a year to make final decisions on grants.

# NORDSAM
# Nordic Co-operation Committee for International Politics
(including Conflict and Peace Research)

**ADDRESS:** PO Box 1253 S-11182, Stockholm, Sweden

**TELEPHONE:** 468 23 4060

**CORRESPONDENT:** Erland Jansson, Research Secretary; Anne-Marie Bratt, Information Secretary

**INFORMATION:** Basic guidelines, twice yearly newsletter.

**GENERAL:** NORDSAM is a joint Nordic body responsible for promoting Nordic research in the field of international politics, including conflict and peace research. The members of NORDSAM represent a broad variety of academic disciplines, such as political science, contemporary history, sociology, international relations, international law, and peace and conflict research. They are appointed by the Ministries of Education of their respective countries. Scholarships and grants are awarded to researchers and advanced students from the Nordic countries. Occasionally support may be given to foreign research within NORDSAM's field of interest. Travel grants are also given for participation in seminars and conferences.

**APPLICATIONS:** Application forms available from the secretariat. Check for new deadlines.

# Olof Palme Memorial Fund for International Understanding and Common Security

**ADDRESS:** Sveavägen 68, S-105 60 Stockholm, Sweden

**TELEPHONE:** 468-7002672

**CORRESPONDENT:** Inga-Lena Wallin, Secretary

**INFORMATION:** Information leaflet, annual report (in Swedish).

**GENERAL:** The fund was established by Olof Palme's family and by the Social Democratic Party to honour his memory. Its purpose is, by scholarships and grants, to

- give opportunities to young people for international exchange and for studies of peace and disarmament
- support work against racism and against hostility towards foreigners and to foster in other ways work for international understanding and common security.

The scholarships are one-time payments of an average of 15-25,000 Swedish Kronor. It is understood that a wide range of proposals can be considered.

**APPLICATIONS:** Contact the fund for further details.

# Fritz Thyssen Stiftung

**GRANT TOTAL:** 22.9 million DM (1991/92)

**ADDRESS:** Am Romerturm 3, 50667 Koln, Postfach 180346, 50506 Koln, Germany

**TELEPHONE:** 0221-257505; Fax 0221-2575092

**CORRESPONDENT:** Dr Rudolf Kerscher, Executive Director.

**INFORMATION:** Annual report, in German, is available.

**GENERAL:** The foundation aims to promote research and learning in universities and research institutes, particularly in the Federal Republic. Special consideration is given to the rising generation of scientists and scholars. It supports particular research projects of limited duration, mainly in basic research in the humanities; international relations; state, economy and society; medicine and the natural sciences. It is known that the foundation has given support in 1992/93 to the Royal Institute of International Affairs for its Russian and CIS programme.

# Volkswagen-Stiftung

**GRANT TOTAL:** DM 158.8 million (1992)

**ADDRESS:** Kastanienallee 35, Hannover-Dohren ; All mail to: PO Box 81 05 09, D-305 05 Hannover, Germany

**TELEPHONE:** 49-511-8381 0/49-511-8381-344

**CORRESPONDENT:** Rolf Moller, Secretary General.

**INFORMATION:** Annual report (in German); Outlines (in English).

**GENERAL:** The foundation was set up in 1961 by the Federal Republic of Germany and the State of Lower Saxony for the promotion of science, technology and the humanities in research and university teaching. It operates nationally and internationally through grants for specific purposes to academic and technological institutions engaged in research and teaching. The foundation is free to support any area of science, as well as the humanities, but has limited its funding programme to a range of specific areas. In the case of applications from abroad, co-operation with German research institutions and scholars is usually essential.

The foundation does not provide funds for peace research in the proper sense of the word. Funding under the terms of the programme area 'Research and Training in International Security' is restricted to three sub-programmes. Applications from foreign research teams are welcomed until 31 December 1994, but the proposed projects must be related to the foundation's own work in this field and must contain a substantial element of German involvement and participation. Further information for applicants can be obtained from the office of the Volkswagen-Stiftung.

To foster East West partnerships the foundation has established two funding programmes:

- 1992: 'Co-operation with Natural and Engineering Scientists in Central and Eastern Europe/Joint research Projects and Summer Schools';
- 1993: 'Common Roads to Europe – Foundations and Examples of Co-operation with Central and Eastern Europe in the Humanities and Social Sciences'.

Further information can be obtained from the office.

APPLICATIONS: It is suggested that initial enquiries and discussions of feasibility be directed to the foundation's advisor in this area. Applications should be presented in German or English. A summary in German will be appreciated. Applications are considered in accordance with their pertinence to programme areas. They must contain sufficient information (including detailed cost schedule) for an objective evaluation by the foundation and its consultants.

# EUROPEAN SOURCES

## Governmental

### Contents

## Commission of the European Communities

**GRANT TOTAL:** About 13.5 million ECUs (1993) About 2 million ECUs for UK development education

**ADDRESS:** Directorate-General for Development, Co-operation with Non-governmental Organisations (VIII/B/2), rue de la Loi, 1049 Brussels 200, Belgium

**TELEPHONE:** (010) 322-299 2972

**CORRESPONDENT:** Karen Birchall, DG VIII.

**GENERAL:** The European Community operates a scheme to co-finance projects run by non-governmental organisations in the member states. The scheme to assist development education started in 1979. Now, some 10% of the overall co-financing budget has been earmarked to educate the public in the EEC countries on development issues, on North/South interdependence and its impact on our daily lives and on those of peoples in developing countries. The EEC can pay up to half the cost of a project. The upper limit from January 1988 is 80,000 ECUs each year (this unit of European currency runs at some £0.75). This contribution ma

Projects must have a European dimension e.g. dealing with EC policies or relations with developing countries, or involving collaboration with NGOs from other Member States, or reaching a European target group. Projects funded in the past have included courses for schools, churches and workers, co-ordination of work at EEC level, production of audio-visual materials, and organisation of campaigns. Organisations must be non-profit making. Those which have received co-financing in the UK between 1979 – 1993 include:

Africa Centre

Bath Development Education Centre

BIAG

BMAC

British Defence and Aid Fund for Southern Africa

Bureau for Overseas Medical Service

Catholic Fund for Overseas Development

Catholic Institute for International Relations

Centre for International Studies

Centre for World Development Education

Change

Christian Aid

Derry Development Education Centre

Development Education Association

Farmers' Third World Network

Federal Trust for Education and Research

Hansard Society

Helpage

International Broadcasting Trust

International Institute for Environment and Development

Intermediate Technology Development Group

Mayday Publications

Merseyside Association for World Development Education

Minority Rights Group

Namibia Support Committee

National Council for YMCAS

One World Action

One World Centre

Oxfam

Oxford House/THIS

Panos

Passe-Partout

Population Concern

Quaker Peace and Service

Returned Volunteer Action

Scottish Education and Action for Development

Shanti Third World Centre

Survival

Third World First

Trade Union International Research and Education Group

Traidcraft Exchange

Voluntary Service Overseas

War on Want

Welsh Centre for International Affairs

World University Service

WWF-UK

**APPLICATIONS:** Criteria of eligibility of NGOs and projects can be found in "General Conditions for the Cofinancing of Projects to raise Public Awareness of Development Issues . . .' (doc. VIII/271/87/EN) Most up-to-date version from Karen Birchall, DG VIII, (see above). Decisions on co-financing are made throughout the year. Applicants can also receive useful information/ exchange services from the NGO-EEC Liaison Committee (which has a sub-committee on education for development) at: 10 Sq. Ambiorix, 1040 Brussels, Belgium (010) 322-736 4087.

# Council of Europe

**GRANT TOTAL:** ECU equivalent: 6,233,000 (41 million francs)(1993)

**ADDRESS:** Division for Pan-European Co-operation Programmes, Directorate of Political Affairs, Council of Europe, B P 431 R6, F-67006 Strasbourg Cedex, France

**TELEPHONE:** 33.88.41.20.00; Fax: 33.88.41.27.14

**CORRESPONDENT:** Jean-Louis Laurens, Head of Division

**INFORMATION:** Synopsis of project; bi-annual report.

**GENERAL:** Since 1989 the Council of Europe has set up several programmes of cooperation and assistance as part of its policy towards countries of Central and Eastern Europe which are committed to the same values and principles of pluralistic democracy, human rights and the rule of law.

The major cooperative activities of the Council for Europe are as follows:

• Dialogue, Awareness-Raising, and Information Activities involving senior level political dialogue through meetings and visits;

information and documentation units in the region of the Council of Europe (at present units are operational in Budapest, Warsaw, Prague, Bratislava, Moscow and Sofia); information seminars and study visits; documentation and translation projects, including translation into Central and Eastern European languages of main Council of Europe texts and sending basic human rights libraries to universities and other institutions; and traineeships at the various Council of Europe Directorates.

• Technical assistance: Since 1993 the technical assistance activities have been divided into two geographically distinct programmes:

1) The Central and Eastern European countries, namely Albania, Bulgaria, Croatia, the Czech Republic, Estonia, Hungary, Latvia, Lithuania, Poland, Romania, the Slovak Republic, and Slovenia and

2) The CIS countries, namely Belarus, Moldova, Russia, Ukraine, and to a more limited extent Armenia, Azerbaijan, Georgia, Kyrgyzstan and Kazakhstan.

The programmes comprise the following sectorial sub-programmes:

– The Demosthenes Programme (for the Central and Eastern European countries) and the Demosthenes Bis Programme (for the CIS countries), covering projects in the fields of human rights (including equality), media, social affairs, health, youth, education, culture and sport, civic society, minorities and legal cooperation (the projects in the legal field are referred to as the Demodroit Programme)

– THEMIS Programme for training of legal professionals

– LODE Programme for the development of local government.

These programmes are financed by the annual budget of the Council of Europe and voluntary additional contributions made by certain member countries. In addition, the Council of Europe is undertaking two joint programmes with the Commission of the European Communities. A Joint Programme for strengthening the respect of human rights and the rule of law in Albania was started in July 1993 and will extend over one year. Another Joint Programme for local government and legal system reform in Estonia, Latvia and Lithuania started in January 1994 and will also extend over one year.

It seems worth quoting a short extract from the bi-annual report dated 1st September 1993: 'a new component has been added at the proposal of the Liaison Committee of the Non-Governmental Organisations to the Demosthenes Programme, namely civil society – democratic participation. Projects undertaken under this heading aim at structuring more effectively and intensifying the scattered actions undertaken since 1989 for the developing and reinforcing the role of NGOs and the voluntary sector in the countries of Central and Eastern Europe'.

# European Youth Foundation

**GRANT TOTAL:** 15,660,000 FF (1992)

**ADDRESS:** Youth Directorate, The Council of Europe, B P 431 R6, F-67006 Strasbourg Cedex, France

**TELEPHONE:** 88 41 23 11; Fax: 88 41 27 78

**CORRESPONDENT:** Executive Director

**INFORMATION:** Grant application guidance booklet; annual report with grants list.

**GENERAL:** The foundation was set up in 1972 by the Council of Europe to provide financial support to international youth activities undertaken by either national or international youth organisations. Its aim is to provide support for youth activities which involve the participation of young people of many nationalities in one project.

The foundation's statute states that it may provide support to such youth activities as serve the promotion of peace, understanding and co-operation between the people of Europe and the world, in a spirit of respect for human rights and fundamental freedoms.

The average age of participants in activities supported is 16-25 years.

The annual endowment is determined by the Intergovernmental Committee which is composed of representatives of the member states of the European Youth Foundation. Projects which may be supported include:

- international meetings for young people or youth leaders;
- documentation and information material on youth issues;
- administrative costs of international non-governmental youth organisations (deadlines for applications 1st October for administrative grants for the following year).

Organisations receiving grants in 1992 included:

Christian Movement for Peace

European Youth Forest Action Foundation

Young Men's Christian Association

Young Europeans for Security

Pax Christi Youth Forum

Northern Ireland Youth Forum

APPLICATIONS: An application form is provided with a guidance booklet about completion. Deadlines: 1st April for projects taking place during the first half of the following year; 1st October for projects taking place in the latter half of the following year. These deadlines do not apply for first applications to the foundation.

# NATO

ADDRESS: Science Affairs Division, B-1110 Brussels, Belgium

TELEPHONE: 32 2 728 4111

GENERAL: **NATO Research Awards**

Candidates are invited to submit subjects of research within the following areas:

- internal and external problems of Atlantic security;
- public perceptions of the Atlantic Alliance and of European security;
- in the context of Article 2 of the Washington Treaty, analysis of the Alliance's role in the development of more stable, peaceful and friendly international relations;
- the European contribution to NATO;
- NATO strategy and emerging technologies;
- the working of democratic institutions, pertaining to the study of the executive, legislative and judicial branches of government, the role of the media and non-

governmental organisations and other political, economic and social dimensions of the democratic system.

**Awards:** Each fellow is awarded the sum of 240,000 Belgian Francs or its equivalent, inclusive of all travel costs. Some 20-25 fellowships are awarded annually.

APPLICATIONS: Forms are obtainable from designated national authorities. For the UK this is the Directorate of Defence Policy, Ministry of Defence, Room 7366, Main Building, Whitehall, London SW1A 2HB (071-218 0787).

Regardless of present residence, applicants should submit their applications to the appropriate authority in the country of which they are a national. Applications should be submitted no later than the end of December. Awards are published the following May.

**NATO Institutional Fellowships**

**Awards:** 250,000 Belgian Francs inclusive of all travel costs

APPLICATIONS: Forms are available from the Ministry of Defence (see address above) and should be returned no later than the end of December.

**NATO Science Fellowship Programme**

Science Fellowships enable scientists to pursue their work or continue their training at institutions in other countries. The scheme is flexible enough to offer support to scientists both at different stages of their careers, and in a broad spectrum of science and technology. Eligibility criteria vary from country to country.

APPLICATIONS: Further details are available from The Royal Society, 6 Carlton Terrace, London SW1Y 5AG (071-839 5561).

**Advanced Study Institutes (ASIs)**

ASIs aim to disseminate advanced knowledge not yet in university curricula and foster scientific contacts through high-level teaching courses. Each course is for ten days, and the level is post-doctoral; lecturer-student ratio is about 1:5 with a participation of 60 to 80 scientists of different nationalities. Applications: Forms are available from NATO Scientific Affairs Division, see address above. Applications can be submitted at any time to be considered by a Selection Panel which meets twice a year. The Panel will usually only consider applications for ASIs to be held the following year.

### Collaborative Research Grants (CGRs)

Their purpose is to stimulate collaborations between research scientists in different countries and thus enhance the effectiveness of research. Funding is for reciprocal visits abroad of one to four weeks. Awards cover international travel and living expenses abroad for members of two or more collaborating research teams. Joint research results are published in scientific journals.

**APPLICATIONS:** Further information and application forms can be obtained form NATO Scientific Affairs Division, see address above.

### Other Activities

The following activities may also receive support in the designated Priority Areas. These direct support to problem areas of particular concern to Alliance Co-operation Partner (CP) countries. The Priority Areas are:

• Disarmament Technologies;

• Environment;

• High Technology;

• Human Resources.

Linkage Grants facilitate co-operation between research teams from CP countries and aim to promote the establishment of strong, lasting scientific links between teams through the undertaking of joint research projects. Funding is for reciprocal short visits abroad for four or five members of research teams over a period of one or two years, and in some cases, for limited equipment costs relevant to the project for the CP country.

Expert Visits allow scientists in CP countries to benefit from the expertise of high level specialists from NATO. On request of group leaders from laboratories in CP countries funding may be provided for travel and living expenses of experts from NATO countries.

Further information is available on these schemes from the Scientific Affairs Division, see address above.

# PHARE

(Programme of Aid for Central and Eastern Europe)

**GRANT TOTAL:** Expenditure total: 1,015 million ECUs (1992)

**ADDRESS:** Commission of the European Communities, PHARE Operational Service (PHOS), 200 rue de la Loi, 1049 Brussels, Belgium

**TELEPHONE:** 32 2 299 1400; Fax: 32 2 299 1777

**CORRESPONDENT:** Peter Kalbe, Conseiller

**INFORMATION:** PHARE Operational Guide; Indicative Programmes; List of Approved Projects, 1990/92

**GENERAL:** PHARE is the European Community's support to the ongoing process of economic reconstruction in the countries of Central and Eastern Europe. PHARE is the acronym for the initial programme, Poland and Hungary Assistance in the Reconstruction of the Economy set up in 1989. It now covers 11 countries: Albania, Bulgaria, the Czech Republic, Estonia, Hungary, Latvia, Lithuania, Poland, Romania, Slovakia and Slovenia. Cross-national or regional projects are supported.

PHARE activities are demand-driven. It is the clear responsibility of beneficiary country governments to define policies, priorities and the sequence and timing of the economic restructuring. Beneficiary countries decide for what particular purposes and measures PHARE aid should be used. PHARE responds to requests by providing financial support, supplies, technical assistance, training and studies for particular programmes of reform in key sectors.

TEMPUS (see separate entry) is that part of the PHARE programme which concerns the development and renewal of higher education in the region. See also the entry for the TACIS programme of European Community assistance to the Commonwealth of Independent States (CIS). PHARE operates both from the offices in Brussels and from within each of the countries receiving PHARE assistance, where National Coordinators designated by the beneficiary countries are responsible for drawing up a sector plan for presentation to PHARE and the Commission.

**APPLICATIONS:** PHARE programmes have to arise from the respective national authorities and presented to the Commission through the designated official coordinators. Ideas for projects should therefore be submitted to these people or governmental authorities in the relevant countries, NOT to the Commission. A list of the National Coordinators is available from PHARE.

# TACIS

(Technical Assistance Programme for the Commonwealth of Independent States)

**GRANT TOTAL:** 510 million ECUs (1993)

**ADDRESS:** Commission of the European Communities, Directorate General External Affairs, DG I-E-TACIS, Rue de la Loi 200, B-1049 Brussels, Belgium

**TELEPHONE:** 32 2 296 6065; Fax: 32 2 296 6012

**INFORMATION:** An Operational Guide (1992); Synthesis of Action Programmes (1992).

**GENERAL:** The TACIS programme set up in 1991 aims to develop the local skills and know-how required for the acceleration of the economic reform process in the Commonwealth of Independent States (CIS) and Georgia. The programme provides the advice, know-how and practical experience needed for the effective functioning and management of a market-based economy and its related institutional structures. The aim is to foster the growth of conditions for the development of the private sector and accelerate integration of the CIS countries and Georgia into the world economy.

Assistance falls mainly into four categories:

• policy advice
• institution building
• design of legal and regulatory frameworks
• training.

Funds are also available for the supply of key equipment e.g. training equipment and materials, computers, demonstration equipment. Priority areas of funding allocated for 1992 were:

– human resources and development;
– food production and distribution;
– energy, transport and telecommunications networks;
– enterprise support services;
– nuclear safety.

Coordinating Units have been established in each Newly Independent State. All projects must be submitted via them.

**APPLICATIONS:** All proposals for the financing of projects must be submitted by applicants from the CIS or Georgia to the relevant Coordinating Unit. Contact the TACIS office for an up-to-date list.

# TEMPUS

(Trans-Europe Mobility Scheme for University Studies)

**GRANT TOTAL:** 93 million ECU (1992)

**ADDRESS:** 14 rue Montoyer, B-1040 Brussels, Belgium

**TELEPHONE:** 32 2 504 0711; Fax: 32 2 504 0700

**CORRESPONDENT:** Ms Lesley Wilson, Director

**INFORMATION:** Annual report, TEMPUS leaflet, TEMPUS Vademecum. List of accepted joint European projects.

**GENERAL:** TEMPUS forms part of the overall programme of Community aid for the economic restructuring of the countries of Central/Eastern Europe (PHARE, see separate entry). The main aims of the scheme are to promote the quality and support the development and renewal of the higher education systems in the countries of Central and Eastern Europe designated as eligible for economic aid and to encourage their growing interaction and cooperation with partners in the European community, through joint activities and relevant mobility.

The EC TEMPUS office was established by the European Cooperation Fund in order to assist the Commission of the European Communities in the implementation of the TEMPUS scheme. The fund acts on behalf of a consortium of nine organisations including: Robert Bosch Stiftung, DAAD (see separate entry); European Cultural Foundation (see separate entry).

Since 1990 the TEMPUS office has awarded grants to a wide spectrum of activities. Grants go to large-scale Joint European Projects involving

European Community institutions and partners in Central/Eastern Europe, individual grants go to staff, some limited support goes to the work of associations, and grants are also available for publications, for studies and surveys, and youth exchange activities.

There are TEMPUS offices in each of the Central/Eastern European countries covered by the programmes with which the EC TEMPUS office works closely. Eligible countries in 1993 were:

Albania, Bulgaria, Czech Republic, Estonia, Hungary, Latvia, Lithuania, Poland, Romania, Slovakia, Slovenia. Expansion to the republics of the former Soviet Union is planned.

**APPLICATIONS:** All applications for Joint European Projects are submitted to the Brussels TEMPUS office. Copies are sent to the relevant offices in each of the eligible countries. Overall assessment is conducted in both the EC and the national TEMPUS offices. Bilateral consultations are then held to reach a common assessment of projects. External experts are then consulted. Discussions follow with representatives of the Ministries of Education and the central PHARE coordinators in the eligible countries. A final list proposed by the Commission is drawn up which is then formally approved by the Ministers of Education in the eligible country concerned.

# JAPANESE SOURCES

## Contents

## Foundation of International Education

**ADDRESS:** 2nd Floor, No 32 Kowa Building, 5-2-32 Minami Azabu, Minato-Ku, Tokyo 106, Japan.

**GENERAL:** The foundation aims to assist educational trusts which establish universities and colleges whose principal object is the training of 'internationalists', to promote research and teaching exchange with other countries, and to deepen mutual understanding in international society.

The foundation has not replied to recent correspondence.

## Honda Foundation

**ADDRESS:** 2-6-20 Yaesu, Chuo-Ku, Tokyo 104, Japan.

**GENERAL:** The foundation aims to contribute to the true welfare and peace of mankind by carrying out an international scholarly re-evaluation of modern civilisation; to tackle the problems of environmental destruction, depletion of natural resources, etc.

The foundation has not supplied further information about its work.

## Japan Shipbuilding Industry Foundation

**GRANT TOTAL:** Current figure not known. US $252 million (1986) of which US $28 million (11%) was for overseas assistance.

**ADDRESS:** Senpaku Shinko Building, 1-15-16 Toranomon, Minato-ku, Tokyo 105, Japan

**TELEPHONE:** 03-502 2371/03-508 2377

**CORRESPONDENT:** Ryoichi Sasakawa, Chairman.

**GENERAL:** The Japan Shipbuilding Foundation was set up by Ryoichi Sasakawa the tycoon/philanthropist determined to 'rid the earth forever of the horror of war', and build 'a heaven on earth where all people can live in harmony as brothers and sisters'. The foundation attempts to fulfil this aim by generous donations to the World Health Organisation, and to the United Nations. The foundation gives grants within Japan and to applicants from over 60 other countries in the field of health, education, social welfare, culture, research and international studies.

The foundation has not supplied up-to-date information about its grant-making. In the 1980s grants included support to: United Nations University for Peace, establishment of the Sasakawa Endowment for Peace, The Friendship Force, Carter Center of Emory University, Chair in International Peace.

**APPLICATIONS:** In writing to the correspondent.

## Mitsubishi Ginko Kokusai Zaidan

(Mitsubishi Bank Foundation)

**GRANT TOTAL:** Current figure no known. 67 million yen(1986)

**ADDRESS:** 2-7-1 Marunouchi, Chiyoda-Ku, Tokyo 100, Japan

**TELEPHONE:** 3 240 3317

**CORRESPONDENT:** Executive Director.

**GENERAL:** The foundation was set up in 1981 by the Mitsubishi Bank, Tokyo, to deepen mutual understanding and promote cultural exchanges between Japan and the rest of the World. It provides grants for research in economics, development studies, international affairs and human rights and for exchanges of groups of people (usually aged between 18 and 39 years) for joint research and other activities. The foundation also organises international conferences. Preference is give to programmes connected with Asia and the Pacific.

No information has been made available about their recent grants.

## Niwano Peace Foundation

**GRANT TOTAL:** 40 million Yen (1992)

**ADDRESS:** Shamvilla Catherina, 5F, 1-16-9 Shinjuku, Shinjuku-ku, Tokyo 160, Japan

**TELEPHONE:** 03-226 4371

**CORRESPONDENT:** Yoshinobu Minami, General Secretary

**INFORMATION:** Niwano Peace Prize, pamphlet, in English; Research and Activity Grant guidelines, in English; Echoes of Peace, quarterly, in English; Peace and Religion, annually, in Japanese; Niwano Peace Foundation Report, quarterly in Japanese.

**GENERAL:** The foundation was established in 1979 'to promote research and activities of peace under the religious spirit in order to contribute to world peace.'

It awards the Niwano Peace Prize (worth 20 million yen) annually to an individual or organisation that is making a significant contribution to world peace through promoting inter-religious co-operation.

Its grants are divided into two categories; research and activity.

Research grants are awarded in the following fields: inter-religious understanding and co-operation, the role of religion today, religious approaches to overcoming impediments to peace, and relationships of science to religion and ethics.

Activity grants are awarded to activities that promote mutual understanding and co-operation internationally or within a country through exchange at a regional level among differing cultures and different religions.

Grants are also awarded to social service, development co-operation, human rights and other activities striving for peace that are being conducted on the basis of religious co-operation and tolerance and transcending religious boundaries.

The foundation positively welcomes applications from overseas. It will not, however, fund research activity for the benefit of a specific group or political ideology. Grants run for one year.

The foundation also conducts or commissions its own research on similar topics, and operates a

Peace Research Institute. It sponsors lectures and symposia throughout Japan, and international exchanges for groups of young people.

Research grants for 1992 included:

Herbert Blumberg, Goldsmiths' College, London University, Summaries, Indexes, and an Organisational Framework for Studies of Religious and Ethical Aspects of Achieving Peace in Today's World (Y200,000);

Masatoshi Kimura, Tokyo University, Palestine Under Mandate (Y300,000);

Activity grants in 1992 included:

International Voluntary Service, Bangladesh, Skill Transfer through Village Volunteer Programmes (Y1million).

**APPLICATIONS:** An application form can be obtained from the foundation. Applications for research grants will be received from August 1 to September 30; applications for activity grants will be received between April 1 and November 10. Obtain the guidelines for applicants for more detail.

# Sasakawa Peace Foundation

**GRANT TOTAL:** 4,872 million Yen expenditure (1991)

**ADDRESS:** Sasakawa Hall, 3-12-12 Mita, Minato-Ku, Tokyo 108, Japan

**TELEPHONE:** 81 3 3769 2081; Fax: 81 3 3769 2090

**CORRESPONDENT:** Akira Iriyama, Executive Director

**INFORMATION:** Annual report; SPF brochure in English and Japanese.

**GENERAL:** The foundation was established in 1986 by Ryoichi Sasakawa, Chairman of the Japan Shipbuilding Industry Foundation, 'to work for world peace through continual and concrete efforts to promote international understanding, exchange, and co-operation'.

Since that time the foundation has set up a series of affiliated foundations and special funds: the Sasakawa Peace Foundation USA, the Foundation Franco-Japonaise Sasakawa and the Sasakawa African Association for it provides the secretariat, and its special area fund, the Sasakawa Central Europe Fund (see below), the Saskawa Japan-China Friendship Fund and the Sasakawa Pacific Island Nations Fund.

The foundation's grantmaking is concentrated on the following programme areas:

- Problem Solving in an Independent World: with emphasis on monitoring global trends and finding solutions to the political and economic problems which arise in the global environment;

- Assisting in the Development of Third World Nations: with emphasis on development projects initiated by the developing countries themselves;

- Forming Networks for International Exchange: at the same time as building up its own inter-organisational network, the foundations seeks to generate other international networks;

- Supporting research: This programme concentrates on support for Japanese scholars studying conditions in the ASEAN, the Middle East, and the former soviet Union, and on fostering conceptual innovation.

- Assisting the Globalisation of Local Communities in Japan: To counteract the concentration of economic activities in the Tokyo metropolitan area, support is given for local communities experimenting in establishing their own overseas links;

- Enhancing Intercultural Communications: support for communication and exchange programmes which contribute to the expression of 'diverse and relevant points of view in the global society'.

- Strengthening the Underpinnings of the Foundation: Priority for training and education for individuals working with the foundation, and also training opportunities for personnel from other private, non-profit organisations in Japan and other countries.

**The Sasakawa Central Europe Fund** was established in 1990 to assist Hungary, Poland, the Czech Republic and Slovakia make a smooth transition to a market economy. It works to promote exchange and dialogue between these countries, to nurture friendly relations through deeper mutual understanding and trust, and to encourage and support environmental protection efforts in the region.

In 1991 support was given to:

Environmental Partnership for Central Europe, support for the organisation's training programme given to the staff of NGOs and municipal environmental agencies in planning, fundraising, organising and working with government agencies and industry (20m Yen/ 140,000 ECU);

'Structure of the Market Economy', an educational TV series for transmission through the national TV stations (124m Yen/868,000 ECU).

For further information about the fund contact: Mr Kotaro Kohata, Assistant Programme Officer, at the above address. (Tel: 81 3 3769 2091; Fax: 81 3 3769 2090).

Support has also been given to projects concerning the Central Europe region from the foundation's main grant programme (see above) specifically concerning networking and global issues.

**APPLICATIONS:** There are no particular deadlines for proposals or limits on the amount of financial support. Proposals can be submitted in any form and summarised in three to four A4 pages.

# AWARDS

## Contents

## Frank Cousins TGWU Peace Award

**GRANT TOTAL:** Award: £4,000 each year.

**ADDRESS:** Transport and General Workers' Union, Transport House, Smith Square, London SW1P 3JB

**TELEPHONE:** 071-828 7788 x 334

**CORRESPONDENT:** Joe Irvine, Secretary to the Award Panel.

**TRUSTEES:** Award panel: Richard Clement, Dan Duffy (Chairman of the TGWU Executive), Joan Ruddock, Bill Harris, Norman Willis, plus another TGWU Executive Committee member.

**GENERAL:** The award is to assist the cost of research, travel and other activities related to projects which promote peace, disarmament and/or arms conversion. The award is made to a person or a project. The awards which started in 1984 have been made to Joan Ruddock, Scientists Against Nuclear Arms and Olive Gibbs.

**APPLICATIONS:** The award is announced during September in the relevant journals and newsheets of the Labour movement calling for applications, from individuals or organisations, detailing the exact way in which the award would be used. There is no application form. The closing date for applications is set out in the announcement.

## Right Livelihood Award Foundation

**GRANT TOTAL:** Annual cash awards: Some US $200,000 (plus honorary, non-monetary awards).

**ADDRESS:** PO Box 15072, S-104 65 Stockholm, Sweden

**TELEPHONE:** 46(0)8 702 03 40; Fax: 46(0)8 702 03 38

**CORRESPONDENT:** Kerstin Bennett, Administrative Director

**TRUSTEES:** Jakob von Uexkull, (Founder/Chairman); Birgitta Hambraeus, Monika Griefahn.

**GENERAL:** The Right Livelihood Awards are popularly known as the 'Alternative Nobel Prize'. They are presented in the Swedish Parliament in Stockholm on the day before the Nobel Prizes in the same spirit as Alfred Nobel, who wanted to honour those who 'during the past year have conferred the greatest benefit on mankind.'

'A crucial feature of the Right Livelihood Award is its holistic approach to the challenges of today. It brings together those who are working for peace and disarmament, human rights and social justice, sustainable economic development and environmental conservation, and for human development, whether through the improvement of health and education, through cultural and spiritual renewal, or through the addition to the stock of human knowledge and benign technologies. The complexities and interdependencies of our world demand such an integrated approach.'

Recipients are chosen by an international jury which includes trustees of the foundation. The award is funded in part from endowment income and by donations from individuals all over the world. The cash award is never given for personal use but for work in progress. The first awards were given in 1990.

Awards in recent years have been made to:

In 1988 –

Dr Inge Kemp Genefke/International Rehabilitation and Research Centre for Torture Victims (Denmark) (Honorary Award)

José Lutzenberger (Brazil)

John F Charlewood Turner (UK)

Sahabat Alam Malaysia/Mohamed Idris, Harrison Ngau, the Penan people (Malaysia)

In 1989 –

The Seikatsu Club Consumers' Cooperative (Japan) (Honorary Award)

Melaku Worede (Ethiopia)

Aklilu Lemme/Legesse Wolde-Yohannes (Ethiopia)

Survival International (UK)

In 1990 –

Alice Tepper Marlin (USA) (Honorary Award)

Bernard Lédéa Ouedraogo (Burkina Faso)

Felicia Langer (Israel)

ATCC- Asociación de Trabajadores Campesinos Del Carare (Colombia)

In 1991 –

Edward Goldsmith (UK) (Honorary Award)

Narmade Bacao Andolan (India)

Bengt & Marie-Therese Danielsson (Polynesia) and Senator Jeton Anjain and the people of Rongelap (Marshall Islands)

MST – Movimento dos Trabalhadores Rurais sem Terra and CPT – Commissao Pastoral da Terra (Brazil)

In 1992 –

Finnish Village Action Movement (Honorary Award)

Gonoshasthaya Kendra/Zafrullah Chowdury (Bangladesh)

Helen Mack (Guatemala) John Gofman (USA) and Alla Yaroshinskaya (Ukraine).

In 1993 –

Arna Mer-KHamis (Israel) and Care and Learning, (Jenin, Occupied Palestine)

Sithembiso Nyoni/ Organisation of Rural Associations for Progress (ORAP) (Zimbabwe)

Vandana Shive (India)

Mary and Carries Dann of the Western Shoshone Nation of North America

**APPLICATIONS:** Nominations need to be made by April 10th. Anyone may nominate a person other than themselves or a project not their own.

# UNESCO Prize for Peace Education

**GRANT TOTAL:** Award: Approximately US $60,000 each year.

**ADDRESS:** UNESCO, Division of Human Rights and Peace, 7 place de Fontenoy, 75700 Paris, France

**TELEPHONE:** (010) 331 45 68 38 17

**CORRESPONDENT:** Janusz Symonides, Director, Division of Human Rights and Peace

**INFORMATION:** Full information on the general rules governing the prize are available from the above address.

**GENERAL:** The UNESCO Prize for Peace Education promotes action designed to 'construct the defences of peace in the minds of men' by rewarding a particularly outstanding example of activity designed to alert public opinion and mobilise the conscience of mankind in the cause of peace.

The prize is awarded annually to an individual, group of individuals or an organisation, and financed from the interest of a large donation to UNESCO by the Japan Shipbuilding Industry Foundation. A jury of nine persons, appointed for 3 years by the Director General, serves as the International Commission for Peace in the Minds of Men.

Laureates of the UNESCO Prize include:

In 1984 –

International Physicians for the Prevention of Nuclear War (IPPNW);

In 1985 –

General Indar Jit Rikhye (India) and the Georg Eckert Institute for International Textbook Research (Federal Republic of Germany);

In 1986 –

Professor Paulo Friere (Brazil);

In 1987 –

Ms Laurence Deonna (Switzerland) and the 'Servicio Paz et Justitia en America Latina';

In 1988 –

Brother Roger de Taizé (France);

In 1989 –

International Peace Research Association (IPRA) and Robert Muller (France);

In 1990 –

Ms Rigoberta Menchu Tum (Guatemala) and World Order Models Project (WOMP);

In 1991 –

Ms Ruth Leger Sivard (USA) and Cours Sainte Marie de Hann (Senegal);

In 1992 –

Mother Teresa;

In 1993 –

Ms Madeleine De Vits (Belgium) and the Graduate Institute of Peace Studies (GIP).

**APPLICATIONS:** The closing date for nominations is fixed each year but is generally 31st March. Nominations may be made by member States of UNESCO, intergovernmental organisations, non-governmental organisations granted consultative status with UNESCO and persons whom the Director-General deems qualified in the field of peace.

# Carnegie-Stichting, Watelerfonds

**ADDRESS:** Vredespaleis, Carnegieplein 2, The Hague 2517K, Netherlands

**TELEPHONE:** (010) 3170-302 4242

**CORRESPONDENT:** The Director

**GENERAL:** The foundation awards the Wateler Peace Prize each year to the person or institution having rendered the most valuable service in the cause of peace or having contributed to finding means of combating war.

This is the only grant the foundation awards. Recent wards have been made to:

Alva Myrdal

Henry Kissinger

International Commission of Jurists, Geneva

UNIFIL contingent

Wilhelm Huber, SOS-Kinderdorf International

# BIBLIOGRAPHY

## UK Sources

'*A Guide to the Major Trusts*', Vols 1 & 2, 1993, (published every 2 years) Directory of Social Change, 129 Queen's Crescent, London NW5 2PG (Tel: 071-284 4364)

'*Directory of Grant-Making Trusts*', 1993-94, (published every 2 years) Charities Aid Foundation, 48 Pembury Road, Tonbridge, Kent YN9 2JD (Tel: 0723-771333)

## USA Sources

'*The Foundation Directory*', 1993, 15th edition, published annually, Foundation Center, 79 Fifth Avenue, New York, NY 10003-3076 (Tel: (800) 424-9836)

'*The Foundation 1000*' (formerly Source Book Profiles), Foundation Center, published annually (see address above)

'*Guide to Funding for International and Foreign Programmes*', 1992, The Foundation Center, NY (see address above)

'*US Foundations Support in Europe*' 2nd edition 1994, Directory of Social Change, (see address above)

## Canadian Sources

'*Canadian Directory of Foundations*', The Canadian Centre for Philanthropy, 1329 Bay Street, Toronto M5R 2C4 (416-515 0764)

## Japanese Sources

'*Directory of Grant-Making Foundations, Guide to Private Grant Sources*', 1992. Contact the Information Officer, The Foundation Library Center of Japan, Elements Sinjuku Building 3F, 2-1-14 Shinjuku, Shinjuku-ku, Tokyo, Japan (Tel: 03-3350 1857; Fax: 03-350 1858)

'*Inside Japanese Support, Japanese Corporate Giving and Foundation Giving Program*', The Taft Group, 12300 Twinbrook Parkway, Suite 450, Rockville, Maryland 20852, USA

'*Directory of Japanese Giving*', 1991, Corporate Philanthropy Report, 2727 Fairview Avenue East, Suite D, Seattle, WA 98102, USA (Tel: (206) 329-0422; Fax: (206) 325-1362) Also available from the Directory of Social Change, see address above.

## South African Sources

'*The Donor Community in South Africa: A Directory*' edited by Ann McKinstry Micon, Institute for International Education, 809 U N Plaza, New York NY 10017-3580

## International Sources

'*International Guide to Funders Interested in Central and Eastern Europe*', 1993, European Foundation Centre, 51 rue de la Concorde, B-1050 Brussels, Belgium (Tel: 32-2-512 8938; Fax: 32-2-512 3265)

'*The International Foundation Directory*', 1991, Europa Publications, 18 Bedford Square, London WC1B 3JN

# INDEX